W9-CUP-840

Easy
Windows XP
troubleshooting

Other Windows XP Titles

Easy
Windows XP
troubleshooting

Robert Penfold

Bernard Babani (publishing) Ltd
The Grampians
Shepherds Bush Road
London W6 7NF
England
www.babanibooks.com

Please note

Although every care has been taken with the production of this book to ensure that any projects, designs, modifications and/or programs, etc., contained herewith, operate in a correct and safe manner and also that any components specified are normally available in Great Britain, the Publisher and Author do not accept responsibility in any way for the failure (including fault in design) of any projects, design, modification, or program to work correctly or to cause damage to any equipment that it may be connected to or used in conjunction with, or in respect of any other damage or injury that may be caused, nor do the Publishers accept responsibility in any way for the failure to obtain specified components.

Notice is also given that if any equipment that is still under warranty is modified in any way or used or connected with home-built equipment then that warranty may be void.

© 2002 BERNARD BABANI (publishing) LTD

First Published - April 2002
Reprinted - August 2002
Reprinted - December 2002
Reprinted - August 2003
Reprinted - January 2004
Reprinted - June 2004
Revised and Reprinted - December 2004
Reprinted - March 2005
Reprinted - September 2005

British Library Cataloguing in Publication Data

A catalogue record for this book is available from the British Library

ISBN 0 85934 521 1

Cover Design by Gregor Arthur

Printed and bound in Great Britain by Cox & Wyman Ltd, Reading

Preface

Although the Windows operating systems are widely regarded as having a lack of stability, this reputation is not entirely fair. Software as complex as any version of Windows is never likely to be fully debugged, but it is not really any built-in bugs that are the major problem with Windows. It is the alterations that are made to the operating system after the basic installation process has been completed. The operating system is added to and altered each time any hardware or major piece of software is added or removed. Windows can be used with an enormous range of software and hardware, but this leaves it vulnerable to problems that originate in hardware drivers, installation programs, and uninstallers. Applications programs can also introduce difficulties if they do not strictly abide by the rules involving memory management, file naming, etc.

Windows XP is more robust that earlier versions of the operating system such as Windows ME, and it does a good job of defending itself against incompatible drivers and applications software. However, Windows XP it is still far from immune to problems. It is doubtful if an operating system can ever be made totally "bomb proof". In order to be usable an operating system must be flexible, but this flexibility inevitably leaves it vulnerable to problems.

Ideally the user would install Windows XP and some applications programs, and then make no further changes to the system. For most users this is not practical though, and new hardware has to be added, software upgrades have to be installed from time to time, and so on. Most modern PCs tend to evolve over a period of time, and the operating system has to change to accommodate this evolution. If Windows XP should cease working it is not usually too difficult to get it up and running again. Most faults introduced into the system are easily reversed, provided you know how. This book details some simple procedures that enable most Windows XP faults to be quickly pinpointed and rectified. You do not have to be a computer expert in order to follow these procedures, but you do have to be familiar with the basics of using the Windows XP user interface.

Where a Windows XP installation becomes seriously damaged it may not be practical to repair it. Even if numerous files have been corrupted or deleted it is probably possible to repair the installation given enough time, but the more sensible approach is to reinstall the operating system. Full instructions for reinstalling Windows are provided, including reinstallation over an existing version and the "from scratch" approach. Either option may seem to be a rather daunting prospect for those of limited experience at Windows troubleshooting, but reinstalling Windows XP is not particularly difficult. It is the guaranteed method of curing Windows XP problems and getting your PC back in full working order again.

Robert Penfold

Trademarks

Microsoft, Windows, Windows XP, Windows Me, Windows 98 and Windows 95 are either registered trademarks or trademarks of Microsoft Corporation.

All other brand and product names used in this book are recognised trademarks, or registered trademarks of their respective companies. There is no intent to use any trademarks generically and readers should investigate ownership of a trademark before using it for any purpose.

Contents

CAW

3

Troubleshooting 123

4

Data rescue 173

5

Backup and restore 219

6

Reinstallation 251

Upgrading problems

Out with the old...

Upgrading from Windows 3.1 to Windows 95 was a big step for those who made the change. A switch was being made from a 16-bit operating system to a 32-bit type. However, to some extent the original operating system was still there, albeit largely hidden away out of sight. Upgrading from Windows 95 to 98 or ME was a relatively minor step, since all three of these operating systems are firmly based on the same program code. Changing from Windows 95, 98, or ME to Windows XP is another big step, and many consider that it is actually a larger change than moving from 16-bit Windows to the 32-bit variety.

The reason for this is that the XP code is not based on a 16-bit version of Windows, and it was written "from scratch" as a 32-bit operating system. It would perhaps be more accurate to say that Windows NT was written purely as a 32-bit operating system, and that Windows 2000 and then XP were derived from this. Windows XP is therefore the successor to Windows NT/2000, and not Windows 9x. Upgrading from Windows 2000 to XP is a small change, but the change from 9x to XP is a major step. As Windows ME is destined to be the last in that series of Windows products, it is a step that all Windows 9x users will eventually have to make.

Upgrading from Windows NT or 2000 to XP should therefore be relatively straightforward. This is not to say that it is possible to upgrade to XP using any PC that is currently running Windows NT4 or 2000. The minimum hardware requirements for Windows XP are more stringent than for earlier versions. Most new PCs at the time XP was launched were up to the task of running the new operating system, but many earlier PCs were not. In fact many PCs less than a year old at the time XP was launched were not adequate to run this operating system properly, although in most cases a memory upgrade was all that was needed to rectify the problem.

Realistic minimum

If you buy Windows XP ready installed on a new PC there should be no problem, and it should have a specification that is high enough to run this operating system very well. The situation is very different when upgrading from any previous version of Windows, and it is essential to check that your PC is up to the task. Only proceed if there is a realistic chance of obtaining good results. This is the minimum specification needed to run Windows XP:

Processor having a clock speed of 233MHz or more

64MB of memory

1.5GB of hard disc space

Video system capable of at least 800 by 600 pixel resolution

CD-ROM or DVD drive

Mouse or other XP compatible pointing device

When looking at the minimum hardware requirements for any software it has to be borne in mind that the specification is the minimum required to run the software, and that a system of this specification might not give usable results. In fact, in most cases the quoted minimum hardware requirements do not represent the lowest specification that provides a usable system. A PC having the minimum requirements will run the software, but will usually perform so badly as to be of little or no practical use.

This is certainly the case here, and although 64MB of memory is sufficient to run Windows XP, it will not enable major applications software to be run once the operating system has been installed. Realistically, 128MB represents the minimum amount of memory that will enable spreadsheets, desktop publishing programs, etc., to be run under Windows XP. Of course, if you intended to use applications software that requires large amounts of memory, or you wish to run several programs simultaneously, 256MB or more of memory will be required. The instruction manuals for Windows applications usually give some guidance regarding the amount of memory needed to run the programs.

Clock speed

The minimum processor clock speed can never be anything more than a rough guide, since a selection of PCs running at a certain clock speed will not provide the same level of performance. The overall speed of the

PC is influenced by other factors, such as the type of processor in use, the chipset on the motherboard, the amount of memory, and performance of the video card. It is unlikely that any PC having a 233MHz processor will run Windows XP well and 300MHz is a more realistic minimum. A processor clock speed of 500MHz or faster is preferable.

Although Windows XP is faster than previous Windows operating systems when used with the latest PCs, the same is not true when it is used with older PCs. Due to increased memory requirements and other factors, Windows XP can run more slowly on older PCs. Consequently, it is not safe to assume that Windows XP will run properly on a PC simply because a previous version of Windows is already working well on that PC. Even if the PC has sufficient resources to run Windows XP, applications programs might run too slowly.

The minimum hard disc figure of 1.5GB is the approximate amount needed to run a typical installation before applications programs and any data are loaded onto the disc. It does not represent a minimum figure for a real world PC running a few applications programs. The minimum hard disc capacity is largely dependent on the number and type of applications that will be used, and the operating system is a less important factor. However, Windows XP requires significantly more hard disc space than Windows 9x. An absolute minimum of about 3GB is needed in order to accommodate Windows XP itself plus two or three typical applications programs.

In order to run Windows XP reasonably well, the minimum specification is therefore something like this:

Processor having a clock speed of 300MHz or more

128MB of memory

3GB of hard disc space

Video system capable of at least 800 by 600 pixel resolution

CD-ROM or DVD drive

Mouse or other XP compatible pointing device

Do not be surprised if you obtain poor results using Windows XP with a system that fails to meet these requirements. Even with this specification, some aspects of performance might not be very good.

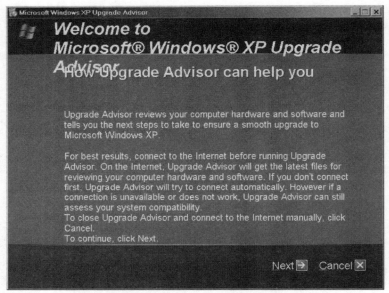

Fig.1.1 The opening screen of the Upgrade Advisor program

Checking

If in doubt, it is possible to run a program that will check whether your PC is suitable for an upgrade to Windows XP. This program is actually part of the Windows XP installation program. The suitability of the PC is checked as part of the normal upgrade process. The purpose of this routine is to warn you of any potential problems with the hardware and the installed software. The standalone version of the advisor program is useful if you wish to upgrade, but would like to check the suitability of your PC before buying the upgrade software. It has been made available on a few "free" discs supplied with computer magazines, and it can be downloaded from the Microsoft web site at this address:

www.microsoft.com/windowsxp/pro/howtobuy/upgrading/advisor.asp

An information screen appears when the program is run (Figure 1.1). This explains what the program will do, and it also points out that for best results the program needs to access the Internet so that it can use the latest information that is available from the Microsoft site. However, the program will still work if no Internet connection is available or you

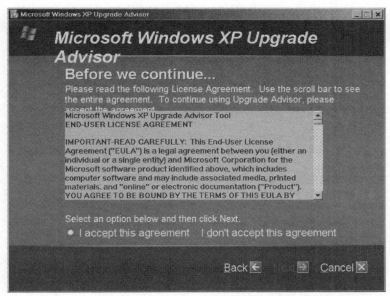

Fig.1.2 You have to accept the licence conditions in order to use the Upgrade Advisor

would rather not allow the program to access the Internet. If you do decide to permit the program to use a Web connection, it is not necessary to connect to the Internet before running the program. It will use a connection that is already active, or try to make the connection if there is no active link.

Operate the Next button to move on to the next screen (Figure 1.2), which is the usual Microsoft licensing agreement. To continue, operate the "I accept this agreement" radio button, and the left-click the Next button. This moves the process on to the information screen of Figure 1.3. The main point of this screen is to point out that Windows XP is compatible with most hardware and software.

Although there are likely to be several problems found by the advisor program, these will probably not prevent Windows XP from being successfully installed on the computer. In most cases it simply means that you will need to make some changes in order to get everything working perfectly. This usually means installing new hardware drivers or reinstalling one or two pieces of software.

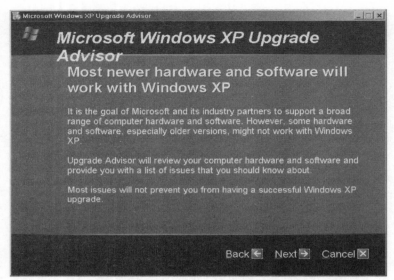

Fig.1.3 As this screen explains, Windows XP is compatible with most software and hardware

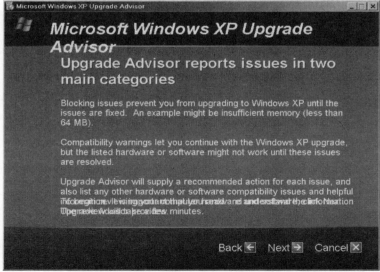

Fig.1.4 An explanation of the problems that can be reported

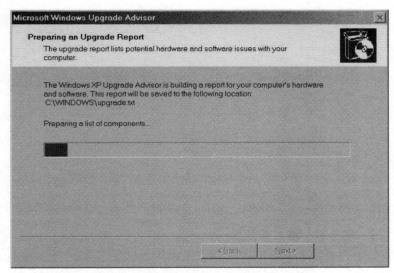

*Fig.1.5 The usual status bar shows how far the checking
has progressed*

Moving on to the next screen (Figure 1.4) provides further information.
This screen does not seem to display properly with all video cards and
screen resolutions, but it is simply explaining the various types of problem
that the program will discover. The most important category is blocking
issues. These problems prevent Windows XP from being installed at all.
The usual causes are shortcomings in the hardware, such as a lack of
memory or processor speed. There should be no blocking issues
provided you have already checked that your PC meets the minimum
hardware requirements. It is virtually certain that compatibility issues
will arise, but in most instances these can be solved fairly easily. The
advisor program gives a recommended course of action for solving
compatibility issues.

Operating the Next button starts the checking process, and the window
of Figure 1.5 then appears. A status bar shows how the checking process
is progressing. The text explains that a copy of the test report produced
by the program will be stored on the hard disc, and the name and location
of the file is given. It will not usually be necessary to refer to this file,
since a summary of the results (Figure 1.6) is displayed once the checking
process has been completed. Although the PC used in this example
has a fair amount of hardware and software installed, the number of

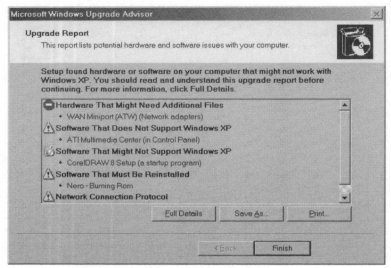

Fig.1.6 A summary of the test results is provided

problems that were reported by the advisor program were quite small. Do not worry if your PC produces a longer list of compatibility issues, because most of them are likely to be minor problems. Operating the Full Details button produces a window that gives more details about compatibility problems (Figure 1.7).

It is likely that a few pieces of hardware will have compatibility problems. Bear in mind that Windows XP uses totally different drivers to Windows 9x, and drivers for Windows NT and 2000 will not necessarily be suitable either. Hardware that was released at about the same time as Windows XP, or later, may include suitable drivers on the installation disc. If not, it is a matter of visiting the manufacturer's web site in search of suitable drivers for Windows XP.

Obviously, there is no guarantee that suitable device drivers will be available for every piece of hardware in your PC. Windows XP device drivers have been produced for most hardware that is no more than a few years old, but support for older hardware is more patchy. No doubt some hardware is unusable with Windows XP. If you are unlucky in this respect, you will have to use an older version of Windows in order to go on using any hardware that is not supported by Windows XP. However,

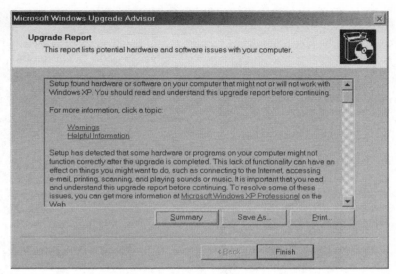

Fig.1.7 Background information is available, if required

many Windows 2000 device drivers will work properly with Windows XP, so it is worth trying Windows 2000 drivers before giving up.

Video

The video card is a common cause of problems when upgrading to Windows XP. If you are upgrading from Windows 2000 or you have a popular video card, it is possible that it will be properly supported by the upgrade version of Windows XP. You should then find that the video system works normally once the upgrade has been installed. It is still worth visiting the web site of the video card manufacturer to see if there is a more recent device driver available for your card. The device drivers for video cards seem to undergo frequent tweaks, particularly in the first year or so of production. It is quite likely that an improved version will be available.

In most cases, the upgrade version of Windows XP will not have the necessary support for the video card you are using. This does not mean that the upgrade can not go ahead. The upgrade program should be able to install generic device drivers for the video card that will at least get the video system operating at relatively low resolution. This will typically be 640 by 480 pixel resolution, but 800 by 600 pixel resolution might be provided. The full colour depth of the video card might be available. Whatever the resolution and colour depth, it will be sufficient to get the new operating system working well enough for the proper video drivers to be installed.

You might find that the generic drivers support higher screen resolutions and colour depths, but it is still advisable to load the manufacturer's drivers for Windows XP. Although the generic drivers will in all probability work perfectly, they will certainly fail to take full advantage of the video card's hardware. Consequently, even software that only uses 2D graphics is likely to run very slowly unless the proper drivers are installed. Odd effects might also be noticed when using generic drivers, such as objects not being erased from the screen properly.

Problem devices

It is unlikely that there will be any major hardware problems provided your PC uses "run of the mill" hardware that is reasonably up to date. As already pointed out, there will not always be XP support for older hardware. Try a Windows 2000 driver if that is the best you can find, but in some cases there may be no suitable driver available. It is then a matter of not upgrading to Windows XP, or upgrading any unsupported hardware. If only one inexpensive item of hardware has to be replaced, it should certainly be worthwhile continuing with the upgrade. Obviously, the upgrade might not be feasible if the PC requires expensive changes in order to accommodate Windows XP. This is a subjective matter and one where you have to weigh up the costs against the advantages and make your own decision. Bear in mind that older hardware is probably nearing the end of its useful life span and will probably have to be replaced before too long anyway.

So-called generic hardware is another likely cause of problems. This is either anonymous hardware that carries no manufacturer's name on the device itself or the documentation, or the name of the manufacturer is given but is one that no one has ever heard of. The problem with this type of hardware is that there is usually no support available from the manufacturer's web site. If you are lucky, a web address will be provided somewhere in the documentation or a search engine will help you locate one. In most cases though, the level of support provided by the big name manufacturers is not available for generic hardware. There is often no ongoing support at all for this type of hardware, which in part accounts for its low cost.

Finding drivers

The fact that a piece of generic hardware lacks a web address for support does not necessarily mean that there is no hope of finding Windows XP drivers. However, it does mean that if the device drivers do exist, finding them will be much more difficult. With generic hardware that came as part of a PC, the Support section of the PC manufacturer's web site might have the drivers you need. A call to the PC manufacturer's help line might also produce some useful information. Provided the PC you are using is not in the "golden oldie" category, the maker should provide ongoing support for all the hardware, including any no-name hardware.

Computer chip manufacturers often produce generic driver software for their products. If your piece of problem hardware is a modem based on (say) a Motorola chipset, the obvious starting point is the Motorola web site. Any search engine should soon locate the manufacturer's web site. This will not always produce a source of suitable drivers. Quite reasonably, the manufacturer of the chips might consider that it is the job of the equipment producer to supply support for their products. However, in practice the sites of chip makers often prove helpful, and it is certainly worthwhile looking to see if there is anything useful on offer.

If a search of the chip manufacturer's site proves to be fruitless, other avenues can be pursued. There are plenty of sites that offer help with device drivers, and using "device drivers" as the search string in the Yahoo search engine will produce a useful list of driver sites. These sites mostly offer a great deal of general information about software drivers, plus advice for beginners on installing them. In most cases there are also search facilities and advice on finding suitable driver programs.

One example of such a site is DriverGuide.com (Figure 1.8). You have to register in order to utilise this site, but registration is free. Amongst other things, it includes search facilities that enable the user to search for a certain manufacturer, drivers for a certain type of hardware, and so on (Figure 1.9). Probably the best know site for device drivers is WinDrivers.com (Figure 1.10). This site provides a lot of general advice together with useful search facilities (Figure 1.11). I have found HelpDrivers.com very useful when tracking down drivers. On one occasion I managed to find the device drivers I needed even though I had nothing more to go on than the markings on the main chip of a modem's circuit board. There is no guarantee that Windows XP drivers will be available for any awkward pieces of hardware, but if they do exist they will almost certainly be available somewhere on the Internet.

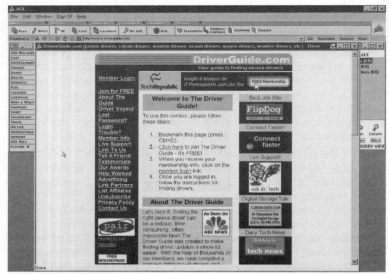

Fig.1.8 DriverGuide.com is one of many sites that deals with device drivers

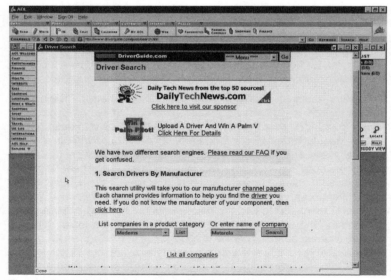

Fig.1.9 DriverGuide.com includes a search facility

Fig.1.10 WinDrivers.com is one of the best known device driver sites

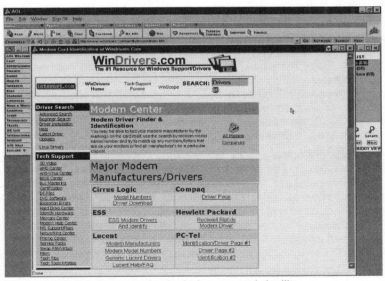

Fig.1.11 WinDrivers.com also includes a search facility

Note that the new drivers must not be installed until after the upgrade to Windows XP has been completed. Some installation programs will detect that the operating system is inappropriate for new device drivers and will refuse to install them. Other installation programs will go ahead anyway, regardless of the consequences.

If the new drivers are installed in the existing version of Windows, it is virtually certain that the relevant hardware will cease to work properly. It is also quite possible that the existing Windows installation will be damaged to the point where it fails to boot correctly. Never try to upgrade any Windows installation that has a serious fault. The upgrade program might detect the problem and refuse to continue. If an upgrade on a faulty Windows installation is allowed to go ahead, the most likely outcome is that things will come to an abrupt halt somewhere during the upgrade. It can then be very difficult indeed to sort things out. In most cases the hard disc has to be reformatted so that Windows can be installed from scratch. This process is described in a later chapter, and it is not something that should be taken lightly.

Integrated hardware

These days a fair percentage of the device drivers used by PCs are for hardware on the motherboard rather than hardware provided by expansion cards. In fact, the majority of the drivers are often for hardware on the main board. These days the sound system is usually built into the motherboard, and so is the graphics system with many business oriented PCs. There can be other integral hardware such as network adapters and modems. Even if a PC lacks any built-in hardware of these types, there will still be ports and other hardware that requires device drivers. In addition to the serial and parallel ports, a modern PC has integral USB, hard disc, and floppy disc interfaces. These all require device drivers in order to work properly.

The ports are unlikely to be troublesome when upgrading, since the Windows XP upgrade program will recognise the popular chipsets and load the appropriate device drivers. Problems are only likely to occur if the motherboard is very recent or very old. If the motherboard hardware is not recognised and the board is several years old, it is likely that the PC is unsuitable for use with Windows XP. With a nearly new PC it is a matter of contacting the PC manufacturer's support centre. They should be able to supply the necessary device drivers or give a source for them.

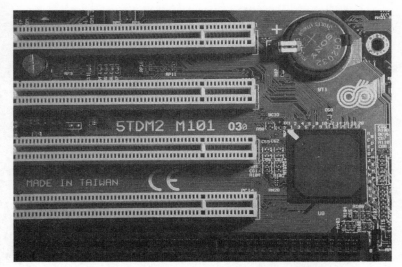

Fig.1.12 Finding the maker's name and the type number for the motherboard is not alway straightforward

The PC manufacturer's support centre should also be able to help with device drivers for integrated hardware such as sound systems and graphics adapters. Again, with an older PC there might be a lack of Windows XP support for the motherboard's hardware, and the upgrade is not a practical proposition unless the necessary drivers can be found. If the PC manufacturer's support centre can not help, or the company has disappeared, it is worth removing the outer casing and looking at the motherboard.

With luck, the name of the manufacturer and the model number for the board will be shown somewhere on the board. Unfortunately, the labels can sometimes be rather cryptic, and there are often spurious labels mixed in with the important ones. The board shown in Figure 1.12 is a Chaintech 5TDM2. In this example the manufacturer's name is not included on the board, but their logo can be seen near the top right-hand corner of the photograph.

Provided you can identify the motherboard, it should be possible to find the latest device drivers on the manufacturer's web site. Failing that, it might be possible to identify the main support chip or chips on the motherboard. Unfortunately, on some boards one of the support chips is covered by a metal heatsink that obscures the manufacturer's name and type number. Provided the support chip or chips can be identified, the relevant web site can be searched for device drivers.

Awkward devices

Most ports, whether on the motherboard or provided by expansion cards, will be recognised by the Windows XP upgrade program and will not give any problems. There are a few exceptions though, and the main ones are serial and parallel port cards that fit into PCI expansion slots. The parallel and serial ports on the motherboard are standard types that fit into the input/output map of the processor in the usual way. The same is true of serial and parallel ports that are provided using ISA expansion cards. The situation is different with ports provided by PCI expansion cards. A PCI slot is really a form of input/output port, and a device that uses one of these slots can not interface direct onto the processor's buses. A serial or parallel port that is provided by a PCI expansion card is therefore non-standard, and can not be installed using the normal drivers.

This problem is overcome using the special drivers provided with the expansion card. This integrates the port into the operating system so that it operates normally, provided the applications programs access the port via the operating system. Some programs try to obtain faster operation by addressing the port directly, but software of this type will not necessarily work with a port provided by a PCI expansion card. It will only work if the card is supplied with re-mapping software that is installed and activated. This software intercepts instructions that try to directly access the hardware, and replaces them with instructions that access the port correctly via the PCI hardware.

A PCI port card should work properly with Windows XP provided the correct device drivers are installed. However, Windows XP, like Windows NT and 2000, does not permit the ports to be accessed directly. Consequently, any re-mapping software should not be used with Windows XP. With modems, mice, and most serial port devices there is normally no need for direct access to the ports. The situation is different with parallel ports, where external disc drives and scanners often utilise direct port accesses in order to maximise the speed of data transfers. Most peripherals of this type are compatible with Windows NT/2000/XP, but will probably have to be reinstalled if you upgrade from Windows 9x to XP. The lack of direct access to the ports might give slightly slower operation with Windows XP. There should be no problems with USB peripherals.

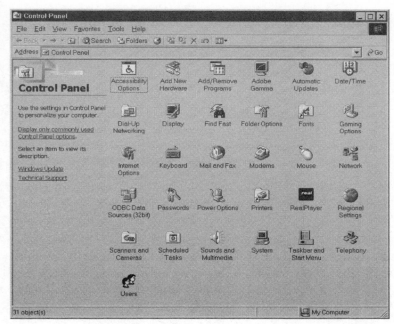

Fig.1.13 The Windows Control Panel with a typical selection of icons

Uninstalling hardware

In general, there is no need to remove any hardware or device drivers before upgrading to Windows XP. It is better to complete the upgrade first and then install the new device drivers. Installing new drivers effectively removes the old ones, which should not adversely affect the new installation. It is not strictly necessary to remove any hardware that is not supported by Windows XP, and will not be used once the PC has been upgraded. However, there is little point in leaving an expansion card in place if it will not be use any more, and uninstalling it ensures that it can not hinder the upgrade. It also makes sure that the card does not use any of the computer's resources.

It is advisable to uninstall the device drivers before physically removing an expansion card. First, go to the Windows Control Panel by selecting Settings from the Start menu, followed by the Control Panel option on the submenu that appears. This produces a window like the one of

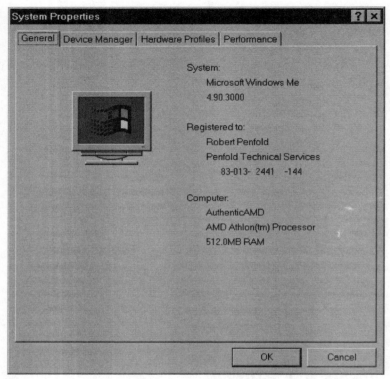

Fig.1.14 The General section of the System Properties window

Figure 1.13. If necessary, scroll the window downward to reveal the System icon, and then double-click this icon. Note that the entries in Control Panel vary somewhat from one PC to another, but the System icon should always be present.

Double-clicking the System icon produces a new window like the one of Figure 1.14. This is the System Properties window, and it defaults to the General section that gives some basic information about the PC. In this case it is Device Manager that is required (Figure 1.15), and it is selected by left-clicking the appropriate tab at the top of the window. The Device Manager window lists the various hardware categories that cover most of the PC's internal hardware, and it will probably include some external peripheral devices. One of these categories should contain the hardware

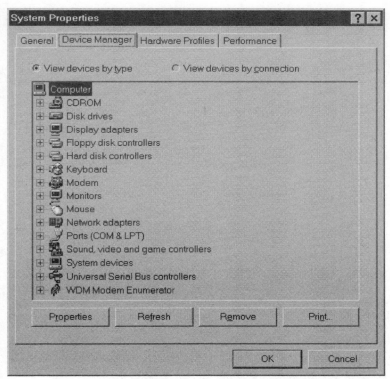

Fig.1.15 Device Manager has sections for most of the PC's hardware

you wish to uninstall, and double clicking the appropriate icon will expand that category to show the individual items it contains. In the example of Figure 1.16 the modem entry has been expanded, and it contains just one item.

In order to uninstall an item of hardware, left-click its entry to highlight it and then operate the Remove button near the bottom of the window. This produces a warning message like the one of Figure 1.17. Left-click the OK button to proceed and remove the drivers for the selected piece of hardware. The appropriate entry in Device Manager should then disappear. If the uninstalled hardware was the only device in its category, the entry for that category will also be removed (Figure 1.18). Note that it is not possible to select and then remove a category. The entry for a

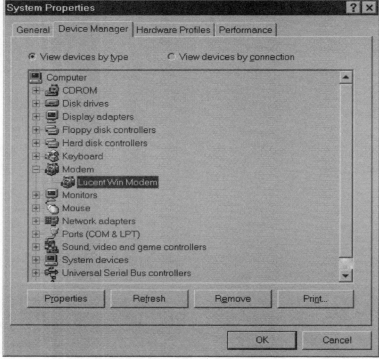

Fig.1.16 Entries in Device Manager can be expanded

category can only be removed by individually uninstalling each piece of hardware it contains.

Note that some pieces of hardware perform more than one function and therefore have multiple entries in Device Manager. An audio card for example, usually provides a MIDI interface and a game port in addition to various audio functions. Consequently, a typical audio card has three or four device drivers listed in Device Manager. I have encountered some that had five or six device drivers listed in Device Manager. All the relevant drivers should be removed when uninstalling any multifunction devices.

Uninstalling in XP

If you do not uninstall incompatible hardware before upgrading to Windows XP, but subsequently feel it would be better to remove it, essentially the same method is used to uninstall the device drivers in Windows XP. However, Windows XP is a classic case of things being "the same but different". The Control Panel can be accessed direct from the Start menu

Fig.1.17 Removing a Device Manager entry

(Figure 1.19). The Windows XP version of the Control Panel is not identical to the Windows 9x version, but it is very similar (Figure 1.20).

If no icons are shown in the right-hand pane, left-click on the Switch to Classic View link in the left-hand section of the window. The usual icons should then appear, including the System icon. Double clicking this icon produces the window of Figure 1.21. The initial window shows some basic information about the computer and the Windows installation. There are several tabs that provide access to various aspects of the system, and the Control Panel is accessed via the Hardware tab. This produces the window of Figure 1.22, and operating the Device Manager button finally brings up the window of Figure 1.23.

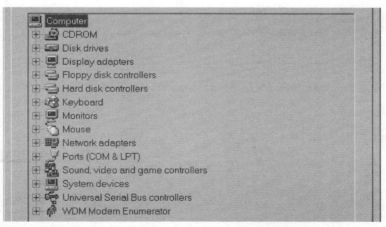

Fig.1.18 Empty categories are automatically removed from Device Manager

Fig.1.19 Launching the Control Panel

This is a minimalist version of Device Manager, but it still permits unwanted hardware to be uninstalled. Like the Windows 9x version, double clicking on an entry expands it to show the individual pieces of hardware in that category. Right clicking on the entry for a piece of hardware produces a menu (Figure 1.24), and one of these enables the device drivers to be uninstalled. There is

Fig.1.20 The Control Panel using the Classic View

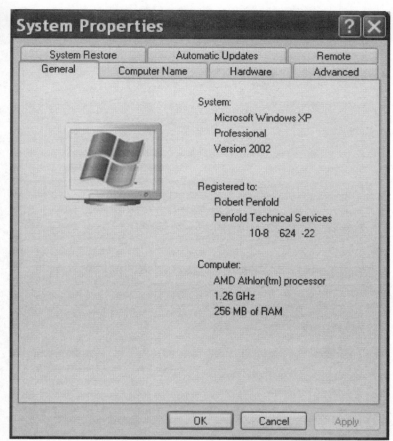

Fig.1.21 The General section of the System Properties window

also the option of disabling the device if you would like Windows to ignore it, but you do not wish to physically remove the hardware from the PC.

Physically uninstalling

With the device drivers uninstalled, it is likely that the computer will try to reinstall the hardware the next time it is booted into Windows unless the hardware is removed from the PC. Shut down Windows and switch off

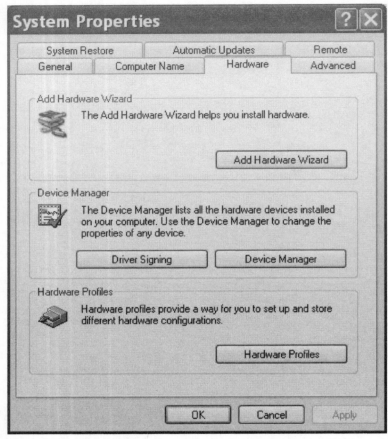

Fig.1.22 The Hardware section of the System Properties window

the computer at the mains supply before doing any work on the computer. In order to remove an expansion card the outer casing (top and two sides) of an AT style case must be removed. With an ATX case, it is only necessary to remove the left-hand side panel. If the serial, parallel, and USB ports are grouped together, possibly with audio and LAN ports as well, the case is an ATX type. The case is an AT type if the ports are liberally scattered over its rear panel. With most AT cases the outer casing is removed by first undoing a few bolts at the rear of the unit, and

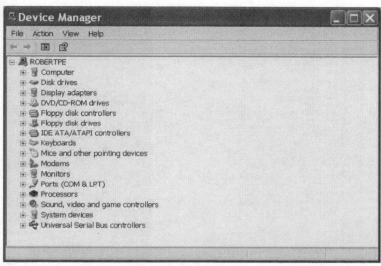

Fig.1.23 Windows XP has a minimalist looking version of Device
        Manager, but the main functions are all present

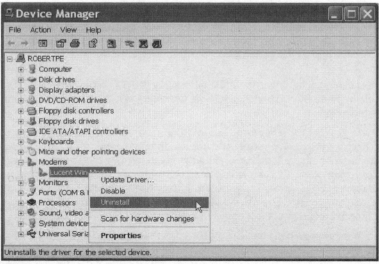

Fig.1.24 Uninstalling a device driver

*Fig.1.25 An expansion card has a metal bracket that is bolted to the
rear of the chassis*

then sliding it backwards until it is free. With ATX cases each panel is
held in place by two or three screws, which are again situated at the rear
of the unit.

There are usually other fixing screws at the rear of a PC, holding in place
things like the power supply and subassemblies of the case. Look at the
way everything fits together and be careful to remove the correct screws.
Note that some PCs have fancy cases that can be difficult to open.
However, if you study the problem for a while it should be possible to
"crack" the case. The PC's instruction should give some guidance on
gaining access to the interior of the case.

Each expansion card has a metal bracket that is bolted to the rear of the
PC's chassis (Figure 1.25). With this bolt removed it not usually too
difficult to pull the card free of its expansion slot, but it can require a fair

amount of force to remove a card that has been in place for some time. Pull steadily on the card using no more force than is absolutely necessary to pull it free. Do not use brute force if the card is difficult to remove. A rocking action will usually loosen an awkward card so that it can be pulled free without having to use excessive force. If your PC was supplied with some spare blanking plates, one of these is bolted in the position formerly occupied by the mounting bracket of the expansion card. Some of these plates clip in place and do not require the mounting bolt. These are easy to spot, because the top section is not flat, but instead has a curved section that is used to clip it in place.

With the card removed and the blanking plate in position, fit the outer casing and boot the computer into Windows. Once Windows has loaded, go to Device Manager and check that the entry for the deleted device driver has not reappeared. If necessary, remove the device driver's entry again, reboot Windows, and then look for the entry once more. You have probably deleted the wrong device driver if it keeps reappearing! The hardware for the driver is still present in the PC, so the Plug and Play system reinstalls the driver each time the computer is booted into Windows. With the hardware removed from the computer, the entry for the correct driver should be easy to spot. It will probably marked with a yellow exclamation mark.

Software problems

There can be problems with software compatibility for a number of reasons. Some software directly controls parts of the computer's hardware rather than going via the operating system. This can give faster operation, but directly accessing the hardware is not permitted under Windows XP, or Windows NT and 2000 come to that. These operating systems are designed to be more stable than Windows 9x, and but this stability is obtained by placing restrictions on the software. Permitting the applications programs to have a free for all with the hardware gives the potential for problems with two programs trying to simultaneously use the same piece of hardware. With the ports, etc., only accessed via the operating system, Windows can ensure that only one applications program uses each piece of hardware at any one time.

Some software is supplied in two versions. The installation program installs one version if Windows 9x is detected on the hard disc, or an alternative version if Windows NT/2000/XP is detected. Software of this type should be usable when upgrading from Windows 9x to Windows XP, but it has to be uninstalled and then reinstalled. This removes the inappropriate version and replaces it with the correct one for Windows XP. The program should then work much as before, but any customisation will almost certainly be lost during the changeover.

Another cause of problems is that some software is only available in Windows 9x compatible form. This is a more serious problem because any software of this type is fundamentally incompatible with Windows XP. This does not necessarily mean that you will be unable to use the software if you go ahead with the upgrade. Windows XP has various compatibility modes that permit most Windows 9x software to be run successfully. Unfortunately, there is no "cast-iron" guarantee that one of the compatibility modes will render the software usable, although this feature is almost invariably successful. Using the compatibility modes is covered later in this chapter. It is probably worth checking with the manufacturer of incompatible software to see if an upgrade to a Windows XP version is available. Using proper Windows XP applications software is better than having to resort to a compatibility mode.

Software for use with CD-RW drives is a common cause of problems when upgrading. With Windows 9x it is necessary to have a program like Direct CD or In CD in order to use a CD-RW disc like a high capacity floppy disc. Windows XP has software of this type built-in, so any existing CD-RW software often has to be removed in order to avoid conflicts. An upgrade to a Windows XP version of the software might be available, or you can just settle for using the built-in facilities.

Uninstalling software

With Windows it is essential to uninstall software properly, rather than simply obliterating any folders that contain the files for the program that you wish to remove. Deleting folders that contain programs and support files is a good way to make Windows unstable, and can even prevent it from booting properly. Virtually all Windows programs are supplied with an uninstaller or they can be uninstalled using the built-in facilities of Windows. The only exceptions are old programs that were written for

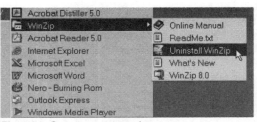

Fig.1.26 Some programs have an uninstall utility

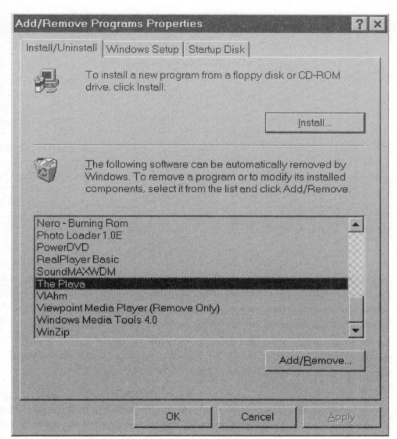

Fig.1.27 Using built-in uninstaller of Windows

Windows 3.1. There are utility programs available that can help with the removal of this type of software. If an old Windows program is not doing any harm, the safest option is to leave it in place and ignore it. If reinstallation is needed, try reinstalling the program without removing the original installation first. In most cases this will get the program working properly again.

Where a program has its own uninstaller, it will be listed in the appropriate section of the Program menu. Figure 1.26 shows the entry for the popular WinZip program, and this includes an option to uninstall the program.

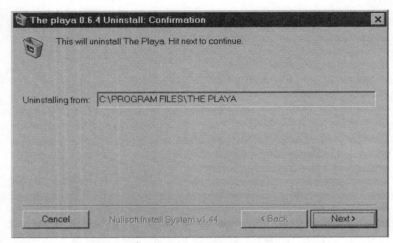

Fig.1.28 Check that you are about to uninstall the right program

The way in which the software is removed using an uninstaller varies from one program to another, but the process is largely automated. In most cases the user has to do nothing more than confirm that they wish to uninstall the program.

Most programs are removed using the built-in facilities of Windows. To remove software via this route, go to the Windows Control Panel and double-click the icon labelled Add/Remove Programs. This produces the appropriate properties window (Figure 1.27), where the program you wish to remove should be listed. Left-click on its entry to select it, and then operate the Add/Remove button. The removal process is customised to suit the particular program being uninstalled, so there is some variation from one program to another.

In this example things are very straightforward, and operating the Add/ Remove button brings up the window of Figure 1.28. This shows the folder containing the program that is about to be deleted, and it provides an opportunity to check that the right program will be uninstalled if you operate the OK button to proceed with the process. If you do opt to proceed, there will be a screen that shows how things are progressing, and this should eventually indicate that the program has been successfully uninstalled (Figure 1.29).

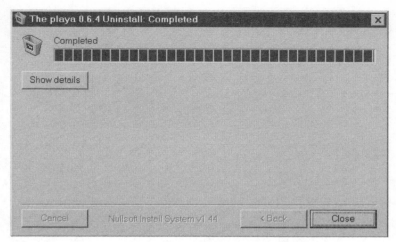

Fig.1.29 The program has been successfully uninstalled

Uninstalling in XP

As pointed out previously, where there is likely to be a problem with a program it is generally better to remove it prior to the upgrade to Windows XP. However, if you should forget to do so, there should be no major problem. The program can be uninstalled from within Windows XP. It is only fair to point out that difficulties can occur with programs that were not listed as potentially problematic by the upgrade advisor program. Due to something going slightly awry during the upgrade process, rather than any compatibility issues, problems can occur with any applications programs after an upgrade. Everything went perfectly on the first PC that I upgraded to Windows XP, apart from Word 97 refusing to run. Fortunately, the upgrade program manages to minimise these problems, and you may well escape them.

If you need to remove a program from Windows XP, either permanently or so that it can be reinstalled from scratch, the process is much the same as under Windows 9x. The route to Window's own uninstaller is slightly different though. Select Control Panel from the Start menu and then double-click on the Add/Remove Programs icon when the Windows Control Panel appears. This produces a window like the one shown in Figure 1.30. Left-click on the entry for the program that you wish to

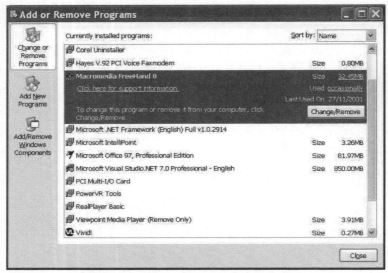

Fig.1.30 The Windows XP version of the uninstall facility

remove. The entry will expand to show some basic information about the program, and the expanded entry will contain a Change/Remove button.

Operating this button produces the warning message of Figure 1.31. Operate the OK button to go ahead and uninstall the program. As in Windows 9x, a new window will appear, showing how things are progressing (Figure 1.32). Eventually, a message should appear, indicating that the program has been uninstalled successfully (Figure 1.33). The uninstaller is slightly different for each program, but things normally follow the steps outlined here. Some programs have a more

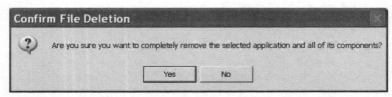

Fig.1.31 Operate the Yes button to go ahead and remove the program

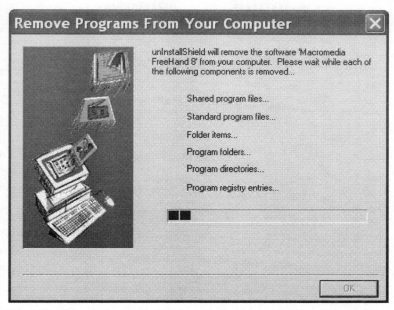

Fig.1.32 This window indicates how far the removal has progressed

complex installer/uninstaller program that permits the program to be deleted or altered in some way. Where appropriate, the Remove option must be selected once into the Setup program.

Sometimes a warning message appears while the program is being uninstalled. This usually explains that a shared file is no longer needed by other programs, and you are asked if you wish to delete it. The file in question is usually a dynamic link library (DLL) type. The safer option is to operate the No button, and leave the file on the disc just in case it is actually needed by another program. In the early days of Windows 95 it did not matter whether you operated the Yes or the No button. Problems would ensue either way! Matters have improved since then, and there should be no risk of problems if the No option is selected. In fact the Yes option is reasonably safe these days, but I would still recommend the cautious approach for those who are something less than Windows experts. If in doubt, always select the No option with this type of thing.

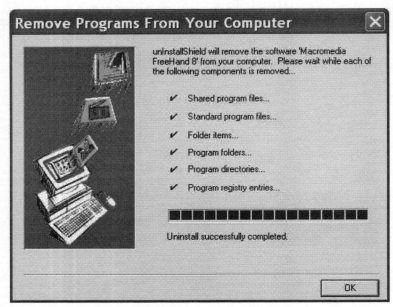

Fig.1.33 The program has been successfully uninstalled

Registering

It is important for Windows XP users to realise that, unlike previous versions of Windows, registering the program is not optional. Strictly speaking, it is not necessary to register Windows XP in order to go on using it indefinitely. It is the Windows Product Activation (WPA) that is essential, but this is normally done as part of the registration process. In

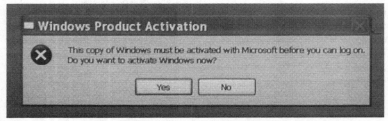

Fig.1.34 Operate the Yes button to go ahead with activation

effect, the Windows XP CD-ROM contains a fully working 30-day trial version of the operating system. If you ignore the onscreen warning messages and do not go through the WPA/registration process, the operating system will refuse to boot properly.

All is not lost if you reach this stage,

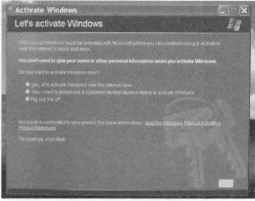

Fig.1.35 Activation can be via the Internet or by telephone

because it is still possible to go through the WPA/registration process and get the operating system working again. When you try to boot into Windows a message like the one shown in Figure 1.34 appears. In order to go on using the operating system it is necessary to operate the Yes button and proceed with the WPA process. Note that you can not log on to Windows by selecting the No option. You can only log off and shut down the computer if this button is operated.

Having opted to go ahead with the activation procedure, the window of Figure 1.35 appears. This gives the option of registering by telephone, over the Internet, or halting the activation process and logging off. It is definitely a good idea to use the Internet option if the PC is suitably equipped, since this is much quicker and easier than verbally exchanging multi-digit product keys and activation numbers over the telephone. It virtually guarantees that the process will be free of errors and will work first time. The Internet method is the only one that we will consider here, but the program provides full instructions if you have to use the telephone route to activation.

After selecting the required option, operate the Next button to move the process on to the next window (Figure 1.36). This gives the choice of activating the program, or activating and registering it at the same time. The obvious choice is to activate the program and also register it while you are at it. If this option is selected, at the next screen the usual registration details are entered (Figure 1.37). Moving on to the next screen (Figure 1.38), your country is selected from the pop-down menu and

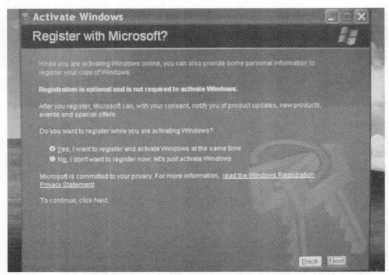

Fig.1.36 You can register at the same time as activating Windows XP

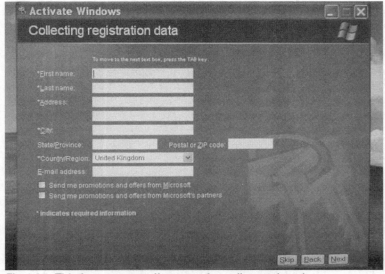

Fig.1.37 This form appears if you opt for online registration

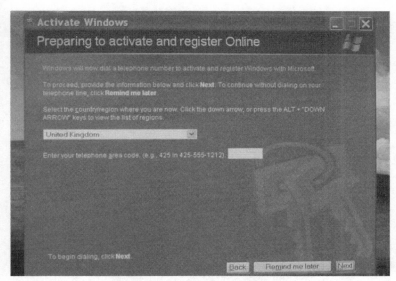

Fig.1.38 Select your country from the pop-down menu

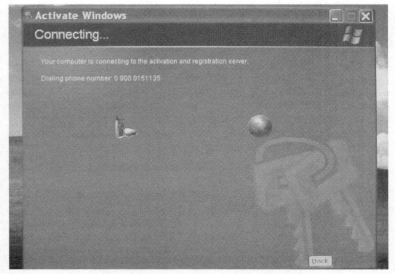

Fig.1.39 The registration/WPA process is then automatic

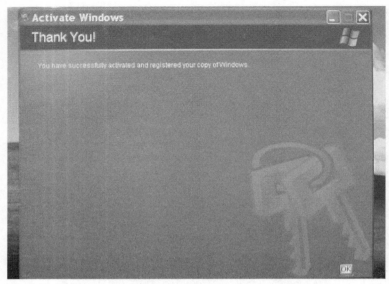

Fig.1.40 This screen will appear if the process is successful

your telephone area code is entered in the textbox. Operating the Next button brings up the window of Figure 1.39, and the program dials the server. The activation and registration processes are fully automated, and after a minute or two the screen of Figure 1.40 should appear, indicating that both processes have been completed successfully. After operating the OK button to close this window, the PC is ready for you to log on to Windows.

Anti-piracy

Windows Product Activation is a new feature of Windows XP, and to say the least, this feature is bit controversial. The idea is to prevent casual piracy of the XP operating system. However, like most anti-piracy systems, it does not make life any easier for legitimate users of the product. It can make life very much more difficult for legitimate users, although it will not necessarily do so. As pointed out previously, the program on the disc when you buy Windows XP is effectively just a 30-day demonstration version. Entering the product identification number during installation was sufficient to get earlier versions of Windows fully working, but with Windows XP it is only the first step in the activation process. You are locked out of the system if you do not activate Windows within 30 days of installing it, so you have to activate Windows or keep installing it from scratch!

Where possible, it is definitely advisable to opt for automatic activation via the Internet. The telephone alternative requires you to read a 50-digit code to a Microsoft representative. This code appears onscreen during the activation process. This is bad enough, but you then have to enter a 42-digit code supplied by the representative. This is clearly an awkward and time-consuming way of doing things, and there is plenty of scope for errors to occur. By contrast, activation over the Internet is quick and there is virtually no chance of errors occurring.

WPA problems

Having to go through the WPA process should be no more than a minor inconvenience, and it is not the necessity for activation that is the main "bone of contention". The activation key is derived from your Windows product identification number and the hardware installed in the PC. To be more precise, it is these items of hardware that are used to produce the number:

Microprocessor type

Microprocessor serial number

Display adapter

SCSI adapter (if fitted)

IDE adapter

Network adapter (if fitted)

RAM amount

Hard drive

Hard drive volume serial number

CD drives

When Windows XP is booted, as part of the boot-up process the installed hardware is checked. The boot process is only completed if the installed hardware matches the full product key that is stored on the hard disc drive during the activation process. On the face of it, two computers having identical hardware could use the same activation key. In practice, this is not possible because the network adapter and processor serial numbers are unique. Two seemingly identical PCs would actually need different activation keys due to the processors and (where appropriate) the network card having different serial numbers.

Hardware changes

There is a potential problem, in that any changes to the hardware will cause a mismatch during the checking process at boot-up. This problem is not as great as it might seem, because you are allowed a certain amount of leeway. Up to four of the items of hardware listed previously can be altered without the need to reactivate the operating system. If more than four items are changed, the activation mechanism will probably assume that the system has been copied to another computer, and it will halt the boot process.

This does not mean that you will have to buy Windows XP again. It will be necessary to call the WPA clearinghouse though, in order to obtain a new activation key. Frequent changes to the computer's hardware and calls to the WPA centre would presumably result in Microsoft refusing to provide further activation codes. You are permitted four changes to the hardware in 120 days or less. This suggests that you can make as many changes to the hardware as you like provided they are made slowly so that there are no more than four changes in each 120 day period. I have not tested this in practice though.

There is little likelihood of problems unless you undertake a massive hardware upgrade. A call to the WPA centre should then get things working again. However, it is best not to be too eager to activate a newly installed copy of Windows XP. This is especially important when upgrading from an earlier version of Windows, if you are unsure about the compatibility of some pieces of hardware. You are given the opportunity to go through the activation process once the upgrade has been completed, but it is best not to do so at this stage.

First, load any new drivers that are required, and try out the new system. If necessary, upgrade some of the hardware, and only go through the activation process when everything is working properly. You have 30 days to get everything working properly, which should be more than ample. It is not necessary to wait for the 30 days to expire before activating Windows XP. The activation process can be started at any time by going to the Start menu, selecting All Programs, followed by Accessories, System Tools, and Activate Windows.

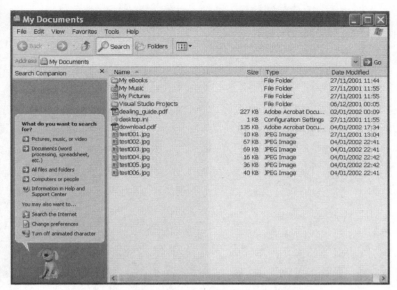

Fig.1.41 The Windows XP version of Windows Explorer

WPA file

Computer hardware is not infallible, and it is possible that it will be necessary to reinstall Windows XP at some point during the computer's operating life. Some PC users reinstall Windows from time to time as a means of clearing out the defunct files that tend to accumulate on the hard disc, and to keep the system working efficiently. There is no limit to the number of times that Windows XP can be reinstalled on the same PC, but reactivation is necessary each time Windows is reinstalled.

There is an alternative to reactivation, and the first step is to make a backup copy of a certain file before deleting the old installation. After Windows XP has been reinstalled, the backup copy of the file is copied to the hard disc. The file in question is called wpa.dbl, and it will normally be placed in the C:\Windows\System32 folder. If it proves to be elusive, track it down using the Search facility of Windows Explorer. Run Windows Explorer and then operate the Search button in the upper part of the window. The screen should then look something like Figure 1.41.

In the left-hand section of the window there is an animated character called Rover, and this is Windows XP's answer to the infamous animated

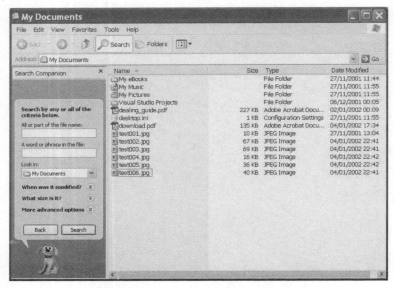

Fig.1.42 Using the Windows Explorer Search facility

paperclip of Word For Windows. Left-click on the All Files and Folders button to bring up the form that enables the search criteria to be defined (Figure 1.42). Type the name of the file (wpa.dbl) into the textbox at the top of the form, and select drive C: using the menu near the middle of the form. Operate the Search button, and after scanning the hard disc the program should produce an entry for the file in the right-hand section of the window (Figure 1.43). The size of the file is only about 10 to 15 kilobytes, so it can be copied to a floppy disc using the Copy and Paste facilities. It can be restored using the same method once Windows XP has been reinstalled.

There is no guarantee that this will always work, but it is merely necessary to go through the activation process if it fails. In the event that the restored wpa.dbl file is not accepted by the system, next time you log on there will be the choice of going through the activation process or logging off again. If you elect to log off it will be possible to log on to the system at the next attempt, but you will then have the usual 30 days before the system times out and locks you out of the system.

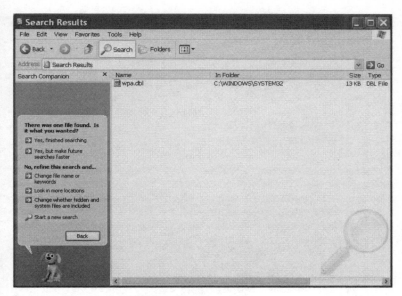

Fig.1.43 The required file has been located

Bundled Windows XP

Product activation is always required when using a retail version of Windows XP. In other words, activation is always needed if you buy a boxed version of Windows XP from a computer shop, rather than getting it bundled with a PC. It makes no difference whether you use the full version or the upgrade, the activation rules are the same. The situation is different with some versions of Windows XP that are supplied with a PC. Rather than using product activation, the program is licensed for use with one PC. That PC is the one with which the operating system was supplied. This system usually works by having the program read the serial number of the BIOS chip in the PC. The operating system will fail to work unless the correct serial number is found, making it unusable on any other PC. PCs covered by volume licences do not usually require product activation either.

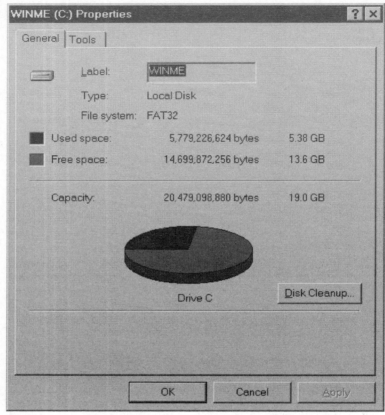

Fig.1.44 The properties of a hard disc viewed in Windows ME

NTFS or FAT32

Windows in general uses three file systems for hard disc drives. These are FAT, FAT32, and NTFS. Windows XP can use all three systems, and after upgrading to XP the file system will the same as the one originally used for the disc. Some users make the assumption that Windows XP will automatically convert the hard disc to NTFS operation as a standard part of the upgrade process, but this is definitely not the case. The conversion might be offered as part of the upgrade process, but it is not essential to make the change at that stage. The conversion to NTFS can be carried out once the upgrade has been completed. NTFS is the file system that Microsoft recommends for use with Windows XP.

FAT is the original disc format used for Windows, but it does not handle large discs efficiently. The minimum size for a sector of the disc is 32 kilobytes, and each sector can only be allocated to one file. This means that 32 kilobytes of hard disc space is used even if a file

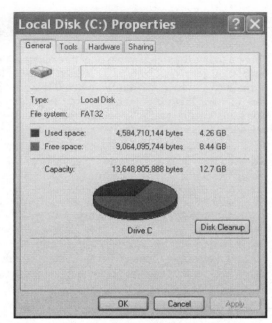

Fig.1.45 Viewing the properties of a disc in Windows XP

containing a few bytes of data is stored on the disc. Also, the final part of each file will occupy 32 kilobytes of the disc, even there are only a few bytes remaining in this section. This means that on average 16K of space is wasted for every file on the disc, and the wastage is even higher for small files. Experience suggests that about 20K per file is wasted in practice. FAT32 permits smaller sectors to be used so that the wastage is greatly reduced, and it has a few other refinements.

A computer that is suitable for upgrading to Windows XP will almost certainly use FAT32. If in doubt about the file system of your PC, it is easy to find out which one is in use. Locate drive C: using Windows Explorer, right-click on its entry, and then choose Properties from the pop-down menu that appears. In Windows 98 or ME this will produce something like Figure 1.44, which includes various information about the disc including the file system. The same method works if you have already made the upgrade to Windows XP (Figure 1.45).

Although Windows XP works well with the FAT32 format, there are some advantages in using the NTFS file system. There is also one circumstance in which converting the hard disc to the NTFS system is not advisable. There can be difficulties with a dual boot system that enables the PC to be booted into Windows 9x or XP. Windows 9x operating systems (including Windows ME) are incompatible with NTFS formatted discs, and they are therefore unable to read any files from them. For most users this incompatibility is not acceptable, as it can make it difficult to use some files with both operating systems.

Apart from these dual boot systems, it is better to use the NTFS file system. This enables access to files and folders to be restricted using the permissions feature. Additionally, files can be encrypted if you are using Windows XP Professional. With the FAT and FAT32 file systems it is possible for anyone to access your files if they have possession of the disc drive. NTFS is more reliable than FAT or FAT32, due to its use of log files to monitor disc activity. This gives a much better chance of the system being able to automatically recover from hard disc problems. Another advantage of the NTFS file system is that disc drives having a capacity of more than 8 gigabytes are handled more efficiently.

Converting

The standard upgrade installation of Windows XP includes a conversion program that will convert FAT or FAT32 hard discs to NTFS operation. However, this is a command line program and not a normal Windows application. It can be run by first selecting the Run option from the Start menu. Then type this line into the textbox in the new Window that appears (Figure 1.46), making sure that it is exactly as shown here:

convert c: /fs:ntfs

It is assumed here that the disc to be converted is drive C:, and the drive letter given in this command must be changed if you wish to convert a different disc. The second part of the command indicates the file system that you wish to use for the disc, which is obvious NTFS in this example. Operate the OK button to run the program, which will result in a DOS box opening and a message like the one shown in Figure 1.47 appearing. The first part of the message simply indicates the current file system used on the disc, which should be FAT or (more probably) FAT32. The second part points out that the program can not run at this stage because the disc for conversion is currently in use.

This message might
not appear if you
are converting
something other than
the boot drive, and
the conversion
process with then go
ahead instead. If you
are trying to convert
the boot disc, it will
inevitably be used by
Windows and
probably numerous

Fig.1.46 *Running the conversion program*

background tasks as well. You are given the opportunity to dismount
the disc, but this option should not be taken. The only way to successfully
use the conversion program on the boot disc is to have it run automatically
at start-up. Presumably, the conversion program runs before Windows
fully installs and the boot disc is properly utilised by Windows.

Programs are run automatically using the often-overlooked Scheduled
Tasks facility. It is not difficult to set up this feature for yourself, and the
first task is to go to the Control Panel and double-click the Scheduled
Tasks icon. This brings up a window like the one of Figure 1.48, and
here the Add Scheduled Task icon is double-clicked. An information
window like the one of Figure 1.49 then appears, and operating the Next
button then moves things on to the window where the required program

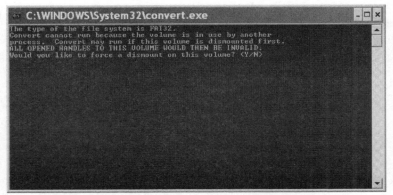

Fig.1.47 *The conversion program is a command line utility*

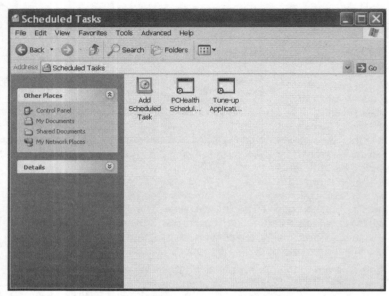

Fig.1.48 Windows XP includes a scheduled task facility

is selected (Figure 1.50). The program can be selected from the list or the program file can be selected using the standard browse feature. Having selected the appropriate program, operate the Next button to move on to the window where the schedule is selected (Figure 1.51). There are several options available via the radio buttons, including one that runs the program when the computer starts.

Fig.1.49 The first step in scheduling a task

In this case it is probably best not to set things up manually, because the switches required by the program complicate matters. Also, Windows will arrange the scheduling for you if you try to run the program and answer "N" when asked if you would like to dismount the disc. Further information appears in the DOS box (Figure 1.52). This explains that the Convert program can not gain exclusive access to the disc,

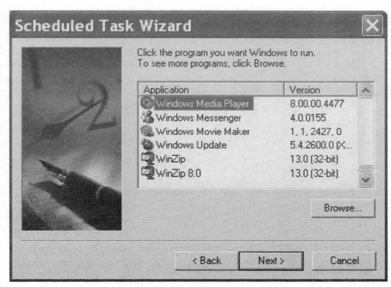

Fig.1.50 Selecting the program to be scheduled

and it asks if you wish to run the program automatically next time the computer is started. Answer "Y" to this question and then restart the computer.

During the boot-up process a screen like the one of Figure 1.53 will appear, explaining that the conversion program is about to run. You have 10 seconds to press any key and abort the process. Assuming that the program is allowed to run, it will start by checking the disc and reporting its results (Figure 1.54).

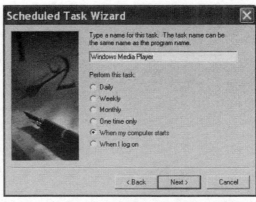

Fig.1.51 Selecting the schedule for the program

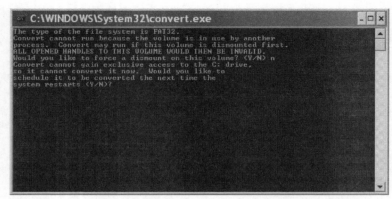

Fig.1.52 The conversion program can be scheduled automatically

If all is well, the conversion process will go ahead and eventually the program will report that its task has been completed successfully (Figure 1.55). At this stage the example system crashed and produced a standard

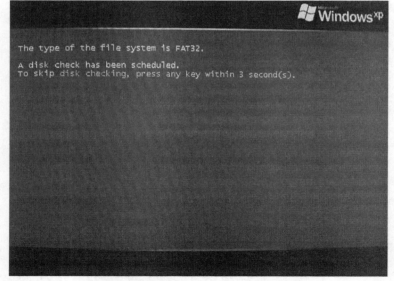

Fig.1.53 The program runs when the computer is restarted

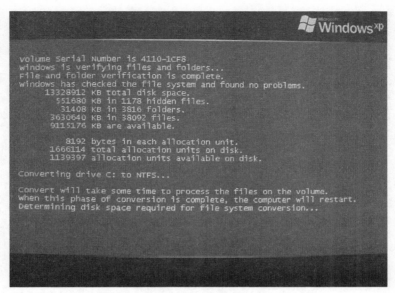

Fig.1.54 The program starts by checking the disc

error screen. However, Windows XP is very robust, and rebooting the computer resulted in it starting up correctly. After some frantic disc activity the process was complete and the disc was fully operational under the NTFS file system. It is as well to check that the conversion has been successful by bringing up the properties window for the disc. This should show that it uses the NTFS file system, as in Figure 1.56.

Fig.1.55 The conversion has been completed successfully

Some programs use files that are cleverly hidden away on the disc in order to store passwords. Using an image of a hard disc or changing its basic structure in some way will usually result in the disappearance of any passwords stored away in hidden files. Changing from one file

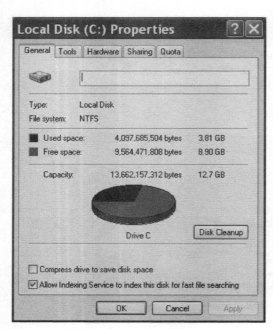

Fig.1.56 The disc is now an NTFS type

system to another is almost certain to result in the disappearance of any concealed passwords, or any other concealed files. For example, if you have an AOL password stored on the disc, changing to the NTFS file system will result in its disappearance. Any loss of stored passwords should not cause any major problems. You will merely have to store them on the disc again in order to resume instant access to the protected files and programs.

Uninstalling XP

It has to be pointed out that having converted the boot disc to the NTFS file system it becomes impossible to uninstall Windows XP and revert to your original operating system and set-up. In all probability you will not need to return things to their pre-Windows XP state, but it is probably best to get the new operating system installed and working well before making the conversion. It should only be necessary to return to the previous operating system if too much of the hardware and (or) software proves to be incompatible with Windows XP, or something vital refuses to work under the new operating system.

Returning to the old operating system is quite straightforward, and the first task is to go to the Control Panel and double-click the Add/Remove Programs icon. An entry for uninstalling Windows XP should appear near the bottom of the program list in the new window that appears (Figure 1.57). Operating the Change/Remove button produces the small

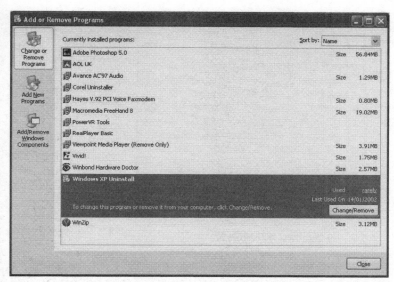

Fig.1.57 Select the Uninstall entry for Windows XP

window of Figure 1.58, where the radio buttons offer two options. In this case it is clearly the Uninstall Windows XP button that should be operated, followed by the Continue button.

If any major changes have been made since the upgrade, a warning window like the one of Figure 1.59 will appear. Any software that has been uninstalled will reappear when the old operating system is restored. Similarly, any software installed since the upgrade will disappear after the change back to the original operating system. In this example a program has been uninstalled, and it will have to be uninstalled again after the old operating system has been restored. There is also a warning

that the changes could produce error messages after Windows XP has been uninstalled, but only if the changes affect any start-up files. Operate the Continue button if you wish to go ahead

Fig.1.58 Choose the Uninstall option here

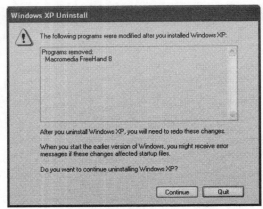

and uninstall Windows XP. This produces the warning message of Figure 1.60, where the Yes button is left-clicked in order to proceed. The old operating system and set-up should be restored after a great deal of hard disc activity and one or two reboots.

Fig.1.59   Major changes will be undone by uninstalling Windows XP

The uninstall facility can be removed if

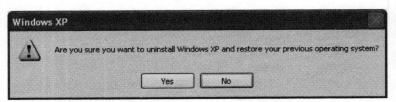

Fig.1.60   Operate the Yes button to uninstall Windows XP

there is no possibility of you wishing to return to the old operating system. Use the lower button at the window of Figure 1.58 in order to remove the backup files for the old operating system. Operating the Continue button produces the warning message of Figure 1.61, and the backup files will be removed if the Yes button is operated. The program then returns to

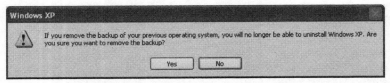

Fig.1.61   Operate the Yes button if you are sure you wish to remove the backup files

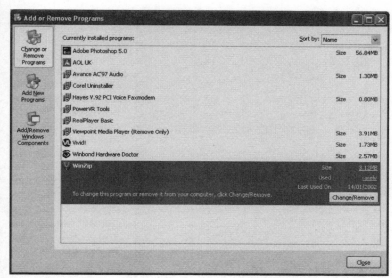

Fig.1.62 The Windows XP entry should have disappeared from the list

the Add or Remove Programs window, with the entry for uninstalling Windows XP will have been deleted (Figure 1.62).

Utilities

There is an unrivalled range of utility software available for the Windows operating system. Whether this software came into being because of numerous deficiencies and faults in these systems, or simply because the software houses wished to sell it to us is debatable. Something that is not debatable is that some of these programs are not compatible with Windows XP. The fact that you have been using a utility successfully for years with other Windows operating systems is no guarantee that it will work properly with Windows XP. Even if you have been using it with Windows NT4 or 2000, that is still no guarantee of compatibility with Windows XP.

In some cases incompatible programs will just produce nonsense results or no data at all. With other programs there is a risk of the operating system being damaged rather than improved in some way. Particularly when using utility programs such as disc defragmenters and cleanup programs, check that they are suitable for use with Windows XP before

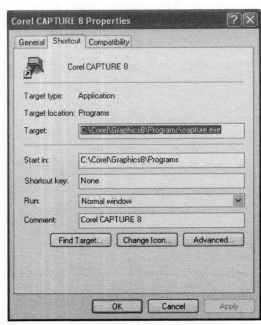

Fig. 1.63 The initial program properties window

using them. The manufacturers' web sites should give up to date information on their utility programs, together with details of any upgrades to XP compatible versions. Apart from the obvious risk of damaging the operating system, with some of these programs there is a danger of losing important data stored on the hard disc.

Software compatibility

As pointed out previously, where an old program gives problems with Windows XP it is possible to set the operating system to give a higher degree of compatibility. It has to be emphasised that this is not a good idea with utility software, or any programs that produce an incompatibly warning message from Windows XP. Ignoring warnings is likely to cause damage to the operating system, and is unlikely to get the troublesome software working properly. If (say) a program uses a DLL file that gives problems with Windows XP, and should not be used with this operating system, setting a greater level of compatibility will not stop it from causing problems. The idea of this facility is to make Windows XP more accommodating to old programs that take shortcuts that are not normally permitted under Windows XP.

The compatibility level can be adjusted manually by right clicking on a shortcut to the program, or on the entry of the program file in Windows Explorer, and the selecting the Properties option. Using either method, a window similar to the one shown in Figure 1.63 should appear. Left-click the Compatibility tab to produce a window like the one shown in

Figure 1.64. The bottom section of the window has checkboxes that can be used to limit the program to basic video modes. In most cases it is the upper section that is needed, and the first step is to tick the checkbox marked "Run this program in compatibility mode for:". This activates the menu that enables the program to be run in modes that give compatibility with earlier 32-bit versions of Windows (Figure 1.65). If the program had previously worked perfectly under Windows ME

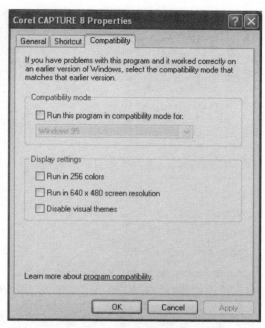

Fig.1.64 The Compatibility section of the program properties window

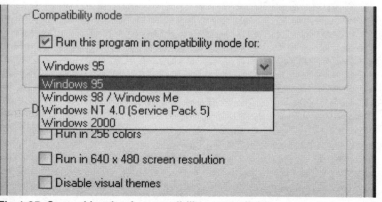

Fig.1.65 Several levels of compatibility are available

1 Upgrading problems

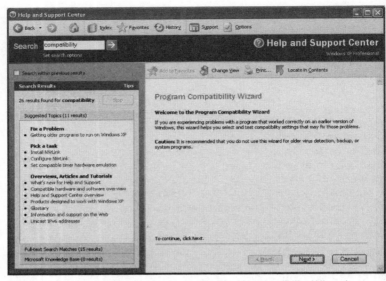

Fig.1.66 Use the Help system to locate the Compatibility Wizard

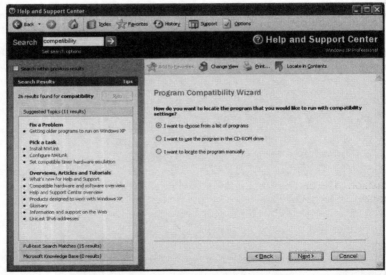

Fig.1.67 The Compatibility Wizard operates in standard wizard fashion

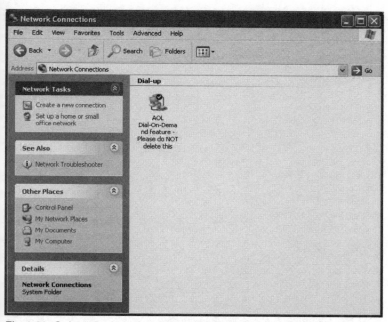

Fig.1.68 Select the icon for the connection you wish to equip with the firewall. In most cases there will only be one icon present

for example, the Windows 98/ME option would be used. Note that it is only necessary to set the level of compatibility once. The correct mode will then be used each time the program is run.

Program compatibility can also be set using the Program Compatibility Wizard. First go to the Start menu and launch the Help and Support program. Use the search system to locate and launch the Program Compatibility Wizard (Figure 1.66). I soon located it using "compatibility" as the search string. It is then largely a matter of answering questions by operating the appropriate radio buttons (Figure 1.67) in standard Wizard fashion. The program should then run in a suitable mode, but with both methods of mode selection there is no guarantee that the program will work properly under Windows XP.

Firewall

Windows XP has a built-in firewall, which is a program that tries to prevent people hacking into your system via the Internet. However, this feature

Fig.1.69 The initial ISP Properties window

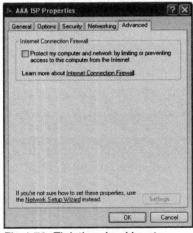

Fig.1.70 Tick the checkbox to enable the firewall

may seem to be conspicuously absent, because it is not enabled by default. To enable the firewall facility, activate the Windows Control Panel from the Start menu, and then double-click on the Network connections icon. This produces a window like the one shown in Figure 1.68. Select the connection you wish to protect by left clicking its icon.

Next, in the Network Tasks panel, left-click the "Change settings of this connection" link. Alternatively, right-click on the icon and select Properties from the popup menu. A window like the one in Figure 1.69 will appear, and operating the Advanced tab will change this to something like Figure 1.70. Tick the checkbox near the top of the window to enable the firewall facility, and then operate the OK button to close the window. The firewall feature can be switched off again by going back to the properties window and removing the tick from the checkbox.

Points to remember

The fact that your computer can run an earlier version of Windows does not mean that it will be able to handle Windows XP. Something well beyond the minimum hardware requirement is needed in order to run Windows XP satisfactorily.

The upgrade advisor program is useful for testing the hardware and software for incompatibility problems before upgrading to Windows XP. A number of potential problems might be found by this program, but it is unlikely that any of them will make the upgrade impossible. In most cases some new device drivers will be needed, or software will have to be reinstalled.

It is advisable but not essential to uninstall any incompatible software and hardware prior to the upgrade. Some software simply has to be uninstalled and then reinstalled in order to provide Windows XP compatibility.

The hardware manufacturer's web site is the first place to look if new device drivers are needed after the upgrade to Windows XP has been completed. There are specialist web sites that can help with the location of device drivers. Where Windows XP drivers have been produced, they will almost certainly be available somewhere on the Internet.

The video card might work with a full range of resolutions and colour depths after the upgrade, but it will almost certainly run very slowly until the proper Windows XP device drivers are installed.

It is not necessary to register Windows XP in order to use it, but it will stop working after 30 days unless it is activated. Reactivation will be needed if it is reinstalled, and might also be necessary if large changes are made to the hardware. Activation via the Internet is much easier than using the telephone method.

By default, the format of the hard disc drive or drives remains unaltered, which means it will use the FAT or (more probably) FAT32 file system. Unless the FAT or FAT32 file system is needed for compatibility reasons it is advisable to convert the discs to NTFS format.

If you are unable to get satisfactory results from Windows XP it is possible to uninstall it and revert to the original operating system and set-up. However, it is not possible to uninstall Windows XP if the hard disc is converted to NTFS format. Therefore, make sure that everything is working properly before converting the hard disc to the NTFS file system.

Troublesome software that worked with earlier versions of Windows can usually be made to work with Windows XP by running the software in a compatibility mode. Do not use a compatibility mode if Windows produces warning messages about incompatible DLL files, or something of this nature. Neither should a compatibility mode be used with utility programs such as disc defragmenters.

Do not use utility programs unless they are designed for operation with Windows XP. If you use old software of this type there is a strong risk of major damage to the Windows installation and other files on the hard disc.

The Windows XP firewall is not activated by default. It must be enabled manually, and separately for each Internet service provider if more than one is installed on the PC.

Prevention is...

Bugs

An installation of the Windows operating system coming to grief is not exactly a rare occurrence, but why should these problems happen at all? I suppose that the chances of removing every single bug from software as complex as this is virtually nil, but genuine bugs in Windows are almost certainly responsible for only a small percentage of the problems. Modern PC hardware is very reliable, and hardware glitches probably have nothing to do with the vast majority of problems either.

Most of the difficulties seem to be due to things that either the user or applications programs do to Windows. Unfortunately, quite minor things can prevent Windows from operating correctly, and it is easily "gummed up" by users making alterations to system settings or deleting essential files. Software that does not strictly abide by the rules can also generate problems.

Windows XP is much more robust than Windows 95, or even Windows ME, but the impression given by some that it is "bomb proof" is certainly misleading. Windows XP places restrictions on software that largely prevent it from using the hardware in such a fashion that the computer will crash or operate unpredictably. It also protects important system files so that rogue software can not alter them.

In fact, there is a whole raft of measures that are designed to prevent accidental or malicious damage to the system. Compared with earlier versions, Windows XP is also much better at recovering from major problems. Even so, problems can still occur and the computer can crash. In most cases, one program crashing will not bring down any others. Each program effectively has its own operating system. Crashing one program and system will leave the others working normally, and any data in the other systems will be safe. However, a catastrophic failure can still occur, and will usually produce a blue screen full of programming data and a suggestion that you contact the system administrator. Fortunately, this type of thing is quite rare.

Do not tweak

Probably the only sure-fire way of preventing Windows from getting into difficulties is to never install any applications programs at all, which is not exactly a practical proposition. However, you can certainly reduce the risk of problems occurring by following some simple rules. Experienced users fiddle around with the Windows configuration files and manage to customise the user interface in ways that are not normally possible. This is fine for those having suitable experience of Windows, because they know what they are doing. They can largely avoid problems and can soon backtrack to safety if something should go wrong.

Inexperienced users are almost certain to damage the operating system if they try this sort of tweaking, and will not have the expertise to quickly sort things out when problems arise. Just the opposite in fact, and one thing can lead to another, with the operating system soon getting beyond redemption. If you are not an expert on the inner workings of Windows it is best not to delve into its configuration files. A great deal of customisation can be done using the normal Windows facilities, and there are applications programs that enable further customisation to be undertaken without having to directly alter files.

Even if you are familiar with Windows 9x and its inner workings, it is not a good idea to start hacking into Windows XP as if it was an early version of Windows. Although there are superficial similarities between Windows 9x and Windows XP, there are also major differences in the inner workings. Things that are acceptable with Windows 9x might not have the desired effect with Windows XP, if they are permissible at all. If you really must tinker with Windows XP, gain some experience with this operating system and learn as much about it as possible before you start altering things.

Careful deletion

In the days of MS-DOS it was perfectly acceptable to delete a program and any files associated with it if you no longer wished to use the program. Matters are very different with any version of Windows from Windows 95 onwards, where most software is installed into the operating system. There are actually some simple programs that have just one file, and which do no require any installation. With others there is a program file and one or two support files, but again, no installation is required. These standalone program files are quite rare these days, but they can be used much like old MS-DOS programs. To use the program you copy it, together with any support files, onto the hard disc. To run the program you use the Run option from the Start menu, or locate the file using Windows Explorer and double-click on it. No installation program is used, and it is perfectly all right to remove the program by deleting the program file.

Most programs are installed onto the computer using an installation program, and this program does not simply make folders on the hard disc and copy files into them from the CD-ROM. It will also make changes to the Windows configuration files so that the program is properly integrated with the operating system. In particular, it will make changes to the Windows Registry. If you simply delete the program's directory structure to get rid of it, Windows will not be aware that the program has been removed. During the boot-up process the operating system will probably look for files associated with the deleted program, and will produce error messages when it fails to find them.

There is another potential problem in that Windows utilises shared files. This is where one file, such as a DLL type, is shared by two or more programs. In deleting a program and the other files in its directory structure you could also be deleting files needed by other programs. This could prevent other programs from working properly, or even from starting up at all. If a program is loaded onto the hard disc using an installation program, the only safe way of removing it is to use an uninstaller program. Uninstalling programs was covered to some extent in chapter one, but here we will consider the subject in more depth. There are three possible ways of uninstalling programs.

Custom uninstaller

Some programs load an uninstaller program onto the hard disc as part of the installation process. This program is then available via the Start menu if you choose Programs, and then the name of the program concerned. When you choose this option there will the program itself, plus at least one additional option in the sub-menu that appears. If there is no uninstall option here, no custom uninstaller has been installed for that program. Uninstaller programs of this type are almost invariably automatic in operation, so you have to do little more than instruct it to go ahead with the removal of the program.

Some uninstallers are quite complex, and these are used where a suite of software rather than just one program has been installed. The uninstaller is then more of a Setup program, that permits more programs to be added in addition to allowing existing ones to be removed. These

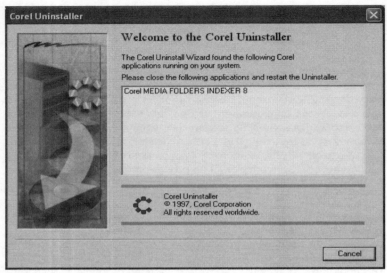

Fig.2.1 Background tasks can prevent an uninstaller from working

Fig.2.2 Using the Windows Task Manager

can be a little more difficult to use than basic uninstaller utilities. Figure 2.1 shows an error message produced by the Corel 8 uninstaller. This kind of error can occur when removing any software, but it is more common with software suites because they often have one or more utility programs running as background tasks. An uninstaller can not be used with

Fig.2.3 Numerous processes are normally listed

software that is in use, so any software it can remove has to be switched off before running the installer.

The easy way of switching off background tasks is to launch the Windows Task Manager. Using the standard Control-Alt-Delete key combination launches this utility, but in Windows XP this feature is more complex than in Windows 9x. With Windows 9x a list of all the programs and tasks currently running is included. With the Windows XP version only the main applications currently running are listed. In the example of Figure 2.2 there is just one program listed, and this is not the one that has to be shut down.

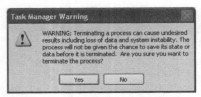

Fig.2.4 There is no risk of data loss with background tasks

In order to see all the tasks and applications that are running it is necessary to operate the Processes tab near the top of the window. This produces what usually be a very long list of programs, as in the Example of Figure 2.3. Here the offending indexing program is third down in the list. In order to halt a process it is first selected by left clicking on its entry, and then the End Process button is operated. This produces the warning message of Figure 2.4, but problems with lost data are unlikely when shutting down a background task. Left-click the Yes button in order to halt the process. The process should then disappear from the list (Figure 2.5). Returning to the Corel Uninstaller program, this time everything is fine (Figure 2.6), and there are no warning messages.

With any uninstaller software you may be asked if certain files should be removed. This mostly occurs where the program finds shared files that no longer appear to be shared. This usually means files with a "DLL"

Fig.2.5 The offending program has been shut down

extension, which are dynamic link library files. It should be safe to opt for removing any files that are no longer shared, but there is a slight danger that the uninstaller will overlook something and remove a file that is still in use elsewhere. This can produce problems with applications programs and can even produce boot problems. Many users prefer to take the safer option and leave the files in place, even if this results in files and

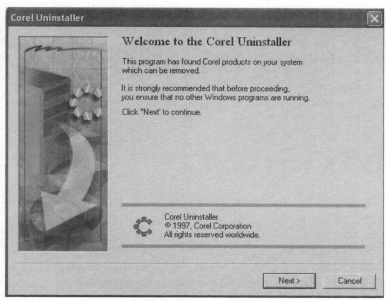

Fig.2.6 This time the uninstaller runs properly

possibly folders being left on the disc unnecessarily. If you are not very expert with Windows it is certainly best to play safe and operate the No button.

Windows uninstaller

Windows has a built-in uninstaller that can be accessed via the control panel. From the Start menu select Control Panel and then double-click on the Add/Remove programs icon. This takes you to the uninstaller, and the lower section of the screen shows a list of the programs that can be uninstalled via this route (Figure 2.7). In theory, the list should include all programs that have been added to the hard disc using an installation program. In practice, there are sometimes one or two that have not been installed "by the book" and can not be removed using this method. Some programs can only be removed using their own uninstaller program, while others have no means of removal at all.

It is mainly older software that falls into the non-removable category, particularly programs that were written for Windows 3.1 and not one of

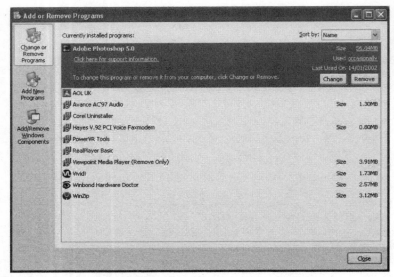

Fig.2.7 The installed programs are listed in the uninstaller

the 32-bit versions of Windows. 16-bit software written for Windows 3.1 is fundamentally incompatible with Windows XP, but it can still be run under this operating system. However, it is run using what is termed a "virtual machine". This means that Windows XP runs a program that emulates the old Windows 3.1 operating system and the enhanced mode of the 80386 microprocessor. One consequence of this roundabout method is that 16-bit software may run more slowly than expected.

Windows 3.1 software does not necessarily conform to the current rules, and may try to directly control the hardware. Software of this type will only run under Windows XP if special device drivers are installed. In general, it is best not to install 16-bit software unless you really do need to use it. If you have 16-bit software installed that you no longer need, third party uninstaller programs might help with its removal. However, the safer option is to simply leave it in place and ignore it. Most software of this type takes up little hard disc space by current standards.

Apart from some 16-bit applications, the only programs that will not be listed in the Add/Remove Programs window are basic standalone programs that did not use an installation process, and were simply copied onto the hard disc. As pointed out previously, these can be deleted manually without any risk of damaging the Windows installation. Where appropriate, the documentation supplied with the program should point out that it does not have to be uninstalled.

Assuming the program you wish to remove is in the list, left-click on its entry to select it and then operate the Remove button. It is then a matter of going through the removal process, which is largely or totally automatic. Eventually you should end up back at the Add or Remove Programs window, with the entry for the program no longer listed.

Third party

As pointed out previously, there are third party uninstaller programs available. These can be used to monitor an installation and then uninstall the software at some later time. These programs are perhaps less useful than they once were, because this feature is built into Windows XP and other versions since Windows 95. Also, the vast majority of applications programs now either utilise the built-in facility or have their own uninstaller software. Most uninstallers will also assist in the removal of programs that they have not been used to install, but this facility is of decreasing relevance to modern Windows computing.

Most of these programs will also help with the removal of things like unwanted entries in the Start menu and act as general cleanup software. Although Windows itself provides means of clearing most of this software debris, these facilities are perhaps of more use to most users than the uninstaller routines. Inexperienced users will probably find this method easier than going through the official Windows channels. Using utility software for "housekeeping" tasks should also involve less risk of damaging the system.

It is worth repeating the warning that some Windows utility programs are not compatible with Windows XP. Using incompatible utility software can seriously damage the system and other files on the hard disc. Always ensure that any utility programs are fully compatible with Windows XP before trying to use them with this operating system. There is otherwise a strong risk that the program will do far more harm than good.

Leftovers

Having removed a program by whatever means, you will sometimes find that there are still some files and folders associated with the program remaining on the hard disc. In some cases the remaining files are simply data or configuration files that have been generated while you were trying out the program. If they are no longer of any use to you there should be

2 Prevention is...

Fig.2.8 Select the Details option from the View menu

no problems if they are deleted using Windows Explorer. In other cases the files could be system files that the uninstaller has decided not to remove because they are needed by other applications. Removing files of this type is very risky because the uninstaller was almost certainly correct. Manually deleting leftover files that are still in use is a common cause of problems with Windows, and files of this type should definitely be left in place.

Sometimes the folders may seem to be empty, but it is best to check carefully before removing them. An important point to bear in mind here is that not all files are shown when using the default settings of Windows Explorer. Using the default settings hidden files will live up to their name, and files having certain extensions are not shown either. In normal use this can be helpful because it results in files that are likely to be of interest

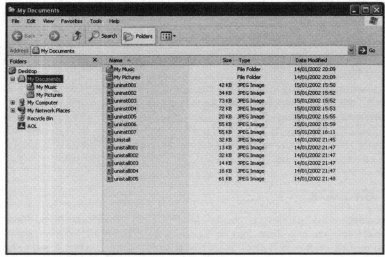

Fig.2.9 The Details view in Windows Explorer

being shown, while those that of no interest are hidden. This makes it much easier to find the files you require in a folder that contains large numbers of files. It is not helpful when Windows troubleshooting because it tends to have the opposite effect to normal. Things like data files that are of little interest are shown, while many of the system files that are of interest are hidden. Windows Explorer should be set to show as much detail about the files as possible.

First go to the View menu and select the Details option (Figure 2.8). This will result in the icons being replaced with text that indicates the size, type, and date of each file (Figure 2.9). With Windows XP you can choose the details that are shown by going to the View menu and selecting the Choose Details option. This produces the window of Figure

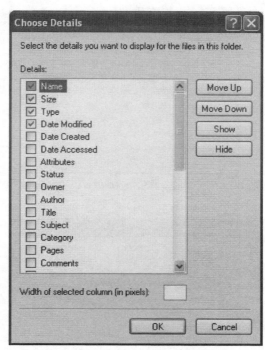

Fig.2.10 Selecting the details that will be displayed

2.10, where the check boxes are used to select the details that will be displayed. The Move Up and Move Down buttons can be used to change the order in which the entries appear in this list, which is also the order in which they appear across the page in Windows Explorer. Figure 2.11 shows files displayed in a customised version of Windows Explorer.

In order to reveal hidden files, go to the Tools menu, select Folder Options, and then left-click on the View tab in the new Window that appears (Figure 2.12). Under the Hidden files and folders entry in the main section of the window, select the Show all files and folders option. The hidden files are certain critical system files, such as those associated with the Windows

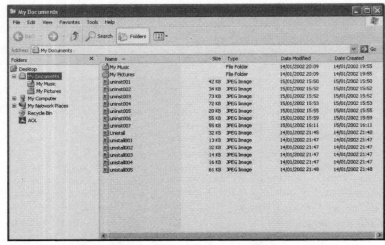

Fig.2.11 File details displayed in a customised Windows Explorer

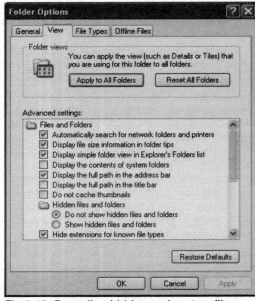

Fig.2.12 Revealing hidden and system files

Registry, that are not normally displayed by Windows Explorer so that they can not be accidentally altered or erased by the user. I would recommend ticking the checkbox for Display full path in title bar. This way you can always see exactly what folder you are investigating, even if it is one that is buried deep in a complex directory structure.

Remove the tick in the checkbox next to Hide the extension for known file types.

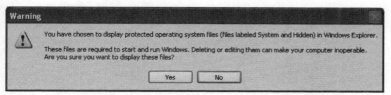

Fig.2.13 Revealing the system files renders them more vulnerable

The extension should then be shown for all file types, which makes it easy to see which one is which when several files have the same main file name. When Windows troubleshooting you might need to view the contents of system folders, but by default these are blocked from view. Tick the Display the contents of system folders checkbox in order to make the system files viewable. In order to see all system files it is also necessary to remove the checkbox labelled "Hide protected operating system files (Recommended)". This will bring up the warning message of Figure 2.13, and it is a warning that should be heeded. By making the system files visible, it becomes easy to seriously damage the operating system, perhaps to the point where there is no option but to reinstall everything from scratch. Never move or delete files unless you know exactly what they are, but be especially careful if Windows Explorer is set to reveal the system files.

Attributes

When viewing the contents of directories you can use either the List or Details options under the View menu, but as explained previously, the Details option provides more information and is customisable. It is therefore the better option when Windows troubleshooting. With Windows 9x there is a checkbox that controls whether file attributes are shown, but in Windows XP this option is selected via the View menu and the Choose Details option. It can be useful to know the attribute of files, since some attributes place restrictions on what can be done with them. These are the letters used for each of the four attributes:

A   Archive

H   Hidden

R   Read-only

S   System

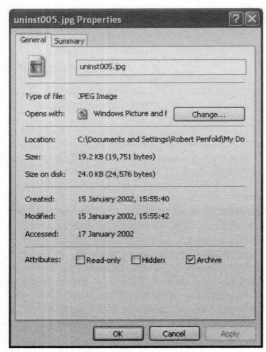

Fig.2.14 Viewing a file's properties

Thus a file that has "R" as its attribute letter it is a read-only type, and one that has "HA" in the attribute column is a hidden archive file. Choose the List option if you prefer to have as many files as possible listed on the screen. Details of any file listed can be obtained by right-clicking on its entry in Windows Explorer and then choosing the Properties option from the pop-up menu. This will bring up a screen of the type shown in Figure 2.14, which shows the type of file, the creation date, when it was last modified, size, etc.

Make sure that the checkbox for the "Remember each folder's view settings" is not ticked. Placing a tick in this box gives each folder its own settings, making it necessary to alter the settings for individual folders rather than altering them globally. Operate the Apply button when you have finished making changes and then the Apply to All Folders button to ensure that the settings are applied globally. There are buttons to permit the default settings to be restored, so you can easily go back to the original settings once a troubleshooting session has been completed. This will hide the system files again and remove the risk of accidentally damaging them.

Deleting files/folders

If any folders are definitely empty, there should be no problem if they are removed. The same is true of data and configuration files that are no longer needed. With other files it may not be clear what their exact purpose is, and it is a bit risky removing files of unknown function. Unfortunately, it seems to be quite common for uninstallers to leave large numbers of files on the hard disc. The uninstaller seems to go through its routine in standard fashion, and reports that the program has been fully removed, but an inspection of the hard disc reveals that a vast directory structure remains. I have encountered uninstallers that have left more than 50 megabytes of files on the disc, removing only about 10% of those initially installed.

Other uninstallers report that some files and folders could not be removed, and that they must be dealt with manually. Some uninstallers seem to concentrate on extricating the program from the operating system by removing references to the program in the Windows registry, etc., rather than trying to remove all trace of it from the hard disc. With most modern computers having large hard disc drives, there would seem to be little point in removing files of unknown worth. Some extra hard disc space will be freed by removing them, but with gigabytes of free space already, this is of no real benefit. If the files do prove to be essential to the wellbeing of the computer, their removal could cause problems. It is best to adhere to the old adage "if in doubt do nowt".

Softly, softly

It might be best to do little or nothing when uninstalling a program leaves a hard disc containing vast numbers of unwanted files, but that is not necessarily the course most people follow. The temptation, and what many people actually do, is to simply drag the whole lot into the Recycle Bin. Sometimes this may be acceptable, but there is the risk that eventually Windows will look for some of the deleted files and start to produce error messages. If you are lucky, the deleted files will still be in the Recycle Bin, and they can then be restored to their original locations on the hard disc. If not, you may have problems sorting things out.

If you really must delete the leftover files, the safer way of handling things is to leave the directory structure and files intact, but change some file or folder names. If only a few files have been left behind, try adding a letter at the front of each filename. For example, a file called "drawprog.dll" could be renamed "zdrawprog.dll". This will prevent Windows from finding the file if it should be needed for some reason, but it is an easy matter for you to correct things by removing the "z" from the filename if problems occur.

Where there are numerous files in a complex directory structure to deal with it is not practical to rename all the individual files. Instead, the name of the highest folder in the directory structure should be renamed. This should make it impossible for Windows to find the file unless it does a complete search of the hard disc, and it is easily reversed if problems should occur. Ideally the complete directory structure should be copied to a mass storage device such as a CD writer, a backup hard disc drive, or another partition on the hard disc. The original structure can then be deleted. If problems occur and some of the files have been cleaned from the Recycle Bin, you can reinstate everything from the backup copy.

As already point out, modern hard disc drives have very high capacities so it is perhaps worthwhile considering whether it is really necessary to remove leftover files. In fact, do you really need to uninstall the program at all? The less installing and uninstalling you do the better the chances of avoiding problems. The downside of leaving programs on the hard disc is that eventually you will end up with a large number of installed programs, and this could generally slow the system down. In particular, the boot-up process can become a very long and drawn out process, and background tasks can use up the computer's resources.

This can be overcome by occasionally wiping the hard disc clean and reinstalling the operating system and applications software from scratch. This is not a particularly quick and easy process, but it is the only totally reliable method of getting Windows back to a lean installation that operates at peak efficiency. Although it is a major undertaking, it should not be necessary to go through this process very often. Some power users routinely install everything from scratch so that their PC is kept at peak performance.

Icon and menu entries

After uninstalling a program you will often find that the shortcut icon is still present on the Windows desktop. If the installation program did not put the icon there in the first place it is very unlikely that the uninstaller will remove it. Shortcut icons that are placed on the Windows desktop manually must be removed manually. This simply entails dragging the icon to the Recycle Bin. Alternatively, right-click on the icon and select Delete from the popup menu. A warning message will appear, explaining that deleting the icon does not uninstall the program. Left-click the Delete Shortcut button to proceed and remove the icon from the desktop. Deleting a shortcut icon can not have an adverse effect on Windows operation, because the icon is all that is being removed. Any leftover files on the hard disc will remain intact.

An uninstaller should delete the entry in the Programs section of the Start menu when removing a program. Unfortunately, this item does sometimes seem to be overlooked, and after removing a number

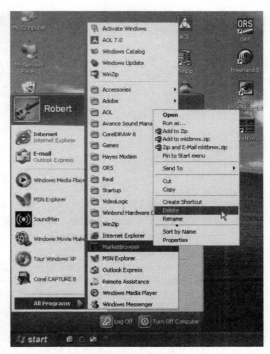

Fig.2.15 Deleting a menu entry

of programs there can be a growing band of orphan entries in the menu. Once again, removing these entries manually should not entail any risk of "gumming up" Windows. However, take care to avoid the complications that could arise if you remove the wrong entry.

To remove an entry go to the Settings entry in the Start menu, and then select the All Programs option. Find the entry that

Fig.2.16 Removing a menu entry does not uninstall the program

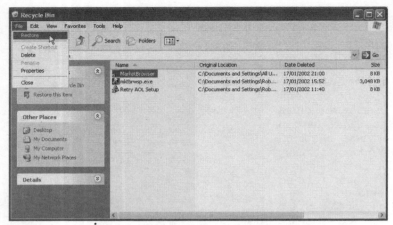

Fig.2.17 A recently deleted menu entry is easily restored

you wish to remove and then right-click on it. Select Delete from the popup menu (Figure 2.15), and a warning message will appear on the screen (Figure 2.16). The message points out that you are removing a shortcut rather than uninstalling the program, and it also gives you a chance to change your mind. The entry will be deleted if you confirm that you wish to go ahead by operating the Delete Shortcut button. A quick check of the Start menu should show that the offending entry has been removed.

It is actually placed in the Recycle Bin, so it can be easily reinstated provided you realise your mistake fairly quickly. To restore the entry, launch the Recycle Bin, then locate and select the file you have just deleted. Select Restore from the File menu (Figure 2.17), and the entry in the All Programs menu should return to its original position.

Beta problems

Both old and brand new software are potential sources of problems with Windows. As already pointed out, old programs can be problematic because they do not adhere to the current rules for Windows software. In the case of brand new software it is the beta test versions or any other versions prior to the commercial release that are the main problem. These are not fully tried and tested, and can not be guaranteed to do things "by the book". In all probability, some sections of the code will contain programming errors and simply will not work properly. People who make a living testing this type of software almost invariably use one PC for testing the software and a second PC for other purposes. That way there is no major loss if the test software runs amok and deletes half the files on the hard disc! If you do not have a second PC for use with dubious software it is best not to try it at all.

At one time the initial commercial releases of programs were not always reliable, and some software publishers seemed to be guilty of getting their customers to unwittingly do the final testing for them. This sort of thing may still go on in some niche markets, but it is thankfully something of a rarity these days. The cost of sending out replacement discs plus the loss of reputation makes it an unsustainable tactic. These days, new software whether it is totally new or an upgrade version, should be very reliable.

In the past it was advisable to let new software mature before buying it, but this should no longer be necessary. New software might contain a few minor bugs, but there should be nothing that will seriously damage your Windows installation. If new software should prove troublesome, there should be a help-line that can give advice on the problem. Software publishers' web sites often have software patches that can fix any obscure problems that have come to light after the final versions of the programs have been sent out to the shops.

Memory

In the early days of Windows 95 it was not unusual for the dreaded red exclamation marks to appear on the screen complete with a brief error message. In fact, there seemed to be one or two of these messages every time someone used a PC. Thankfully, this type of thing is relatively rare these days. There were probably two main reasons for these early problems, and one of them was a lack of memory in the PCs of the day. At that time memory was quite expensive. Eight megabytes of RAM was quite typical, and 16 megabytes was considered to be a large amount of memory.

Software manufacturers were eager for their programs to appeal to as many people as possible, which often led them to be overoptimistic about the system requirements. If the requirements listed 8 megabytes of memory as the minimum and recommended at least 16 megabytes should be used, then 16 megabytes was probably the minimum that would really give trouble free and usable results.

These days memory is relatively cheap, and PCs are mostly well endowed in this respect. On the other hand, programs, including operating systems, seem to require ever more memory. Also, many users now have two or more programs running simultaneously, probably with several background tasks running as well. If you run memory hungry programs on a computer that has a modest amount of memory and error messages keep on appearing, it is worth investing in some extra memory. Even if it does not cure the problem, Windows and your programs will almost certainly run more quickly. If you wish to run a couple of major applications under Windows XP there is a lot to be said for having at least 256 megabytes of RAM installed in your PC.

Another problem when Windows 95 came along was that most of the Windows software available at the time was really intended for use with Windows 3.1. In theory, most of this software was fully compatible with Windows 95, but in practice there often seemed to be odd incompatibility problems. Most of this software is now long gone, but as already pointed out, it can usually be used with Windows XP. However, there is no guarantee that these old 16-bit programs will run properly under Windows XP. The only way to find out is to use the "suck it and see" method. It is advisable not to press on regardless if error or warning messages keep appearing on the screen.

Old Windows 3.1 software may be a rarity, but there is still plenty of Windows 9x software that is not recommended for use with Windows XP. There is also some software for Windows NT and 2000 that will not work properly with Windows XP. To avoid problems, check that software is Windows XP compatible before installing it, and never use programs that are not compatible. Windows XP will do its best to intercept and disable incompatible files such as certain DLL types, but the best way of avoiding problems is to keep incompatible software off the system. As explained previously, it is necessary to take extra care with utility software such as disc defragmenters that have the potential to cause considerable damage to the Windows installation. Incompatible software of this type can and probably will do extensive damage to the files on the hard disc.

Windows problem?

Some users tend to jump to conclusions when there are problems with a PC running Windows. Probably most problems are the result of the operating system becoming damaged, but by no means all problems are caused in this way. I have often been asked to help with supposed Windows problems that turn out to be due to some other cause. A crucial consideration when locating the cause of a PC fault is where in the proceedings is it that things go awry? If the PC fails to start up at all, with no initial messages, etc., from the BIOS's POST (power-on self-test) program, the fault is clearly not a Windows problem. The fault is occurring long before the PC starts to boot into Windows, and there is certainly a hardware problem.

Matters are less clear cut if the PC gets through its initial checking, starts to boot into Windows, but rapidly comes to a halt. When this happens there will often be an error message along the lines that the boot disc is missing or has a corrupted boot sector, and you will be asked to insert a system disc and then press any key. This means that the computer has looked at the boot drives specified in the BIOS Setup program but has not found a bootable disc. An obvious first step is to check the BIOS settings by going into the Setup program. The manual for your computer should give at least brief details of how to enter the BIOS and change the settings. This is also covered in more detail in a later chapter. Assuming the settings are suitable, the problem could be due to hardware fault with the disc or the IDE interface on the motherboard, or it could be caused by corruption of the data in the boot sector of the disc.

Sometimes the PC will start booting, but it will stop almost immediately. When this happens there will not necessarily be an error message displayed on the screen. In fact there will probably be no message, with the computer instead "freezing". The Control-Alt-Del key combination might reset the computer so that it tries to boot again, but a hardware reset will probably be needed. In other words, operate the reset button on the computer if it has one, or switch off, wait a few seconds, and then switch the PC back on again. If the boot process almost instantly falters again it is possible that there is a hardware fault, but a corrupted boot sector on the disc is the most likely cause of the problem. If you are unlucky, the hard disc has failed and will have to be replaced.

System files

If the system files in the boot sector of the disc have become damaged, the obvious first step is to replace them. In order to do this in Windows 9x the computer is booted using the Windows Startup disc in drive A:. Windows XP does not rely on booting from a floppy disc in an emergency. It is possible to produce an MS-DOS boot disc using Windows XP, but this is likely to be of little or no use when troubleshooting. In an emergency the normal approach is to first try to boot into Safe Mode, which is much like its equivalent in Windows 9x. The computer boots into Windows XP,

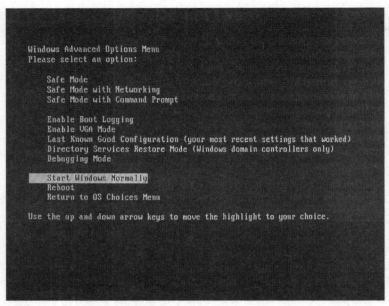

*Fig.2.18 The Advanced Options menu enables the computer to be
         booted in Safe Mode*

but with a basic video driver and probably with some of the hardware
not installed. Although the computer is something less than fully
functioning, it should work well enough to permit some troubleshooting.
If you can get the computer into Safe Mode it can probably be restored
to full working order without too much difficulty.

A menu giving a number of boot options can be obtained by pressing F8
as the computer starts to boot into Windows. This is essentially the
same method that is used with Windows 9x, but the available options
(Figure 2.18) are somewhat different. The various boot modes will not
be considered at this stage, and the standard Safe Mode is all that is
needed here. Use the up and down cursor keys to highlight the Safe
Mode entry and then operate the Return key. This moves things on to
the screen of Figure 2.19 where the required operating system is selected.
Obviously, Windows XP is selected here, but in most cases it will be the
only operating system available. Operate the Return (Enter) key to boot
the PC in Safe Mode.

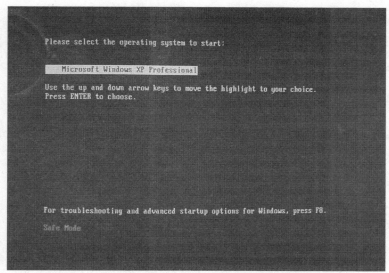

Fig.2.19 Where appropriate, select the correct operating system

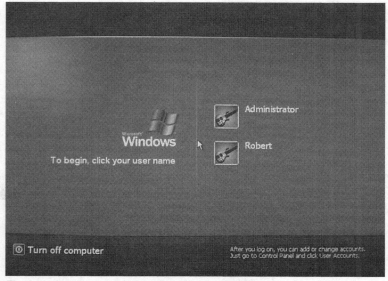

Fig.2.20 Logon to the system in the usual manner

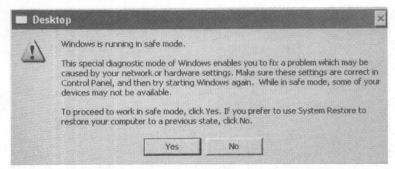

Fig.2.21 This warning message appears on entering Safe Mode

Initially the screen will fill with text that shows the drivers that have been loaded, and then the logon screen should appear (Figure 2.20). Logon in the normal way, and the warning message of Figure 2.21 will appear. This explains that Windows is running in a diagnostic mode and that some devices will not be available. It also gives the option of using the Restore feature, which is something that will not be considered further

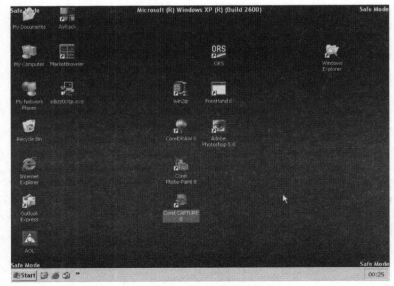

Fig.2.22 The screen when booted into Safe Mode

here. Operate the Yes button to complete the boot into Safe Mode, which will give a screen something like the one shown in Figure 2.22.

Recovery Console

It is virtually certain that the basic system files are intact if the PC manages to boot into Safe Mode. There is a good chance that these files are damaged if the boot process fails, especially if it fails well before the logon process. When the computer can not even boot into Safe Mode there are basically two choices. One is to simply abandon the current installation and reinstall everything from scratch. It is a bit early in the proceedings to consider this option, and the more normal course of action is to resort to the Recovery Console. This is a more sophisticated recovery set-up than the Startup floppy discs used with Windows 9x. In order to run the Recovery Console the computer must be booted from the Windows XP installation disc.

Any modern PC should have no difficulty booting from a CD-ROM drive, although it might be necessary to boot from the drive having the lowest letter if your PC has two or more CD-ROM drives. In other words, if the CD-ROMs are drives D: and E:, it will probably be necessary to boot from drive D:. A PC that has Windows XP installed might be set to boot from the CR-ROM drive first, and to then try the hard disc if no bootable CD-ROM can be found. In this case, it is merely necessary to switch on the PC, put the XP installation disc in the CD-ROM drive, and wait for the system to boot from this drive.

If the computer is not set to boot from the CD-ROM drive at all, it will be necessary to change some settings using the BIOS Setup program. The same is true of the computer is set to boot from the hard disc drive first. While it is possible that the BIOS will detect that it can not boot from the hard drive, and then move on to the CD-ROM drive, this is unlikely. It is odds on that the BIOS will try to boot from the hard drive, and that things will grind to a halt somewhere during this process. The only way to tell whether it is possible to boot from the CD-ROM drive is to use the "suck it and see" approach. It is clearly not possible without some adjustment to the CMOS settings if the computer ignores the CD-ROM drive and tries to boot from the hard disc. Altering the settings stored in the CMOS RAM using the BIOS Setup program is covered in detail in a later chapter.

If everything is set up correctly, a message saying "Press any key to boot from CD-ROM" will appear on the screen. The message appears only briefly so you have to press a key almost immediately in order to

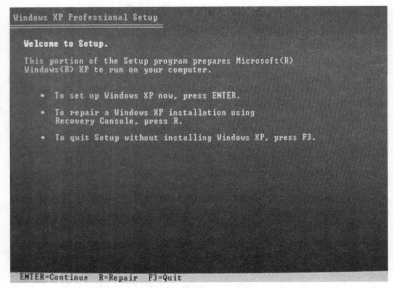

```
Windows XP Professional Setup

 Welcome to Setup.

 This portion of the Setup program prepares Microsoft(R)
 Windows(R) XP to run on your computer.

    • To set up Windows XP now, press ENTER.

    • To repair a Windows XP installation using
      Recovery Console, press R.

    • To quit Setup without installing Windows XP, press F3.




 ENTER=Continue   R=Repair   F3=Quit
```

Fig.2.23 The initial menu of the Setup program

boot from the CD-ROM drive. The computer will try to boot from the
hard disc if you are too late. It is then a matter of resetting or restarting
the computer and trying again. An onscreen message will appear when
the computer starts to boot from the CD-ROM, and this simply explains
that the computer's hardware is being scanned. Eventually the boot
process should finish and a screen like the one in Figure 2.23 will then
appear. The problem is almost certainly a hardware fault rather than a
Windows problem if the PC will not boot from the hard disc or a CD-
ROM.

Password

In order to run the Recovery Console it is merely necessary to press the
R key. This produces a screen like the one shown in Figure 2.24, where
the installed systems are listed. In most cases there will only be one,
which is the Windows XP installation. It is then just a matter of operating
the 1 key and then the Return key to go into the Recovery Console.
Operate the appropriate number key and then press Return if more than
one system is installed on your PC. You will need the administrator

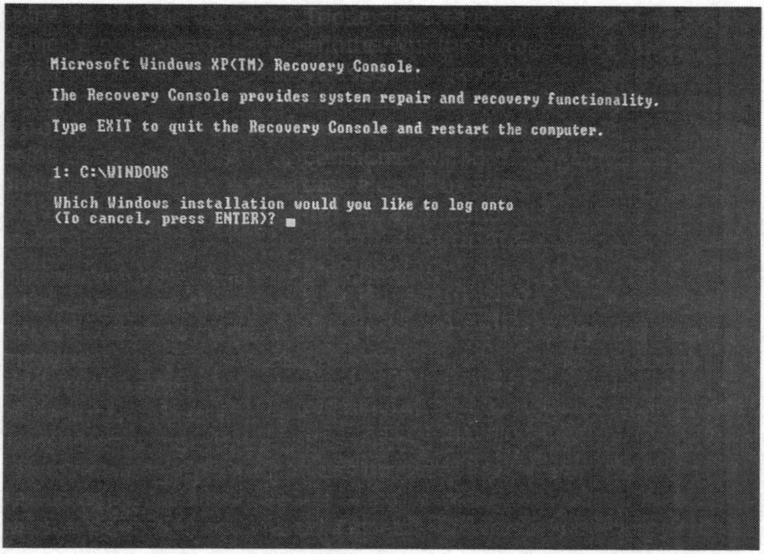

```
Microsoft Windows XP(TM) Recovery Console.

The Recovery Console provides system repair and recovery functionality.

Type EXIT to quit the Recovery Console and restart the computer.


1: C:\WINDOWS

Which Windows installation would you like to log onto
(To cancel, press ENTER)? ▪
```

Fig.2.24 *Select the correct operating system from what will usually be a list of one*

password in order to log into the Recovery Console program. If the system has been upgraded to Windows XP, by default the administrator password will be the same as the one for the user at the time the upgrade was made.

Once into the Recovery Console the screen looks more or less like a normal MS-DOS type (Figure 2.25). With MS-DOS and Windows 9x the SYS command is used to place the system (boot) files onto a disc, but this command is not used with Windows XP. Instead, the FIXBOOT command is used to copy the boot files to the specified disc or partition. For example, in order to copy the boot files to drive C:, this command would be used:

fixboot c:

After pressing the Return key to issue the command, the computer will respond with a message asking if you are sure that you would like to write a new boot sector to the specified drive. Press the Y key followed by the Return key in order to proceed. This should result in the computer almost instantly responding with another message indicating that the new boot sector was successfully written to the disc. Reboot the computer

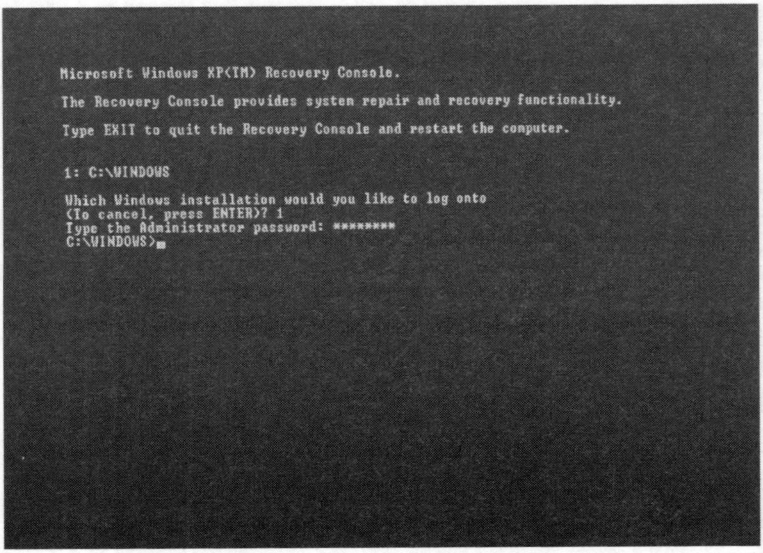

Fig.2.25 The Recovery Console uses a command line interface

by operating the reset button or switching it off and on again. The computer will then boot into Windows XP, provided the problem was actually due to a damaged boot sector.

If the PC still fails to boot properly into Windows it is a matter of delving further into the problem using the techniques described in chapter 3. If there is wholesale damage to the Windows files it may be a matter of reinstalling Windows. In an extreme case any important data on the hard disc that has not been backed up must be rescued, and then the hard disc is wiped clean so that Windows can be installed "from scratch". Emergency rescue of data, backing up the hard disc, and reinstalling Windows are covered in chapters 4, 5, and 6.

Emergency boot

It is worthwhile making an emergency boot floppy disc when the system is functioning properly. It is then possible to use this disc if the boot sector of the hard disc becomes corrupted. The floppy disc is only used for the initial part of the boot process, after which the computer boots from the hard disc in the normal way. A disc of this type will not get the computer into Windows XP when there are problems with things like device drivers or other system files that are used later in the boot process.

To make an emergency boot disc, first use Windows XP to format a floppy disc in the normal way. This can be done by locating the floppy drive in Windows Explorer, right clicking on its entry, and then selecting the Format option. This brings up the window for the Format program, and the default options should be suitable. Operate the Start button, which will produce a warning message explaining that all data on the disc will be lost. Left-click the Yes button if you wish to go ahead and format the disc. Using Windows Explorer, copy these files from root directory of the boot drive to the newly formatted floppy disc:

Boot.ini

Ntldr

Ntdetect.com

Bootsect.dos

Ntbootdd.sys

The first three files should always be present, but one or both of the last two might be absent. They will only be present if they are actually needed. Bear in mind that Windows Explorer will only show these files if it is set to show hidden files. When using the boot disc the BIOS must be set to boot from the floppy drive (drive A:) before drive C: or the emergency boot disc will just be ignored at boot up. Apart from the fact that the boot process starts from drive A;, the system should boot normally when the emergency boot disc is used.

Late problems

Sometimes Windows seems to get 90 percent of the way through the boot-up process before it comes to a halt. When this happens it is likely that the problem is in the Windows installation and not due to a hardware fault. When things come to a halt with an error message stating that a certain file or files could not be found, this indicates that the problem is within Windows itself. Matters are less clear cut if any error messages refer to an item of hardware, or Windows tries to reinstall an item of hardware that was previously installed correctly. It could be that the trouble is due to problems with a corrupted driver program, but it is also possible that a faulty item of hardware is giving the Windows Plug-N-Play facility some difficulties.

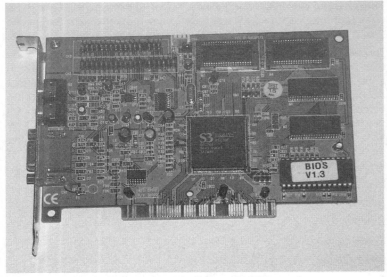

Fig.2.26 The fixing bracket is at the left end of this card

On the cards

Fixing hardware problems goes beyond the scope of this book, but it is covered in "Easy PC troubleshooting (BP484)" from the same publisher and author as this book. However, if the item of hardware that seems to be giving problems is an expansion card, it is probably worthwhile checking that it is properly seated in its expansion slot. To do this you will have to remove either the outer casing or a side panel, depending on the style of case used for your PC. An expansion card has a metal bracket that is used to secure it to the rear of the PC's chassis, and connections on the bottom edge that fit into the expansion slot. The metal bracket can be seen at the left end of the card shown in Figure 2.26, and the connections can be seen on the extended part of the card at the bottom.

Before the card can be removed, the fixing bolt for the mounting bracket must be fully unscrewed (Figure 2.27). The card can then be pulled free of its expansion slot. Many PC expansion cards are vulnerable to damage from static charges, even if those charges are of modest voltages. A certain amount of care must therefore be exercised when pulling the card free of the expansion slot. In this case things are eased by the fact that the card does not need to be completely removed from the PC. It is just a matter of pulling the card free of the expansion slot and then pushing it firmly back into position again. This makes sure that the card is fully pushed down into place in its slot. Removing and replacing the card also tends to clean the connectors so that any connections that were previously a bit iffy make good contact once more.

Fig.2.27 *Fully remove the fixing bolt before extracting an expansion card*

In order to avoid damage from static charge it is advisable to leave the PC connected to the mains supply, but to switch it off at both the mains socket and the PC's on/off switch. Although the PC is switched off, it will be earthed to the mains earth connection. Touch the metal chassis of the computer before pulling the card from its slot. This will remove any static charge in your body and should be sufficient to ensure that no harm comes to any of the PC's hardware.

Make sure that the card is parallel to the slot as in the upper view of Figure 2.28, and not at an angle to it as in the lower view. The bend at the top of the mounting bracket is often something less than a perfect right angle, which tends to skew the card slightly as the fixing bolt is screwed into place. Therefore, make quite sure that the card stays parallel to the expansion slot when the card is fixed in place. If necessary, remove the card again and carefully bend the top of bracket to produce a better approximation to a right angle.

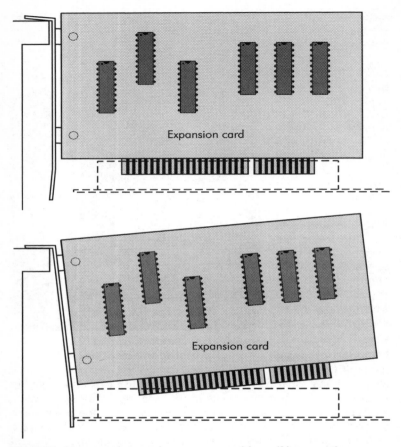

Fig.2.28 An expansion card can cause problems if its mounting bracket does not have the correct right-angled bend

Diagnostics software

Diagnostics software intended to help locate the source of hardware problems can be useful if you are unsure if a problem is due to an obscure Windows fault or an intermittent hardware problem. Suppose you have a PC that is largely working but seems to be a bit erratic or unreliable. Perhaps it sometimes boots into Windows all right but it hangs up on other occasions. Once into Windows, things may go perfectly well for a few minutes and then the computer suddenly crashes. This sort of thing can be caused by a software fault, but it is often due to something like a memory, processor, or disc problem.

If a problem only occurs when a certain applications program is run, it probably has its origins in that piece of software. Running hardware checks is then a little pointless, and it is matter of contacting the software publisher in search of a solution to the problem. Similarly, if the problem only occurs after a particular program has been used, it is very unlikely that either Windows or a hardware fault is the cause of the problem. It is again a matter of contacting the software publisher to see if there is a known problem with the applications program.

You may have some hardware diagnostics software, and if so it is certainly worthwhile running the software on a PC that is giving intermittent problems. In my experience, if a PC has a tendency to simply grind to a halt with the display freezing, the problem is more likely to be in the hardware than the software. This is also the case where things come to a halt with the screen going blank. The fault is more likely to be in the software if the dreaded Windows error messages ("This program has performed an illegal operation and will shut down", etc.) keep appearing. However, this is only a general rule and there are exceptions.

Diagnostics programs will run tests on many parts of the system, including hard and floppy disc drives, the main memory, video memory, the processor, and the ports. Programs of this type sometimes operate under MS/DOS. This is primarily so that they can take control of the memory when making memory tests. Windows places restrictions on the way memory is allocated to programs, and would therefore place much of the memory beyond the reach of the diagnostics software. Note that it is no use trying to use this type of program by running it under any version of Windows using a DOS box. Windows would still be running and would not permit the program to function properly.

MS-DOS boot disc

Normally this type of software is run by booting into DOS mode and then running the program from the DOS prompt. There is no real equivalent of booting into DOS mode when using Windows XP, so it is usually a matter of booting using a MS-DOS system disc or a Windows 9x Startup disc. Windows XP does not use a Startup disc, and can not produce a true equivalent of a Windows 9x Startup disc. It relies on booting from

Fig.2.29 The Format program

the installation CD-ROM when things go seriously awry. However, it is possible to produce an MS-DOS boot disc using Windows XP.

Start by double clicking on the My Computer icon. Then right-click on the icon or entry for the floppy drive in the new window that appears. Alternatively, launch Windows Explorer, double-click the My Computer entry, and then right-click the entry for the floppy drive. Either way, select the Format option from the popup menu that appears. This launches the Format program (Figure 2.29), where most of the default options can be accepted. However, make sure that the checkbox labelled "Create an MS-DOS startup disk" is ticked.

Operate the OK button when the Format Completed message appears on the screen. The disc is then ready for testing, but note that the computer will only boot from a floppy disc if it is set to boot from drive A: before it tries to boot from the hard disc. Also note that booting into MS-DOS gives access to drive C: if it is formatted using the FAT or FAT32 file systems, but not if it is an NTFS type. In fact drive C: will not be recognised at all if it uses the NTFS file system. This clearly makes it impossible to boot into MS-DOS and then run MS-DOS programs on the hard disc.

Of course, in cases where the checking program is small enough to fit onto a floppy disc there is no problem. Simply copy it to the floppy disc and run it from there. Where it is too large, copy the files to a CD-R disc, boot from the floppy drive, and then run the program from the CD-R disc. Note that you will have to install the MS-DOS drivers from the CD-ROM drive on the boot disc. MS-DOS will not even recognise standard IDE/ATAPI CD-ROM drives unless suitable device drivers are installed. These drivers, together with installation instructions, should have been supplied with your PC or with the drive if it was added later.

Many diagnostics programs that run under Windows reboot into MS/DOS to perform some of the tests, and then go back into Windows to

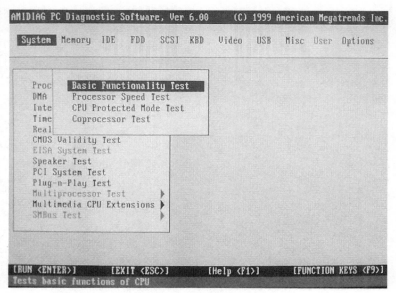

Fig.2.30 Amidiag 6.00 running under MS-DOS

display the results. Programs of this type generally lack compatibility with Windows XP, and are totally unusable with this operating system. In fact, at the time of writing this there is very little diagnostics software that is compatible with Windows XP. No doubt this situation will soon change, but in the mean time there may be no alternative to using MS-DOS based programs. Do not be tempted to use diagnostics software under Windows XP unless it is fully compatible with this operating system. Apart from the fact that it will not work properly with Windows XP, if it works at all, incompatible software has the potential to damage the system further rather than help cure existing problems.

Making tests

When you manage to get some diagnostics software working with Windows XP, what will it actually do? This obviously depends on the particular software in question, but there are a number of features that are common to most diagnostics programs. Most of these programs will perform a series of tests on the drives, the microprocessor, the memory, and most aspects of the hardware. Fig.2.30 shows Amidiag

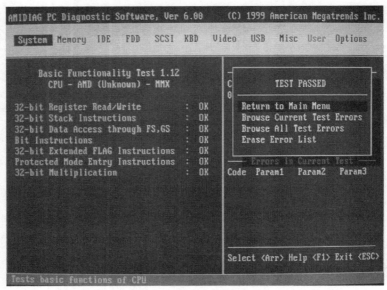

Fig.2.31 The processor has passed this test

6.00 in operation, and this program is being run using a floppy boot disc with the program files on a CD-R disc. It is therefore running in MS-DOS and it is completely independent of Windows XP.

There are various hardware categories available from the menu bar across the top of the screen. The cursor and Return keys are used to select the required category, and items from the menus and submenus. In this example the processor is being tested for basic functionality, and Figure 1.31 shows the result of the test. No errors have been detected. Fig.1.32 shows a set of memory tests in progress, and again there have been no errors reported so far. Clearly, a wide range of tests can be performed using a diagnostics program such as Amidiag 6.00.

If a fault only occurs intermittently it might be necessary to repeat the test procedures a few times in order to coax the system into an error while the diagnostics software is running. Obviously you should try to concentrate on tests that are likely to bring results, and not bother too much about tests on parts of the system that are unlikely to be causing the problem. Faults associated with the ports and the floppy disc drive are unlikely to be responsible for bringing the system to a halt at times

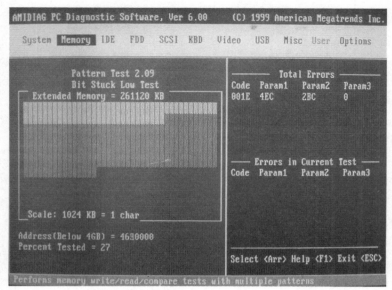

Fig.2.32 Memory testing in progress

when none of these are in use. On the other hand, you may as well give every part of the system a "quick once over" while you are using the diagnostics software, just in case the problem does actually lie in an unlikely part of the system. If the system has a tendency to hang up periodically, the memory, processor and video card are probably the most likely sources of the problem.

What is a virus?

Do not overlook the possibility of problems being caused by a computer virus. There are actually several types of program that can attack a computer system and damage files on any accessible disc drive. These tend to be lumped together under the term "virus", but strictly speaking, a virus is a parasitic program that can reproduce itself and spread across a system or from one system to another. A virus attaches itself to other programs, but it is not immediately apparent to the user that anything has happened.

A virus can be benign, but usually it starts to do serious damage at some stage. It will often infect the boot sector of the hard disc, rendering the system unbootable. It can also affect the FAT (file allocation table) of a disc so that the computer can not find some of the files stored on the disc. The partition table can also be affected, so that the reported size of a disc does not match up with its true capacity. The disc might even be rendered totally inaccessible. The less subtle viruses take more direct action such as attempting to erase or overwrite everything on the hard disc, or erasing the system files while flashing an abusive message on the screen.

A virus can be spread from one computer to another via an infected file, which can enter the second computer via a disc, a modem, or over a network. In fact, any means of transferring a file from one computer to another is a potential route for spreading viruses. A program is really only a virus if it attaches itself to other programs or files and replicates itself. A program is not a virus if it is put forward as a useful applications program but it actually starts damaging the system when it is run. This type of program is more correctly called a "Trojan Horse" or just a "Trojan". Either way, these programs can cause immense damage to the files on the disc, but there should be no risk of any hardware damage occurring.

Virus protection

This is a case where the old adage of "prevention is better than cure" certainly applies. There is probably a cure for every computer virus, but identifying and eradicating a virus can take a great deal of time. Also, having removed the virus there is no guarantee that your all your files will still be intact. Unfortunately, there is a good chance that some damage will have been done. Unless the virus is treated early in the proceedings there is a likelihood of massive damage to the files on the hard disc.

The ideal approach is to avoid doing anything that could introduce a virus into the system, but for most users this is not a practical proposition. These days computing is increasingly about communications between PCs and any swapping of data between PCs provides a route for the spread of viruses. It used to be said that PC viruses could only be spread via discs that contained programs, and that data discs posed no major threat. It is in fact possible for a virus to infect a PC from a data disc, but only if the disc is left in the drive and the computer tries to boot from it at switch-on.

These days there is another method for viruses to spread from data discs, and this is via macros contained within the data files. Obviously not all applications software supports macros, but it is as well to regard data discs as potential virus carriers. Some of the most

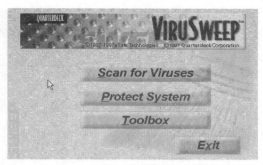

Fig.2.33 The ViruSweep startup screen

widespread and harmful viruses in recent times have been propagated via Emails containing macros infected with a virus, so this problem is one that needs to be taken very seriously.

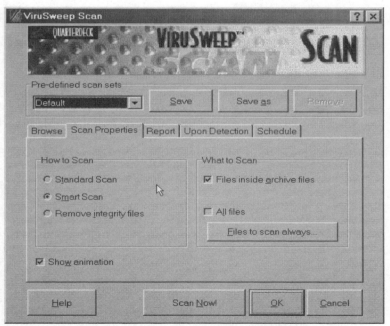

Fig.2.34 The first ViruSweep screen when scanning for viruses

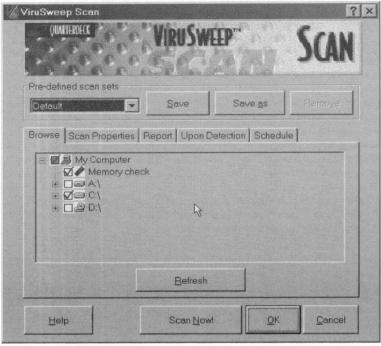

Fig.2.35 This screen enables the type of scan to be selected

Given that it is not practical for most users to avoid any possible contact with computer viruses, the alternative is to rely on anti-virus software to deal with any viruses that do come along. Ideally one of the "big name" anti-virus programs should be installed on the system and kept up to date. This should ensure that any infected disc is soon spotted and dealt with. Software of this type is designed for use before any problems occur, and it normally runs in the background, checking any potential sources of infection as they appear.

There is usually a direct mode as well, which enables discs, memory, etc., to be checked for viruses. Figure 2.33 shows the startup screen for the Quarterdeck ViruSweep program, which is not running under Windows XP incidentally, but it still demonstrates the basic method of using anti-virus programs. Selecting the "Scan For Viruses" option takes the user into further screens that permit various options to be selected.

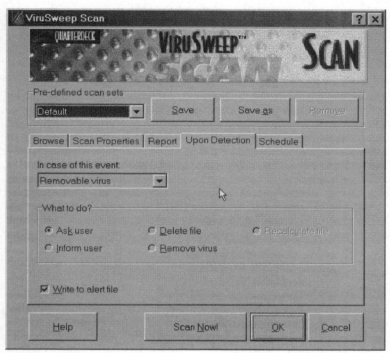

Fig.2.36 This screen gives control over the action taken when a virus is detected

The first screen (Figure 2.34) permits the user to select the parts of the system that will be checked. Viruses can exist in memory as well as in disc files, so checking the memory is normally an option.

Virus removal

Further screens enable the type of scan to be selected (Figure 2.35), and the action to be taken if a virus is detected (Figure 2.36). Most anti-virus software has the option of removing a virus rather than simply indicating that it has been detected. Note though, that in some cases it might not be possible to automatically "kill" a virus. The program will then usually give details of how to manually remove the virus. Follow the removal instructions "to the letter", or you might make things worse rather than better.

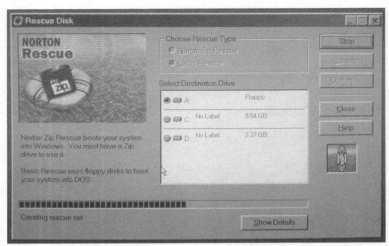

*Fig.2.37 Most anti-virus programs can make recovery discs. Norton
Anti-virus 2000 makes a set of five recovery discs*

Things are likely to be very difficult if you do not use anti-virus software
and your PC becomes infected. On the face of it, you can simply load
an anti-virus program onto the hard disc and then use it to remove the
virus. In practice, it is definitely not advisable to try this method, and
most software of this type will not load onto the hard disc if it detects that
a virus is present. This may seem to greatly reduce the usefulness of the
software, but there is a good reason for not loading any software onto an
infected system. This is the risk of further spreading the virus by loading
new software onto the computer. With a lot of new files loaded onto the
hard disc there is plenty of opportunity for the virus to spread.

Most viruses can actually be removed once they have infected a system,
but not usually by loading a major piece of anti-virus software onto the
hard disc and using it to remove the virus. The method offered by many
anti-virus suites is to boot from a special floppy disc that contains anti-
virus software. With this method there is no need to load any software
onto the hard disc, and consequently there is no risk of the anti-virus
software causing the virus to be spread further over the system. With
the Norton Anti-virus 2000 program a boot disc plus four support discs
are made during the installation process (Figure 2.37). If boot problems
occur at a later date, the PC can be booted using the Norton boot disc,
and with the aid of the support discs a comprehensive range of virus

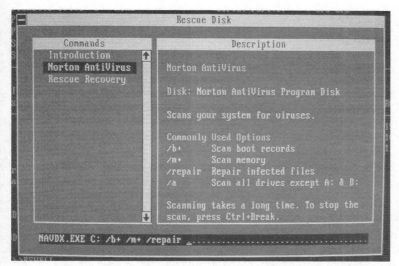

Fig.2.38 Virus scanning with the aid of the Norton Anti-virus 2000 recovery discs

scans can be undertaken (Figure 2.38). In some cases the virus can be removed automatically, and it might also be possible to have any damage to the system files repaired automatically as well.

Firewall

Do not make the mistake of thinking that the built-in firewall of Windows XP is a suitable alternative to anti-virus software. The purpose of a firewall is to stop hackers from gaining access to the files on your PC via a network connection, which usually means the Internet. A firewall does not provide protection against viruses, which are mainly spread by computer users unwittingly introducing them to their PCs, rather than someone hacking into their PCs and introducing the viruses. Ideally, both a firewall and anti-virus software should be used so that your PC is protected from both types of attack.

Bashful viruses

Often it soon becomes clear if a virus or similar program is the cause of Windows problems. The virus will proudly proclaim its presence with an onscreen message. In other cases it will not do so, making it difficult to determine whether the problem is due to a virus or a genuine problem with Windows. If there are repeated problems with the boot files becoming damaged or erased, it is very likely that a virus or similar program is responsible. A lot of inexplicable changes to the Windows Registry and other system or configuration files is also good grounds for suspicion.

There is plenty of anti-virus software available commercially, on the Internet at low cost or free, and it is often given away on the cover-mounted CD-ROMs supplied with computer magazines. If you suspect there may be a virus causing the problem it is best to use at least two and preferably three up to date anti-virus programs to check the PC's hard disc. Where applicable, download updates for the software so that you are using the most up to date versions. These should detect any new viruses. There is no guarantee that the problem is not due to a virus in the event that the programs fail to detect one. On the other hand, it becomes an outside chance and it is probably better to follow other avenues of investigation rather than pursue a virus that is probably not there.

It is only fair to point out that even if the anti-virus software does find a virus and kill it, you may still need to do some work in order to get the computer up and running again. The anti-virus program may be able to repair all the damage inflicted by the virus, but there is a fair chance that the damage will be too great for everything to be fixed. Anyway, with the virus killed off you are at least in a position to start repairing the damage and return things to normality.

Before continuing with this it is not a bad idea to give some thought to the way in which the virus found its way into your PC. There is otherwise a risk that it will soon return and undo the repairs you have made. If you had been using some discs from another computer prior to the problem occurring, check all those discs using the anti-virus programs. Bear in mind that many viruses have a sort of gestation period, and that there can be a substantial gap between the virus program finding its way into your PC and the program actually starting to do its worst. Ideally, you should check all discs that have been used with the PC in the previous few weeks or even months.

Closing notes

It helps to avoid problems if the PC is closed down in the approved fashion at the end of each session. Simply switching off with Windows XP still running is unlikely to do any major harm, but is certainly not a good idea. Switching off with applications programs running is worse, and can lead to problems with Windows XP or the applications programs. One potential cause of difficulties is that Windows XP itself and many applications programs place temporary files on the hard disc drive. When Windows and the applications programs are shut down in the correct manner, these files are deleted. If you simply switch off with things still running, or the PC is suddenly switched off due to a power failure or hardware fault, these files are left on the disc. This may not matter, but there is a risk of the files confusing matters when the PC is switched on again.

Windows XP is very good at dealing with the computer being shut down improperly, and the computer will probably appear to start up normally the next time it is used. There is no equivalent to the Scandisk startup routine of Windows 9x. Although there is no outward sign of anything out of the ordinary, Windows XP is certainly dealing with the leftover files in the background. Do not rely on Windows XP expertise at dealing with problems to always get you out of trouble. Usually it will, but there is certainly no guarantee that it will always sort things out. Try to avoid problems by doing things properly. Always go through the logoff routine when you have finished using the computer.

Even if you do try close down Windows correctly every time, it is still possible to run into difficulties with problem software. With earlier versions of Windows you soon encountered programs that just "froze" and would not respond to the mouse or keyboard. A more interesting but less common variation was the program that started to behave erratically with commands having the wrong effect, odd things happening on the screen, etc. Often when this occurred, the program failed to close down when the cross icon in the top right-hand corner of the screen was operated. Once an application program had gone seriously awry it was not uncommon for Windows itself to behave erratically, and it would often fail to close down properly.

Windows XP is much better at spotting potentially risky programs and it often takes measures to avoid problems occurring. However, there is no guarantee that it will always head off problems, and it is best to avoid dodgy software in the first place. If you do run into problems with erratic or "frozen" programs, wherever possible applications and Windows itself should be shut down properly, or in a reasonably orderly fashion, rather than simply resorting to the on/off switch or Reset button.

Task Manager

Windows does provide an escape route that will usually do the trick if the PC becomes seriously "gummed up". As explained previously, the Control-Alt-Delete key combination launches the Windows Task Manager (Figure 2.39), and by default this list the applications programs that are currently running. To be more precise, it list programs that have taskbar buttons. If you launch something like a screen capture program that runs in the background and does not have a button on the taskbar, it will not be listed as an application by the Task Master program.

Fig.2.39 The Windows XP Task Manager

A program can be shut down by left clicking its entry in Task Manager to select it, and then operating the End Task button. Note that this is not intended to be a normal method of shutting down programs, and this method should only be used if the usual methods fail. In other words, where selecting Exit from the File menu or left clicking the cross in the top right-hand corner of the window fails or is not possible for some reason.

When a program is in trouble there is usually a "(Not Responding)" message next to its entry in Task Manager. Bear in mind that a lack of response from a program does always mean that it has crashed. Similarly, the "(Not Responding)" message in Task Manager is not a cast-iron guarantee that something has gone wrong. The problem can simply be that the program is carrying out a complex task that is taking so much processing time that there are not enough resources left to permit periodic contact with the Task Manager program. It is therefore a good idea to wait a while before forcing a program to close down.

The waiting time depends on the type of task that the program is undertaking. If it is not doing anything particularly demanding there is probably no point in waiting more than a few seconds. If it is sorting the names of everyone in the world into alphabetical order it would probably be worthwhile waiting a few minutes. It is generally worth waiting a while if the program is still producing hard disc activity. This is not always a sign that everything is working properly but slowly, and some programs get stuck in a loop where the same disc activity is repeated ad infinitum. Therefore, if several minutes of waiting fail to resolve the problem it is probably time to force the program to close.

Saving data

Using the End Task button in Task Manager is operationally much the same as closing a program via the usual routes. You should be presented with an opportunity to save any open files. It is possible that operating the End Task button will not have the desired effect, and it is then necessary to resort to the Processes section of Task Manager. In order to switch to this section it is merely necessary to operate the Processes tab near the top of the window. Most of the listed Processes are background tasks (Figure 2.40), but any applications that are running will also be included. For instance, in this example there is an entry for PhotoShop.

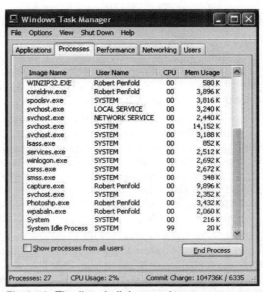

Fig.2.40 The list of all the running programs

A program can be forced to close by selecting its entry and operating the End Process button. Operate the Yes button when the warning message appears on the screen. This method is more or less guaranteed to end the program, but it will not give an opportunity to save any data that was in use by the program. Consequently, this method should only be used as a last resort. The applications program might

Fig.2.41 The Users section of Task Manager

rescue all or most of your data. It will then give the option of opening the saved data the next time the program is run. Failing that, you have to return to the last version you saved to disc. This will probably mean the loss of some work, but the loss should not be too great provided you save data at frequent intervals.

When unstable applications software makes it impossible to signoff normally, Task Master can again provide a possible solution. Operating the Users tab brings up a list of the current users, and in the example of Figure 2.41 there is just one user logged on to the system. In order to logoff, select the appropriate user and operate the Logoff button. It is possible to take things a step further by going to the Shut Down menu and selecting Restart or Turn Off. These respectively shut down the computer and restart it, and shut down the computer and switch it off.

If the system has well and truly hung-up and fails to respond to any user input, or you get an error screen explaining that Windows has been halted, there is no alternative to using a hardware reset. Operate the computer's reset button if it has one, or switch off the PC, wait a few seconds, and then switch it on again. Of course, any unsaved data will be lost if you have to exit the system in this way.

Where the system is showing signs of instability it is advisable to save your data to disc, using a new name rather than overwriting the existing file. This way, if anything should go wrong while saving the file, the existing version will not be damaged. If necessary, you can then resort to the existing version and salvage most of your data. Having saved the file, close all applications and shut down the system. Then restart it again, launch the applications, load the data files, and hope that everything then works more reliably.

It is definitely not a good idea to keep using an unstable system in the hope that things will get better. They might, but the more likely scenario is that the problem will get worse until things go seriously awry. Exiting the system and restarting is a much better strategy and it will often produce better results at the second attempt. Exiting at the first sign of trouble greatly reduces the risk of losing any data.

Customising

It is worth noting that the Processes section of Task Manager can be customised to show the required information fields. With the Processes tab selected, go to the View menu and choose the Select Columns option. This produces the window of Figure 2.42, where a tick is placed in the checkbox for each field you wish to include. Operate the OK button when you have finished, and the changes should then take immediate effect (Figure 2.43).

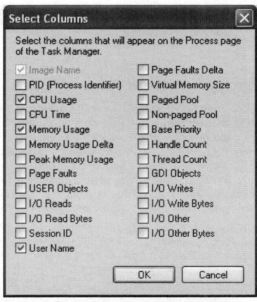

Fig.2.42 Customising the Processes section of Task Manager

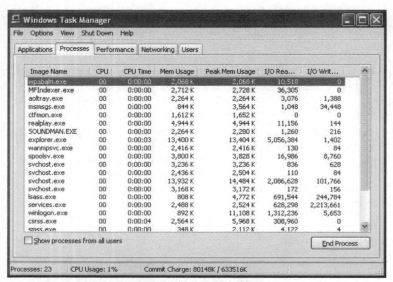

Fig.2.43 The customised version of the Processes window

Background information

As pointed out previously, most modern PCs usually have a number of background tasks in operation, and not just Windows plus any applications you are running. If you use the Control-Alt-Delete immediately after a PC has booted into Windows, you will probably find quite a long list of programs in the Processes section of the Windows Task Manager. In fact a tally of about 30 is "par for the course". Some of these programs are probably providing essential Windows functions, while others are media players, anti-virus monitoring routines, etc.

In theory, there should be no problem in having numerous background tasks provided the PC has enough memory to accommodate everything. In practice, the PC might not have sufficient memory to accommodate all the programs if there are a large number of them and you use memory hungry applications. Also, if your PC has only the minimum recommended amount of memory for the version of Windows in use, having large numbers of background tasks is inviting problems. The appearance of error messages mentioning illegal operations, fatal

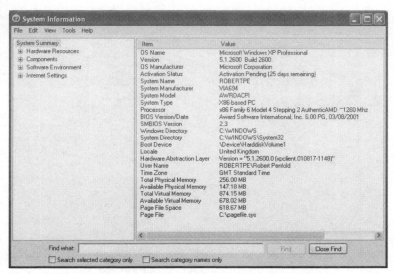

Fig.2.44 The initial screen of the System Information utility

exception errors, and page faults are often indicative of faulty or inadequate memory.

With any version of Windows you can check the amount of free memory by running the System Information utility. From the Start menu select All Programs, Accessories, System Tools, and then System Information. The Windows XP version of this utility is shown in operation in Figure 2.44. The initial page provides some general information about the processor, operating system, amount of memory, and so on. The total physical memory is the amount of RAM installed in the computer, but obviously this is not all available for applications. A substantial amount is used by Windows itself, background tasks, and another section is set aside as temporary storage space. In some versions of Windows the amount of free system resources is given as a percentage, but with Windows XP the available physical memory is quoted in megabytes instead. This is the important figure, and problems could result if this figure is very low.

Try running a couple of major applications and loading some data files into them, and then return to the System Information window. It does not automatically update the figures, so the amount of free physical memory should be the same as before. In order to update the figure go

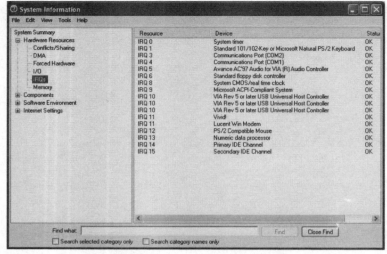

*Fig.2.45 A list of IRQ assignments provided by the System
Information program*

to the New menu and select the Refresh option. The information screen
will go blank for a fraction of a second and it will then be updated with
the new figures. These should include a reduced value for the amount
of memory available. Incidentally, the figure for virtual memory includes
hard disc space that can be used as a sort of slow alternative to RAM.

It is perhaps worth mentioning that a wide range of facts and figures can
be obtained from the System Information program. Try double clicking
on one of the entries in the left-hand section of the window, and then
select the subcategories one by one. Information on the running tasks,
memory, and many other aspects of the PC can be obtained from this
program. In Figure 2.45 the program is providing a list of the IRQ
assignments.

Dynamic information

As pointed out previously, the System Information utility does not
automatically update the information, which can sometimes produce
misleading results. The amount of memory used by a program can
change massively from one instant to the next. The amount of memory
used will often be relatively small while the program is idling and waiting

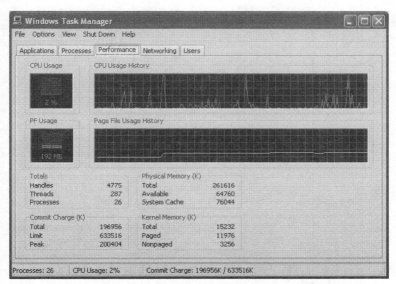

Fig.2.46 The Performance section of Task Manager in operation

for user input. A huge and almost instant increase in memory can occur if the program is then set a complex task. The same is true of microprocessor usage, which is generally minimal while a program is idle but can be very high when certain tasks are being undertaken.

The Processes section of the Windows Task Manager is usually a better source for information on memory and processor usage. This program does automatically update the information, and three refresh rates (high, normal, and low) are available from the View menu and the Update Speed submenu. There is also an option that permits the program to be paused. Remember that the information fields can be customised by way of the View menu and the Select Columns submenu.

The Peak Memory Usage is probably the most useful for checking the amount of memory used by applications. You can go through a typical session with a program and then check to determine the maximum amount of memory that it used. This is more practical than trying to manually monitor memory while using the program. The amount by which memory usage varies is often quite surprising. PhotoShop 5.0 was found to use only about 15 megabytes of memory initially, but over 128 megabytes was used when processing a large bitmap.

In order to monitor processor usage it is best to operate the Performance tab in the Windows Task Manager, which produces a display like the one shown in Figure 2.46. The top section of the window includes a graph that shows how processor use varies over time. Note that by default the Task Manager will be displayed on top of other windows, so it is reasonably easy to monitor processor usage while using applications programs. If the Task Manager is minimised, its button appears towards the right-hand side of the Windows taskbar where it acts as a simple bargraph display that shows processor usage.

The lower graph in the Performance section of Task Manager shows page file usage. The page file is what used to be known as a swap file, and it is still sometimes referred to by this name. By either name, it is a hidden file on the hard disc that the computer uses to swap data in and out of memory. In other words, it is used as an extension of memory, but data has to be placed back into the real memory for processing. This means that data is frequently swapped between the disc file and the real memory, and it is from this that the swap file name is derived. By default, the size of the page file is set at a minimum of 1.5 times the size of the real memory, or physical memory as it is usually termed. The default for the maximum size is three times the amount of physical memory. With Windows Explorer set to show hidden files, the page file can be found in the root directory of the boot drive as "pagefile.sys".

Interpretation

Figures provided by Task Manager can be misleading, and the page file usage is a good example of this. On the face of it, this figure shows the amount of data stored in the page file. Actually, it is the amount of space that is committed for use, and there is not necessarily any data stored in the file. Hence, this figure can be quite high at around 75 megabytes or more even if there are no applications running. A sudden jump in the page file usage figure is a fair indication that the file is in use and that more space has had to be committed.

The Commit Charge figures are useful where you wish to know how much of the computer's resources are in use, rather than how much a particular process is using. As well as appearing in the Performance section of Task Manager, these figures are always shown along the bottom of the Task Manager window. The Total figure is the total amount of physical and virtual memory in use by the processes that are running at the time. The Limit figure is the total amount of memory (physical and virtual) that is available to the system. Preferably, the first figure should never be near to the second one, as this would mean that the system was in danger of running out of memory. Ideally, the Total figure should not be greater than the amount of physical memory installed in the computer. There will then be little or no use of the page file, and the computer should run at maximum speed.

Solutions

It is usually pretty obvious when a computer is lacking in memory, because things slow very noticeably and the hard disc is accessed at practically every mouse click. A lack of processing power usually manifests itself by the computer seeming to hang-up when any major task is performed, although normal operation is restored when the processor eventually manages to complete the task. The Task Manager is useful in identifying the processes that use large amounts of memory or processing time.

Where a computer is lacking in speed, memory, or both, the only zero cost solution is to avoid running so many processes that it can not cope. Instead of running two or three major applications simultaneously, only run them one at a time. Memory is relatively cheap these days, so a memory upgrade is probably worthwhile in situations where a shortfall is seriously hampering performance. A processor upgrade is generally more expensive and difficult, where it is possible at all. The only solution to a serious lack of processing power might be to buy a new and much faster computer!

Reducing the number of background processes that are running can help to reduce both memory and processor usage, but do not expect this to have a dramatic effect on performance. Most background tasks do not use much memory or processor time, and switching off one or two of them will not produce a huge increase in performance. Also, bear in mind that many of these tasks are essential to the normal running of the computer. Switching off one of these essential tasks will probably result in the computer rapidly coming to a halt. Only switch off tasks if you are sure that they are nonessential. Of course, where there are large numbers of these programs and the computer has a limited amount of memory, switching off several tasks could produce a very worthwhile boost in performance.

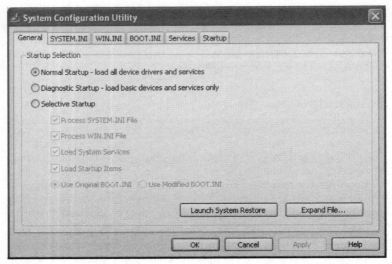

Fig.2.47 The General section of the System Configuration Utility

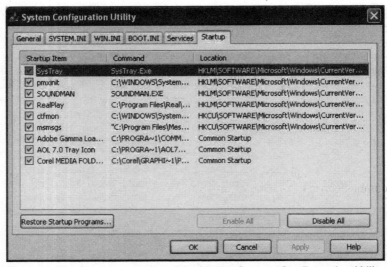

Fig.2.48 The startup programs listed in the System Configuration Utility. Unticking a checkbox blocks the relevant program at startup

Non-starters

Rather than switching off non-essential tasks once the computer is underway, they can be prevented from starting up by removing their entries in the System Configuration utility. The programs can then be run when and if they are required. In order to start the System Configuration utility, select Run from the Start menu, type "msconfig" (without the quotation marks) into the textbox, and operate the OK button. This will produce a window like the one shown in Figure 2.47. By default the General section is shown, and this is a useful diagnostics tool. In this case though, it is the Startup section that is required (Figure 2.48), and this is brought up by operating the appropriate tab.

A list of startup programs is shown, and each one has a checkbox. Removing the tick from a checkbox results in that program not being loaded at startup. By removing a tick you are not uninstalling that program and it can still be launched manually. In addition, a program can be reinstated by going back to the System Configuration utility and restoring the tick to its checkbox. For the sake of this

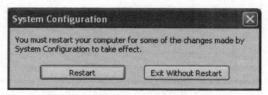

Fig.2.49 Operate the Restart button to check that the changes have taken effect

example, the ticks for the Soundman and Realplay programs were removed. The Apply and Close buttons are operated once the required changes have been made.

The deselected programs will not be switched off by the System Configuration utility, and a warning message to this effect will be displayed on the screen (Figure 2.49). These programs will not be launched on subsequent occasions when the computer is booted. It is advisable to operate the Restart button so that you can check that the changes have taken effect. Once back in Windows XP, use the Control-Alt-Delete key combination to launch the Windows Task Manager and then operate the Processes tab to produce a list of running processes. This should not include the startup programs that have been suppressed. Figure 2.50 shows the list of running processes on the example system, and both the Soundman and Realplay programs are missing from the list.

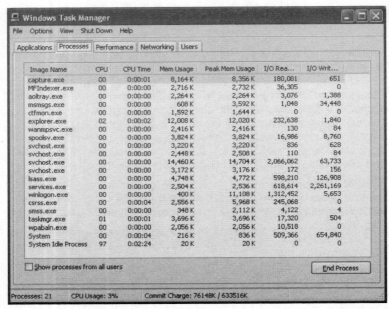

*Fig.2.50 With the computer rebooted, the two suppressed programs
are no longer listed, indicating that they have been
successfully prevented from running at startup*

Points to remember

Do not mess around with the Windows Registry, configuration files, or any part of the system unless you know exactly what you are doing.

Do not delete files manually unless you are sure it is safe to remove them. Where possible, programs should be removed using their own uninstall utility or the built-in facility of Windows.

Avoid using any form of beta or test software. If you wish to experiment with software of dubious stability, have a PC specifically for this purpose.

Do not blame Windows if things grind to a halt before the boot-up sequence starts. A failure this early in the start up sequence is due to a hardware fault or an error in the BIOS settings.

A hardware fault can be responsible for the boot-up process failing almost as soon as it starts, or never actually starting. However, it could be due to damaged or missing boot files, so try replacing them using the Recovery Console and the Fixboot command.

If you have access to some diagnostics software, use it to check that the problem is not due to a hardware fault. Be careful to use Windows XP compatible utilities, or MS-DOS programs run with the aid of an MS-DOS boot disc.

Make sure the expansion cards are fitted into their expansion slots correctly.

If the boot process stalls late in the boot sequence check that the hardware drivers are properly installed. One of the programs that runs at start up could also be the cause of the problem.

The fact that a virus has not announced its presence does not mean it is not there. If there are inexplicable problems with the system, use anti-virus programs to scan the files on the hard disc, recently used floppy discs, etc. Ideally an anti-virus program should be installed on the PC and used to make regular checks of the system.

Do not switch off your PC while Windows is still running. Shut down Windows first, and then switch off your PC if it is a type that does not switch off automatically.

Even if the operating system or applications software is behaving abnormally, try to close down the system properly.

Do not get your computer to "bite off more than it can chew". There is a limit to the amount of software that a PC can have running at the same time. The operating system can be damaged if the computer keeps running out of resources and crashing. The Windows Task Manager is useful for monitoring running processes and their use of system resources.

Preventing unnecessary programs from running automatically at startup can help to conserve system resources. Most startup programs are easily blocked using the System Configuration utility.

Troubleshooting

Booting problems

Many users of MS-DOS were surprised at the ease with which the new operating system could be halted in its tracks when they moved to Windows 95. A relatively simple operating system such as MS-DOS does not usually fail to boot unless there is damage to one of the boot files. Normally when things go wrong it will throw up a few error messages during the boot process, and some entries in the configuration files will be ignored. The operating system might not operate exactly as you would like once the system has booted, but the system will usually boot. Having booted, it will to a large extent be functioning and usable.

The situation is different with a complex operating systems such as Windows 95 and the subsequent Windows operating systems, including Windows XP. These are all dependent on numerous files being present and correct on the hard disc. If any of these files is damaged or absent, or a configuration file erroneously specifies a file that is not present, the boot process will often stop about half way through. When Windows does manage to boot successfully despite such problems, it is likely to be unstable and come to a halt later in the proceedings.

Windows XP is more robust than previous versions of Windows, but it does not operate under the "boot anyway" philosophy of MS-DOS. The cautious approach of Windows operating systems could be by accident rather than design, but it is probably a safety measure to ensure that the system only boots if it can do so reliably. With a complex operating system such as Windows XP, the last thing you need is the system booting but then running amok.

Not all Windows faults centre on boot problems, but it is probably true to say that the vast majority of serious problems involve the boot process stalling at some point in the proceedings. Windows can boot normally and then give difficulties, but this is often the result of problems elsewhere in the system. Hardware faults and bugs in applications software can both produce this kind of behaviour. Much of this chapter is therefore devoted to boot problems, and it is this topic that is covered first.

Safety first

Do not jump to the conclusion that the system has become unusable because Windows crashes during the boot-up sequence. There could be a major problem, but it is worth resetting the computer a couple of times to see if the problem clears itself. Also, try switching off, waiting a few seconds, and then turning the PC on again. There can be an occasional problem with a piece of hardware failing to reset properly at switch-on. Switching the PC off and on again will usually clear this sort of problem. If that fails, boot in Safe Mode (as described in detail in the next part of this chapter), shut down Windows in the usual way, and then try rebooting normally.

When repeated attempts to boot the system result in the boot process coming to a premature end, Windows should be booted in Safe Mode again. This is a sort of very basic "boot at all costs" mode that can be used when troubleshooting. There are other modes that can be useful when Windows troubleshooting. In order to boot into one of these modes the F8 function key must be pressed as soon as the BIOS start up routine ends and the boot process begins. There is only a very brief gap between the BIOS finishing its start up processes and the system starting to boot, so you must press F8 as soon as the BIOS has finished its routine. In fact with some systems the only reliable way of entering Safe mode is to repeatedly press F8 as the end of the start up routine approaches. Pressing F8 when using Windows XP brings up the simple menu system shown in Figure 3.1. This is a summary of the options:

Start Windows Normally

Booting using the Normal option takes the PC through a normal Windows XP boot-up process, but it is obviously of no use if the computer has a major boot problem. Selecting this option will simply result in the computer rebooting and hanging up gain.

Safe Mode

Safe Mode boots into Windows XP, but only a minimalist version of the operating system. The display is a basic type that usually offers a minimum of 640 by 480 pixel resolution in up to 24-bit colour depth. However, depending on the video card installed in your PC and the set-up, the resolution might be higher at 800 by 600 pixel resolution, and the normal colour depth might be available. This mode should be familiar to anyone familiar with Windows 9x troubleshooting, and it is much the same as the Windows 9x equivalent. In general, the Windows XP version

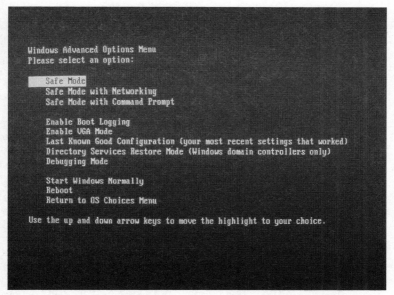

Fig.3.1 Safe Mode is selected from the Advanced Options Menu

of Safe Mode is better because less of the hardware is disabled. Even with the basic 640 by 480 pixel resolution and the other limitations of this mode, it is often possible to use it to fix Windows problems.

Although more functional than the Windows 9x Safe Mode, there are still some items of hardware that do not work in this mode. Items such as the soundcard, CD-ROM drive and modem might not be operational in this mode. Some hardware drivers are not loaded during the boot process in order to increase the chances of booting into Safe Mode. In Windows 9x Safe Mode the CD-ROM drives are always disabled, but standard IDE types will normally be operational in Windows XP's Safe Mode. This is more than a little helpful. Peripherals connected to the USB ports do not normally function, but USB keyboards and mice will do so provided the computer's BIOS provides the necessary support. Startup programs are not loaded when Safe Mode is used.

Most of the usual Windows fault-finding and configuration facilities are available from Safe Mode. System Restore, Device Manager, the Registry Editor, and the Backup utility are all available. Obviously in a minimalist Windows environment there can be some restrictions on services available, but they work more or less normally. Boot problems are often caused by faults in the drivers for new hardware, and having access to Device Manager and System Restore means that most problems of this type can be rapidly sorted out.

Safe Mode with Networking

This is essentially the same as the normal Safe Mode, but the drivers, etc., needed for Windows networking are loaded.

Safe Mode with Command Prompt

Despite the name of this mode, it is nothing like the normal Safe Mode. The computer is booted using a basic set of drivers, but it is booted into an MS-DOS style environment, complete with a command prompt. In most cases it is much easier to undertake troubleshooting using the normal Safe Mode with its graphical user interface. However, the command line version of Safe Mode might be usable when it is impossible to boot into the standard version.

Enable Boot Logging

This mode boots the computer normally, but a log file showing the name and status of each driver is placed on the hard disc. The log file is updated as each driver is loaded, and the idea is that the last entry in the file will identify the driver that is causing the system to crash. In practice, things are not quite as simple as that, but it is nevertheless a useful feature if the problem is proving to be elusive.

Enable VGA Mode

The VGA mode is not a normal troubleshooting mode, and it is not intended as an aid to locating faults. It boots the computer normally, but into the standard VGA mode rather than the normal startup mode of the video card. This is useful if there is a problem with the video settings, such as a refresh rate that is too high for the monitor. Boot in this mode and then adjust the video settings to restore proper operation.

Directory Services Restore Mode

This is only available with Windows XP Professional, and it seems to be of very limited practical value.

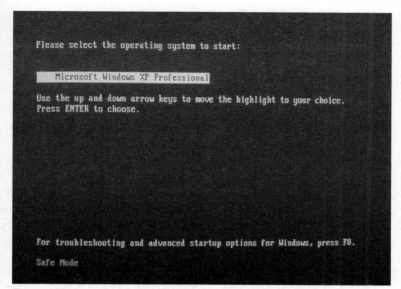

Fig.3.2 This menu will usually list a single operating system

Debugging Mode

This is another mode that you will probably never need to use. The computer is booted into Windows kernel mode, and the debugging is then achieved via another computer running a suitable debugger program, with a serial link use to provide communication between the two computers.

Last Known Good Configuration

Similar in concept to using the System Restore facility, but more limited in its scope. It effectively takes the computer back in time to the last settings that enabled it to boot successfully. Unlike the System Restore facility, this mode does not erase or restore files. The file structure remains unchanged, but an earlier version of the Registry is used when booting the computer. Obviously, this mode will only be successful when the cause of the problem is an error or errors in the Registry. The System Restore facility is more likely to restore normal operation.

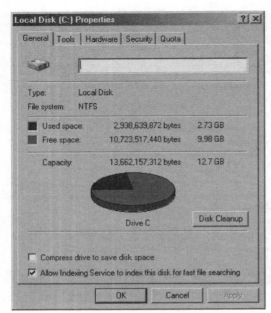

Fig.3.3 Obtaining disc drive information

Using Safe Mode

Safe Mode is the usual starting point when boot problems occur. Use the cursor keys to highlight this option in the Windows Advanced Options menu, and then press enter to start the boot process. A screen like the one of Figure 3.2 will then appear. Where appropriate, select the correct operating system and then press the Return key to continue booting into Safe Mode. At the logon screen, sign in as the Administrator so that you have maximum freedom to make adjustments to the system.

A warning message towards the end of the boot process explains that Safe Mode provides a simplified version of the operating system. It is only intended to permit problems with the system to be traced and fixed, and it is not designed to permit the system to be used normally. I suppose that in an emergency it might be possible to run applications programs in Safe mode, but this is something that should only done when suitably desperate. Operate the Yes button to remove the button and complete the boot into Safe Mode.

Once the PC is booted in Safe mode you can undertake some basic checks, and the usual starting point used to be the Windows Scandisk utility. However, this has not been included with Windows XP, which instead uses the Check Disk program. This is supplied in two versions, which are a graphical user interface program and a command line utility (Chkdsk.exe). For most purposes the graphical user interface program will suffice, and this is easily accessed. In My Computer or Windows

Explorer, right-click the entry for the drive you wish to check and then choose Properties from the popup menu. This produces a window like the one of Figure 3.3, that gives some basic information about the drive.

Operate the Tools tab to switch to a Window like the one in Figure 3.4, which includes an error checking facility. Left clicking the Check Now button produces the small window of Figure 3.5, where two options are available via the checkboxes. Initially

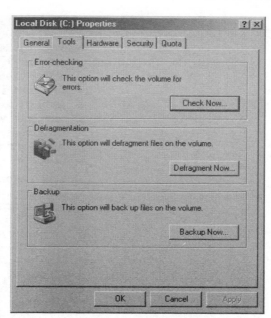

Fig.3.4 Operate the Check Now button

it is probably best to leave both checkboxes blank, and to go ahead with the checking process by operating the Start button. The program will then check the disc for errors, showing its progress in the lower section of the Window (Figure 3.6). Once the process has been completed, the program will either report that there were no errors or give a list of the problems that were detected.

If faults were detected it is advisable to run the program again, but using one or both of the options provided by the checkboxes. One option sets the program to automatically fix any errors that are detected. This is the quicker of the two options. The second option results in the

Fig.3.5 Two options are available from this Window

program going through a very thorough checking process. It will try to recover locate bad sectors in the disc and recover any data contained by those sectors. Using this option helps to minimise the damage caused by disc errors, but with large drives it can many hours for the task to be completed. Once underway there is no way out of the program other than switching off the computer, which has the potential to increase the number of disc errors and is definitely not a good idea.

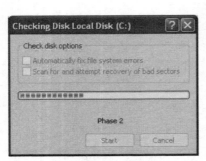

Fig.3.6 The bargraph plots the program's progress

The program is unable to fix errors in a disc that is currently in use, which means that it can not check the boot drive while Windows is running. Trying to check a disc that is in use produces the error message of Figure 3.7. To go ahead with the checking and fixing process, operate the Yes button and restart the computer. The checking program will be launched during the boot process, before the boot drive is left with any open files. The screen will show how things are progressing (Figure 3.8), and the boot process will continue once the disc checker has completed its task.

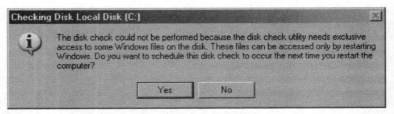

Fig.3.7 An error message is produced if the disc is in use

Users of Windows 9x operating systems soon become used to Scandisk running automatically during the boot routine if the computer has not been shout down properly. Check Disk is likely to run automatically at boot-up if a system having a FAT32 boot disc is shut down abnormally, but it is unlikely to run automatically in systems that have a NTFS boot

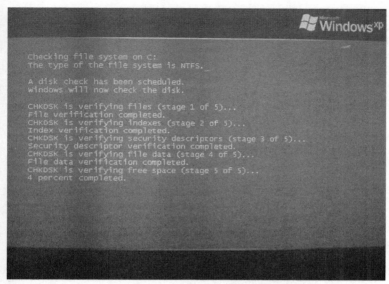

Fig.3.8 The program can be run automatically at startup

disc. This is because the NTFS system is better able to recover from abnormal disc activity, making it unnecessary to run Check Disk at the slightest excuse. There is probably no point in running Check Disk manually if the computer was not shut down properly, because it is unlikely that any disc writing errors would have been produced.

Hardware drivers

Devices such as soundcards, video cards, and even the built-in interfaces of the PC such as the parallel and USB ports require drivers to integrate them with the Windows operating system. Problems with Windows drivers are not exactly a rarity, and it is best to check for driver faults sooner rather than later. The normal way of doing this is to go into Device Manager. In Windows XP it can be launched from the Start menu by first selecting the Control Panel option and then double clicking on the System icon. This launches the window of Figure 3.9, where the Hardware tab should be operated. In the new window (Figure 3.10), left-click on the Device Manager button, and you will then have a screen something like Figure 3.11.

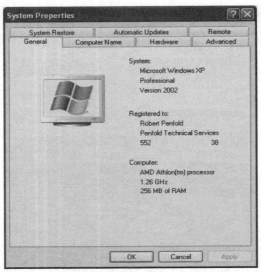

Fig.3.9 The System Properties window

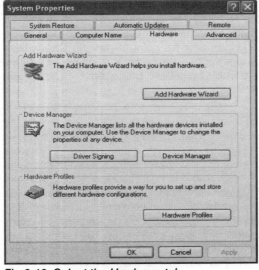

Fig.3.10 Select the Hardware tab

Normally there will be a yellow exclamation mark (!) against an entry if the program has detected a problem with the item of hardware in that category. Double clicking on an entry in the table expands it to show all the drivers in that category, and where appropriate there will be an exclamation mark against an entry. In fact Windows will usually expand a category for you if it contains an item of hardware that seems to have a problem. In the example of Figure 3.12, the section for Sound, video and games controllers has been expanded, but there are no problems shown with any of the devices. In normal operation it is possible to double-click on an entry that has a question or exclamation mark in order to get further details on the problem.

Unfortunately, in Safe Mode Device Manager is not fully

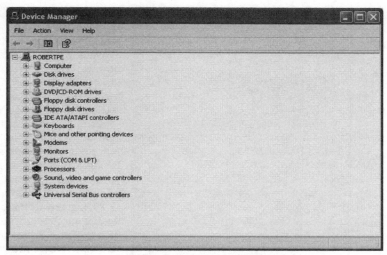

Fig.3.11 The Windows XP version of Device Manager

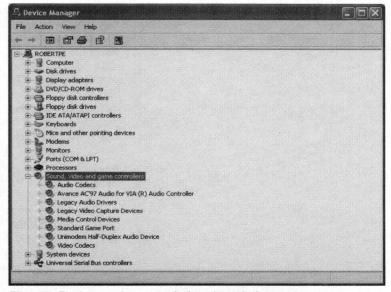

Fig.3.12 Entries can be expanded to show their contents

Fig.3.13 Status information is often unavailable in Safe Mode

Fig.3.14 Some status information is available

operational, and its diagnostic abilities are rather limited. No device drivers are loaded for several items of hardware, so no errors will be reported for these devices. If you try to get status information in Safe Mode you simply get a message of the type shown in Figure 3.13, explaining that status information is not available in Safe Mode. Note that Device Manager should provide status information for any hardware that is fully available in Safe Mode, such as the keyboard and floppy disc drive. For example, Figure 3.14 shows the properties window for the floppy disc drive, and it is being reported as working properly.

If you think an item of hardware might be causing the problem, operate the Troubleshoot button in the General section of its properties window. This starts the appropriate

Hardware Troubleshooter, as in the disc drive example of Figure 3.15. This tries to locate and cure the problem in standard wizard fashion. The Hardware Troubleshooter is considered in more detail later in this chapter.

Despite its limitations in Safe Mode, Device Manager can still be useful. It might indicate a problem with an item of hardware that is supported in Safe Mode. Often boot problems occur when a new piece of hardware has been added to a computer. It is not a foregone conclusion that the new hardware is the cause of the boot failure, but it is very likely that it is the culprit. Using Device Manager the device drivers for the new hardware can be removed, and with luck the computer will boot normally again. You are then in a better position to deal with the troublesome hardware. Going through the installation process again might produce better results, but in most cases an updated device driver will have to be obtained from the hardware manufacturer.

Old hardware

It is best not to jump to conclusions where the PC is one that has been in use for some time and it has undergone some changes to the hardware over the years. Is the "faulty" hardware actually something that was removed when you upgraded the computer a year ago? Is it something that is no longer in use because it ceased working when you upgraded the computer to Windows XP? Windows XP is good at automatically adjusting to changes in the hardware, but it might not always get it right.

Problems with hardware will not necessarily prevent Windows from booting, so the computer might have been working properly for some time although there was a perceived problem. With things such as mice and soundcards the PC will often boot-up even if there is a problem, but the hardware concerned will not work properly. If the hardware is no longer in use or has actually been removed from the system, you will probably remain blissfully unaware of the problem reported in Device Manager. The drivers for more crucial items of hardware such as the hard disc drive and the video card are more likely to bring the boot process to a halt. Although they might not be doing any harm, it is a good idea to remove or disable any drivers for hardware that is no longer in use. This makes sure that the unnecessary drivers can not cause any problems.

Where hardware problems are found in Device Manager it certainly makes sense to sort them out before trying to proceed further. This might get the system working properly again or there could still be boot problems,

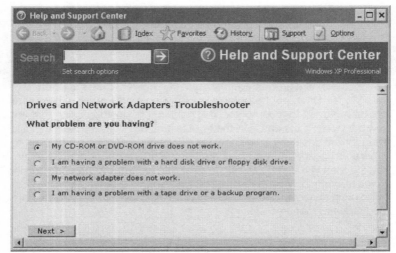

Fig.3.15 An example of a Hardware Troubleshooter

but it at least clears away some potential causes of
the problem. Reinstalling drivers can be problematic with the old drivers
still in place. Even though there is a suspected problem with the existing
ones, Windows can be reluctant to replace them with drivers that do not
have a later date. It is best to remove the existing drivers and then shut
down Windows and reboot the system.

Removing drivers

Device drivers are easily removed using the Windows XP version of Device
Manager, but you will notice some differences if you are used to the
Windows 9x version. Left clicking on the relevant entry to highlight it and
then operating the Remove button is not possible due to the lack of a
Remove button! Instead, right-click on the relevant entry to produce a
popup menu (Figure 3.16). The options available from the menu depends
on the type of hardware concerned, but there are Disable and Uninstall
options for normal hardware such as modems and game ports.
Essentially the same facilities can be obtained by double clicking on an
entry in Device Manager. This produces the property window for the
device (Figure 3.17), and selecting the Driver tab switches the window to
look something like Figure 3.18.

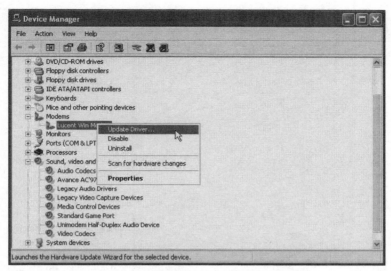

Fig.3.16 This popup menu has an Uninstall option

The Uninstall option is equivalent to the Remove button in Windows 9x, and it is used to remove the device driver. Note that with Plug and Play devices the drivers can only be uninstalled if the hardware is present in the PC and active. With the hardware absent or disabled, it will not have an entry in Device Manager. A warning message like the one in Figure 3.19 appears when the Uninstall button is operated. Left-click

Fig.3.17 A hardware property window

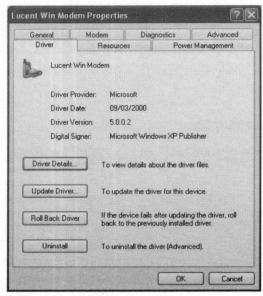

Fig.3.18 The Driver section of the window

the Yes button in order to proceed and uninstall the device drivers. The entry for the uninstalled device should then disappear from the list in Device Manager.

A Disable option is available from the popup menu or the menu at the bottom of the General section of the Properties window. This option differs from uninstalling the drivers in that they remain on the disc and are ready for use. Windows will ignore them though, and the hardware becomes "invisible" to the system without the drivers installed. The relevant entry will remain in Device Manager, but with a cross over its icon to indicate that the device has been disabled (Figure

3.20). An enable option is then available, so that the device can be reinstated again.

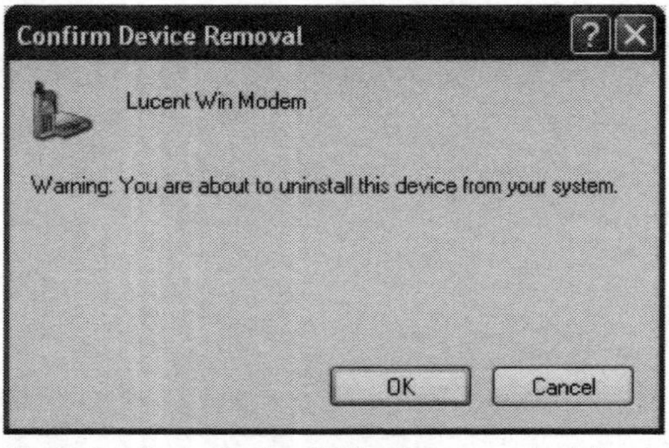

This facility is not designed solely as an aid to troubleshooting, but it is clearly useful to be able to temporarily disable a device that is suspected of causing problems. If the

Fig.3.19 Operate the OK button to uninstall the drives

computer will boot perfectly well with the suspect device disabled, but not when it is enabled, it is certainly the source of the problem. If the problem persists when the suspect device is disabled, it is highly unlikely that it has anything to do with the boot failure. Note that it is not possible to select a category from the Device Manager list and then remove or disable it. Each entry has to be managed individually. A category will be removed if all the devices it contains are uninstalled.

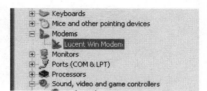

Fig.3.20 *The cross means that the device has been disabled*

Roll back

In addition to Uninstall and Disable options, Device Manager may also permit drivers to be rolled back. The Roll Back Driver feature is for use with recently installed device drivers that were supposed to give improved performance but actually make matters worse. This is unlikely to happen when using signed (Microsoft approved) drivers, but is quite likely to occur when testing beta versions. Unless you are suitably expert, using any sort of beta test software is not a good idea, and signed device drivers should always be used wherever possible.

If things do go badly awry with an updated driver, using the Roll Back Driver option is an easy way to remove the new drivers and reinstate the old ones. Incidentally, this feature is new to Windows XP and it is not available in earlier versions of Windows. Obviously, this feature is only available where the original drivers have been updated, and an error message will appear if it is used with the original device drivers. It is otherwise just a matter of following the onscreen prompts until the roll back is complete.

Multiple drivers

Where (say) just one out of four drivers for a soundcard is not working properly, it is best to remove all the drivers and reinstall everything "from scratch". Note that it is not safe to equate each category in Device Manager with a single piece of hardware. For example, the category that has the entries for a soundcard might also contain entries for a modem. The entries in Device Manager usually make it clear which

piece of hardware each one is related to, but if in doubt you can always right-click on an entry and select the Properties option. The information in the General section should be specific about the piece of hardware linked to each entry. In the example of Figure 3.21 the driver is clearly related to a modem, even though it was grouped with the soundcard entries and was not in the Modem section.

Fig.3.21   The hardware associated with each driver should be indicated

Updating

Reinstalling drivers sometimes has the desired effect, but the problem is often due to a fault in the driver software. In some cases reinstallation seems to cure the problem, but before too long it returns again. In other instances the problem returns immediately when the drivers are reinstalled. If you have an Internet connection it is a good idea to check the manufacturer's web site to see if a more recent version of the driver software is available. There are usually frequent updates to the drivers for newer items of equipment.

In general, it is not a good idea to install an updated driver with the old version still in place, so use Device Manager to remove the original driver before installing the new one. One exception to this is where the updated driver is not actually a full set of driver software. Sometimes the new version uses some of the original files, while changing other files and (or) adding new ones. As always, read the installation instructions before installing the new software. This should state whether the original drivers should be left in place or removed. If it is does not, then the old drivers should be removed prior to installing the new ones. It might give other warnings, and it is often necessary to switch off anti-virus software before installing new drivers, for example.

The standard method of updating drivers is to use the Update Driver facility of Device Manager. This is straightforward in use, but many manufactures provide a Setup program with new drivers. This program is located using Windows Explorer, and then run by double clicking its entry. Installation is then largely automatic, although there will be the usual licensing agreements to agree to. The new drivers will take effect as soon as the computer has been rebooted. Either method should work, but where a Setup program is included with the drivers, it is advisable to use it rather than try to install the drivers using Device Manager.

Hardware problems

If repeated reinstallation of the drivers fails to clear the yellow exclamation marks, and updated drivers do not help either, it is quite likely that the cause of the trouble is a hardware fault. In the case of an expansion card, check that it is fitted in its expansion slot using the simple method outlined in chapter 2. If the PC can be booted in normal mode, use Device Manager to check the cause of the problem. Double-click on the entry for the troublesome device to bring up its Properties window. The program may be vague in its reporting of the fault, stating something along the lines that the device is not working properly, and that the hardware is faulty or the drivers are not installed.

Sometimes the reporting is more specific, perhaps stating that there is a hardware conflict. This means that the device needs to use resources of the computer that are already used by another piece of hardware. A problem of this type should not occur if the PC has been in use and working well for some time. It is more the type of thing that happens when new hardware is added to a PC, particularly if it is already fitted with some older expansion cards. A hardware conflict is not strictly speaking a Windows problem, and goes beyond the scope of this book.

Windows provides some built-in help for dealing with this type of thing in the form of the Hardware Troubleshooter. As pointed out previously, this can be launched by operating the Troubleshoot button in the device's Properties window. Wizards will then guide you through the process of sorting things out. With luck, the problem will soon be cured, but if inadequate resources are available for all the hardware there will be no

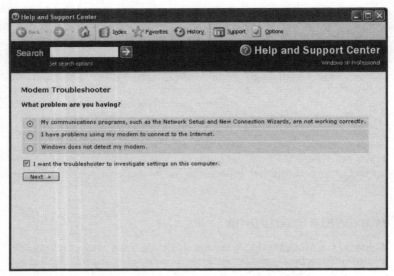

Fig.3.22 The initial window of the Modem Troubleshooter

alternative to disabling one of the devices producing the conflict. The Troubleshoot option is available for any item of installed hardware, and it will help to solve a wide range of problems via a simple question and answer routine.

Figure 3.22 shows an example of the Troubleshooter in action, and in this case it is helping to cure problems with a modem. The first questions try to broadly define the fault, while later ones look for specific problems. For the sake of this example we will assume that the basic problem is that Windows is not detecting the modem, and the appropriate radio button is therefore operated, followed by the Next button. The next window (Figure 3.23) gets you to establish that the modem is connected correctly. The appropriate radio button is selected after some simple checks have been completed, and the process then moves on to the next stage. The Troubleshooter facility is sometimes criticised for being too simplistic, but it can be useful for those lacking experience in hardware troubleshooting.

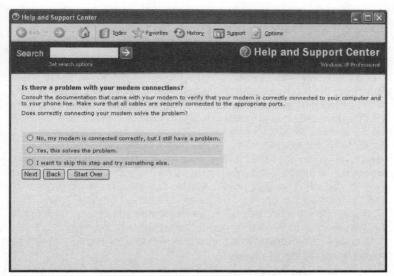

Fig.3.23 The second screen has a further question to answer

Logging

If no problems can be found with the hardware, or sorting out the problems that are found makes no different to the boot problems, it is time to look elsewhere for the fault. Newly installed software that makes a mess of a configuration file is probably the most common cause of Windows start up problems. If the system refuses to boot just after some new software has been installed it is odds-on that the installation program has made a mistake somewhere in the process. There are two options in the Windows 9x start up menu that help you to discover the root cause of the fault when the system refuses to boot. These are the logged start up and step by step confirmation modes. Windows XP offers a logged start up but no step by step confirmation mode is provided.

In the past, it was normal for PCs to display a long string of messages detailing what was happening during the boot process. These messages are not normally displayed on a modern PC unless it is booted in some sort of diagnostics mode. The basic function of the logged boot up is to write these messages to a file called Ntbtlog.txt that is placed in the Windows directory of the boot disc. This file can be read using any text editor or word processor. Note that this is different to the equivalent start up mode of Windows 9x where the log file was called Bootlog.txt and stored in the root folder of the boot drive. With Windows 9x the previous version of the file, if there is one, is saved as Bootlog.prv. There is no equivalent of this in Windows XP, so you must rename log files if you wish to avoid having them overwritten by any subsequent log files.

Apart from the fact that the log file is generated, Windows boots normally when the logged mode is selected. With Windows failing to boot properly, it is therefore necessary to boot in logged mode and let the boot process fail, reset the computer, restart it in Safe Mode, and then examine the contents of the log file. One of Window's built-in text editors can be used to examine the Ntbtlog file if your PC is not equipped with a word processor. From the Start menu choose All Programs, Accessories and then Wordpad. This produces a simple but effective word processor, and the Ntbtlog file can be loaded by selecting File and Open. This produces the standard Windows file requester that can be directed to the Windows directory. Make sure that either text (txt) files or all files (*.*) is selected in the lower part of the window, or Ntbtlog.txt will be "invisible" to the file requester.

Once loaded, there is no difficulty in making a detailed examination of the file's contents. The list of messages is comprehensive and provides a full list of every action during boot up. The file also shows whether each action was successful. This is just a small sample from a long Ntbtlog file:

```
Microsoft (R) Windows (R) Version 5.1 (Build
2600)
 1 17 2002 23:42:37.500
Loaded driver \WINDOWS\system32\ntoskrnl.exe
Loaded driver \WINDOWS\system32\hal.dll
Loaded driver \WINDOWS\system32\KDCOM.DLL
Loaded driver \WINDOWS\system32\BOOTVID.dll
Loaded driver ACPI.sys
Loaded driver
\WINDOWS\System32\DRIVERS\WMILIB.SYS
Loaded driver pci.sys
Loaded driver isapnp.sys
Loaded driver viaide.sys
Loaded driver
\WINDOWS\System32\DRIVERS\PCIIDEX.SYS
Loaded driver MountMgr.sys
```

```
Loaded driver ftdisk.sys
Loaded driver dmload.sys
Loaded driver dmio.sys
Loaded driver PartMgr.sys
Loaded driver VolSnap.sys
Loaded driver atapi.sys
Loaded driver disk.sys
Loaded driver
\WINDOWS\System32\DRIVERS\CLASSPNP.SYS
Loaded driver sr.sys
Loaded driver Fastfat.sys
Loaded driver KSecDD.sys
Loaded driver NDIS.sys
Loaded driver viaagp.sys
Loaded driver Mup.sys
Did not load driver Advanced Configuration and
Power Interface (ACPI) PC
Did not load driver Audio Codecs
Did not load driver Legacy Audio Drivers
Did not load driver Media Control Devices
Did not load driver Legacy Video Capture
Devices
Did not load driver Video Codecs
Did not load driver WAN Miniport (L2TP)
Did not load driver WAN Miniport (IP)
Did not load driver WAN Miniport (PPPOE)
```

As with all faultfinding, resist the temptation to jump to conclusions. In this short extract from the log file there are several lines that indicate something was not loaded. However, it is obvious that things did not come to an immediate halt because the boot process continued for hundreds more lines and processes. Most boot log files, whether for Windows 9x or XP, seem to show a few failed processes that turn out to be of no consequence. With a Windows XP upgrade it is very likely that there will be a large number of lines indicating that files were not loaded. Any "leftover" Windows 9x files that no longer serve any purpose because they are incompatible with Windows XP will not be loaded. Even where Windows XP has been installed from scratch, it seems to be quite normal for numerous files not to be loaded.

It is conceivable that an error early in the proceedings could result in failure later in the boot process, but it is towards the end of the boot log file that the cause of the problem is most likely to be found. Ideally, you should make a boot log file when the computer is functioning normally, and then save it on the disc under a new name. This file can then be compared with a new boot log file if boot problems should develop. This should reduce the risk of being misled by failed processes that are not completed during a normal boot into Windows. It is perhaps worth pointing out that unlike Windows 9x, Windows XP does not boot MS-DOS and then load Windows on top of MS-DOS. It is DOS-free and boots straight into Windows. Hence, the initial part of a Windows XP boot log looks very different to a Windows 9x type, with no sign of the usual MS-DOS start up files.

Error message

The cause of Windows stalling during start up is something you will not necessarily have to strive to discover. More often than not Windows will halt with a message stating the reason for everything suddenly grinding to a halt. Sometimes the problem will be due to a missing file. In fact, it seems to be due to a damaged or missing file in most instances. A damaged file could be one that has become corrupted, or perhaps it has been overwritten by a rogue installer program. Some of the error messages are rather cryptic, but the Microsoft web site gives information on error codes that should help to clarify the likely cause of the problem. Using part of the error code in the search engine should be sufficient to produce some useful information on the problem.

If the problem occurs after a piece of software has just been uninstalled, it is likely that the uninstaller removed a file that is needed by another program. The easy solution is to boot in Safe Mode and reinstall the software, which should reinstate the file that Windows considers to be essential. Assuming that this is successful, you can either take the easy option and leave the reinstalled program in place, or try removing it again. The fact that the original removal of the program did not go entirely according to plan does not necessarily mean that a second attempt will also fail. On the other hand, it will not be a great surprise if it does fail.

It is worth making the point that installing and uninstalling software tends to be less troublesome if you always opt for the default directory rather than choosing another directory. I am not entirely sure why this should be, but it is probably due to minor errors in some installer and uninstaller programs. Anyway, unless there is a good reason to do otherwise, always settle for the default directory.

In the event of the boot process failing again, reinstalling the software once more should restore normal operation. You are not necessarily stuck with the program for life, and normal operation should be possible if the program is removed again and the contentious file is reinstated. The file causing the problem could be in the program's directory structure or in the Windows directory structure. Either way, using the file search function of Windows Explorer should soon locate it. Copy the file to a temporary directory and then uninstall the program.

If the file was copied from somewhere in the Windows directory structure, copy it back to that location. If it was it the program's own directory structure, the directory it came from might have been removed by the uninstaller. One approach to the problem is to remake part of the erased directory structure so that the file can be copied back to its original location. This might not be necessary though, and in most cases Windows will find the file if it is placed in the Windows directory structure where files of a similar type are located. In the case of a DLL file for example, Windows should find the file if it is copied to the Windows/ System and Windows/System32 folders.

File hunt

In cases where reinstalling a recently uninstalled program is ineffective, or there is no recently uninstalled software to put back, reinstalling Windows is probably the best option. If Windows is reinstalled on top of the existing installation there should be no problems with your applications software. Any programs that are correctly installed with Windows should remain so after Windows itself has been reinstalled. This assumes that the existing Windows installation is not totally wrecked, and that it is repairable. Where large numbers of important files have been wiped out, there may be no option but to rescue as much of your data as possible and then reinstall everything from scratch.

Although one might think that reinstalling Windows would always cure any boot problems, it is only fair to point out that it is not a universal panacea. In a fair proportion of cases it will get things back into working order, but sometimes the problem with the old installation is carried through into the new one. When Windows is installed over an existing installation, some of the settings from the old installation are copied to the new one. This is necessary in order to integrate installed programs into the new Windows installation, but it provides a route for an existing problem to find its way into the new installation.

If no easy solution can be found to a Windows boot problem it is certainly worthwhile trying reinstallation before spending large amounts of time trying to precisely identify and cure the problem. Reinstalling Windows does not take all that long and there is a reasonable chance that it will get the operating system fully operational again. If the problem is due to a missing file, and it is a standard Windows file that has gone "absent without leave", reinstallation should get Windows running properly again. Similarly, if a standard Windows file has become corrupted, reinstalling Windows should overwrite the damage file with a sound version and cure the problem. Installing Windows "from scratch" and on top of an existing installation are both covered in chapter 6.

Problems with missing and corrupted files often involve dynamic link library files, or DLL files as they are usually termed. These files are easily spotted when browsing the hard disc as they all have a "dll" extension. Some users make a backup copy of all the DLL files on the hard disc so that any files of this type that are accidentally erased or overwritten by an earlier version can be easily replaced. Windows XP does its best to protect system files, including DLL types. If you are feeling brave, try using Windows Explorer to locate a DLL file in the Windows/System directory,

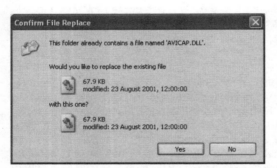

Fig.3.24 This warning message is produced because the original file is still in place

and then delete it. Next go to the Recycle Bin and try restoring it. This will produce something like Figure 3.24, asking if you wish to overwrite the existing (and identical) file of that name. In other words, the file was not actually deleted. It was simply copied to the Recycle Bin.

It is unlikely that any protection system will 100 percent effective while still permitting necessary changes to be made to the system. In addition, a hardware glitch could result in damage to any files. Consequently, it can still be worthwhile backing up DLL files. The subject of backing up DLL files is covered in chapter 5. There will be a vast number of DLL files on the backup disc or directory, but if the one you require is actually there it should not take too long to locate it using the Find Folders or Files facility in Windows Explorer. It can then be copied to the appropriate folder using Windows Explorer.

Searching Windows

On the face of it, if a DLL file is damaged or missing and you think it might be on the Windows XP installation disc, browsing the disc should bring it to light. In practice there is a minor complication in that most of the Windows files are not stored on the installation disc as individual files. Instead you will find a number of cabinet files on the disc, and these are the ones that have a "cab" extension. Many of the Windows files are compressed and grouped together in these cabinet files, but if you double-click on one of them using Windows Explorer the files within each one will be shown as if they were separate entities. Note that some file compression/decompression programs will automatically launch if you try to open a cabinet file. Where appropriate, this program can be used instead of the built-in facilities of Windows Explorer.

The files within a cabinet file can be copied using the normal Windows Explorer methods such as Copy and Paste. Therefore, it is possible to copy a file from the installation disc so that a missing or damaged file can be replaced. Finding a specific file on the installation disc could be difficult, but the search facility of Windows Explorer is equal to the task. It will find files even if they are archived in cabinet files. Having located the file using the search facility, it can then be copied and pasted from there in the usual way.

Note that many DLL files are installed by applications programs. They are also installed together with device drivers. Consequently, not all DLL files required for a given Windows installation will be found on the Windows installation disc. It is for this reason that many Windows users make backups of all the DLL files on their system. It is then easy to locate any DLL file, regardless of its source. If you known which piece of software or hardware is associated with the missing or damaged DLL file, it is probably best to uninstall and reinstall it. This is likely to be quicker and easier than trying to find the file on the installation disc, where it will probably be in compressed form. It also stands a better chance of success. There may actually be a problem with more than one file associated with the troublesome software or hardware. Reinstallation should repair all the files that are damaged or missing.

Where it is impossible to boot the computer into Windows, even in Safe Mode, it is possible to use the Recovery Console to copy files from the Windows installation disc, or any other accessible disc, to the hard disc. Those with memories that stretch back to the days of MS-DOS should have little difficulty in copying files from the command line, but it is trickier for those who only have experience with graphical user interfaces. If you are not used to command line interpreters it is best to locate the file or files you require using Windows XP on a system that is functioning correctly. Make a note of the path to the files or files.

The Copy command is used to copy files, and one way of using this command is to specify the full path to the source file and the destination directory, as in this example:

copy D:\support\xyz.dll C:\temp

This command copies the file called "xyz.dll" in the "support" directory of drive D: to the "temp" directory on drive C:. An alternative method is to make the directory containing the source file the current one, and then give the basic name of the file as the source. Of course, any extension to the file name must still be specified. This leaves no room for confusion when several files have the same name but different extensions. This command would have the same effect as the previous example:

copy xyz.dll C:\temp

The Copy command can not be used with files that are contained within cabinet files, and the Expand command must be used instead. For example, this command would decompress the file called "xyz.dll" in the cabinet file called "sysfiles.cab", which would have to be in the current directory:

expand sysfiles.cab /f:xyz.dll C:\

The /f: switch is used to specify the file that must be decompressed. After decompression, the file is copied to the root directory of disc C: (C:\). Note that there are restrictions on the destinations for cabinet files, but there should be no problems if files are copied to the Windows\System32 directory or the root directory of the boot drive. It is not possible use the normal commands to enter and display the contents of a cabinet file. However, it is easy to get the Expand command to display the contents of a cabinet file in the current directory. This command would list the contents of the cabinet file called sysfiles.cab:

expand sysfiles.cab /f:*.* /d

In this case the "/f:" part of the command uses wildcard parameters to specify all files in the cabinet file. The "/d" switch indicates that a directory of the files should be listed, but the files should not be expanded and copied.

When using the Recovery Console it is possible to obtain help on any command by issuing that command with the "/?" switch. For example, this command will produce the help screen for the Expand command:

expand /?

System File Checker

In Windows 9x the purpose of the System File Checker is to check for errors in the system files, and to permit specified files to be restored from the installation disc. A similar facility exists in Windows XP, but it scans all the protected files for errors and automatically repairs any errors that are found. It is run by first selecting the Run option from the Start menu and typing this into the textbox:

sfc /scannow

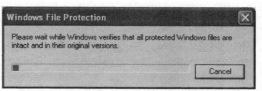

Fig.3.25 The system File Checker in action

There are various switches available for this program, as detailed in the Windows XP Help system. In this case the /scannow switch is used to make the program operate immediately. Once running, the program uses a small window to show how far the process has advanced (Figure 3.25). Then Windows XP installation disc must be inserted into a CD-ROM drive when prompted (Figure 3.26). The scanning and correcting process is not particularly fast, and it might take several minutes for the program to completed its task.

Fig.3.26 The program needs the Windows installation disc

Windows Registry

The Windows Registry seems to be regarded by many as the place to go in order to cure any Windows problem, but matters are not as simple as that. Problems with Windows are not necessarily due to anything amiss in the Registry. If a hardware driver is not installed properly or is faulty, the Windows Registry is unlikely to provide an answer to the problem. Perhaps of greater importance, even where editing the Registry can clear a problem, unless great care is taken it is likely that the problem will be made worse rather than better. Making any changes to the registry has to be regarded as a high-risk activity.

Windows automatically produces backup copies of the Registry and other system files from time to time. It is possible to resort to one of these using the System Restore facility if the Registry becomes seriously damaged. Also, you can make your own backup copies of the Registry files, which can be restored if you somehow manage to get the Registry files beyond redemption. If you are determined to go ahead and experiment with editing the Registry I would certainly recommend making backup copies just in case things go seriously awry. Even if the Registry is well and truly backed up, it is still not a good idea to start making changes unless you are sure you know what you are doing. You can probably resort to a backup copy if things go seriously awry, but realistically, unless you know what you are doing your chances of success when tinkering with the Registry are minimal.

What is it?

Probably most Windows users have heard of the Registry, but there are relatively few that know its exact nature and purpose. It is a database that contains all manner of Windows system settings. If you change settings via the Control Panel, you are actually making changes to the Windows Registry. The same is true when you install or remove software or hardware, or make practically any changes to the system. It is not just the Windows settings that are stored in the Registry, and it can be used to store configuration information for applications programs as well. The device drivers for items of hardware can also use the Registry. This factor probably increases the risk of the Registry being corrupted when software or hardware is installed or uninstalled. The Registry files can easily be damaged if the installer or uninstaller gets it slightly wrong.

Windows experts often edit the Registry as a means of customising their Windows installation. Obviously many aspects of Windows are easily changed via the standard routes, such as using the Control Panel to change things such as screen colours, resolution, etc. Hackers often prefer to go direct to the Registry because they can make some changes that are not possible via the approved channels. This is fine for those having the necessary expertise to make this type of change. Presumably, they also have the necessary expertise to repair any damage they cause. This type of thing it is definitely not to be recommended for occasional dabblers.

Editing

Many computer configuration files can be edited by simply loading them into a text editor or word processor and making the required changes.

This method is not normally used with the Registry files, and instead they are edited via the special editing utility. This program is called Regedit, and it can be found in the Windows directory. One way to run Regedit is to go to the Start menu, choose Run, type "regedit" in the text

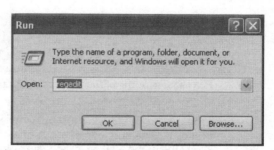

Fig.3.27 Running the Regedit program

box, and then operate the OK button (Figure 3.27). There is no need to include the path to the Regedit.exe file since Windows will know where to find it.

Alternatively, use Windows Explorer to find the Regedit.exe file and then double-click on it to run the program. Either method will bring up the rather blank looking initial screen of Figure 3.28. Note that there is no Regedt32 in Windows XP. If you type "regedt32" into the Run textbox, Windows XP will actually run the standard Registry Editor program.

The Windows XP Registry should pose few problems if you are used to dealing with the Registry in previous versions of Windows. Both the Registry itself and the Registry Editor operate along broadly the same lines as their predecessors. It will probably require some intense effort if you do not have any previous experience with the Registry. In operation, the Registry Editor is designed to be much like Windows Explorer. There

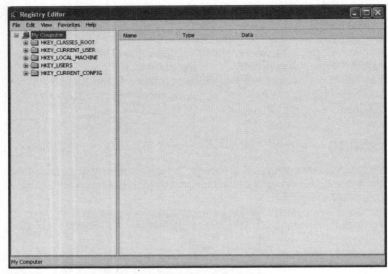

Fig.3.28 The initial window of the Regedit program

are what appear to be files and folders, but you need to bear in mind the program is showing the contents of a database, and that it can not be used in exactly the same way as Windows Explorer. For example, the drag and drop approach does not work when using Registry Editor.

Double clicking on one of the entries in the left-hand section of the screen expands it, as in Figure 3.29, to show what appear to be subfolders. In Windows Registry terminology the left-hand section of the screen shows keys, and double clicking on one of these expands its entry to show the sub-keys. With subfolders, double clicking on an entry will sometimes reveal further subfolders.   Likewise, double clicking on sub-keys will sometimes reveal a further layer of the key structure. A "+" mark beside a key icon indicates that a further layer of sub-keys is available. In normal Windows Explorer fashion, left clicking the "+" mark expands the key or sub-key. The mark then changes to a minus sign, and left clicking it contracts that section of the key system.

Once the lowest level in the key structure has been reached, double clicking on an entry produces something like the window of Figure 3.30. Including the icons on the left, the right-hand section of the screen breaks down into three sections. The icon indicates the type of data stored in

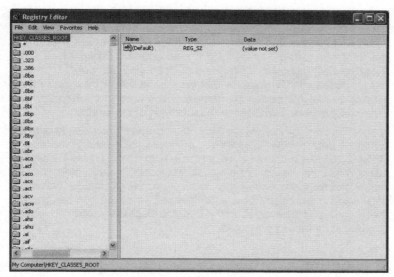

Fig.3.29 The keys can be expanded, like folders in Windows Explorer

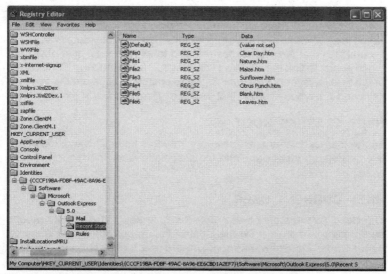

Fig.3.30 Registry data is displayed in the right-hand panel

the key. An icon containing "ab" indicates that the key holds a string, which means that it contains letters and (or) numbers. An icon containing "011110" indicates that the key holds a numerical code, which is often in the form of a binary number and not an ordinary decimal type. The hexadecimal numbering system is also used, and numbers of this type are preceded by "Ox" to show that they are in this numbering system. This column also includes the name for each entry in the Registry, and the names usually give clues to the functions of the entries.

Next along from the icons is the Type column, and there are eight different types of data. REG_BINARY for example, is a binary value, and REG_DWORD is a double word, which is term used to describe a 32-bit value. The third column is the actual data stored in each value. You will notice that for many entries the Data column simply states "(value not set)". This means that not even default values have been assigned to these entries. However, should it become necessary to do so, values can be set for these parameters.

Navigation

You do not have to move around the Registry for long in order to realise that the number of values stored there is vast. I do not know how many values are to be found in an average Windows Registry, but it must be many thousands. There are five main Registry keys in the "root directory", which are known as hive keys incidentally. The Registry data is stored in several files that are sometimes referred to as hive files. It is obviously much easier to find the required value if you understand the significance of the hive keys, and know which one to search. These are the five hive keys and the types of value that each one contains:

HKEY_CLASSES_ROOT

All the file associations are stored within this key. This includes OLE information, shortcut data, and file associations for the recognised file types.

HKEY_CURRENT_USER

The desktop preferences are stored in this key. This mainly means parameters that are set via the Control Panel, but other data is stored here. Under the Software sub-key there is a further sub-key for each item of installed software, so there can be a vast number or entries here as well.

HKEY_LOCAL_MACHINE

Machine in a Windows context means the PC that it is running on. This hive key therefore contains data that is specific to the particular PC concerned. As one would expect, there is a Hardware sub-key here, but there are others such as a Network sub-key and a Security type. There is a Software sub-key here as well, but it is different to the one found under the HKEY_CURRENT_USER hive key. The information stored in this Software sub-key seems to be largely associated with hardware configuration and uninstalling the software, rather than things like screen colours.

HKEY_USERS

If the PC has more than one user, this hive key is used to store the preferences for each user. In most cases the users feature of Windows is not utilised, so the information here will simply duplicate that stored in the HKEY_CURRENT_USER hive key. Perhaps more accurately, HKEY_CURRENT USERS will duplicate the data stored in HKEY_USERS.

HKEY_CURRENT_CONFIG

This key contains the current software and hardware configuration data. In the likely event that you are only using one configuration, it will contain the same data as HKEY_LOCAL_MACHINE.

Registry backup

It is a good idea to make a backup copy of the Registry before undertaking any editing. One way of doing this is to use the System Restore facility to take a so-called snapshot of the system's state. If anything should go wrong, the Restore facility can be used to take the system back to this state, which should get it working again. Using the System Restore facility is covered later in this chapter. The Windows XP Backup utility can also be used to save and restore essential system files. This topic is covered in chapter 5.

The Registry checker also has the ability to save and restore the Registry, or individual hives, via the Export and Import options in the File menu. The entire Registry can be exported by selecting the My Computer entry in the left-hand section of the window prior to selecting the Export option. Individual hives can be exported by selecting the hive's entry prior to using the Export facility. There are several Registry file formats available from the file browser that appears when the Export command is selected (Figure 3.31).

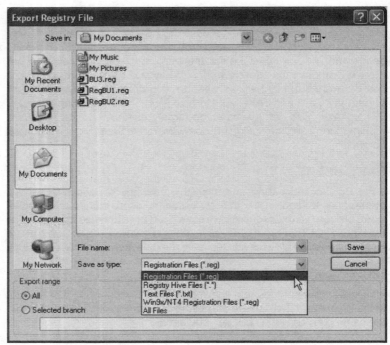

Fig.3.31 Several Registry file formats are available from the menu

The default "reg" format can be used for individual hives or the entire Registry. The "Registry hive files" option saves individual hives only, and an error message will be displayed if this format is used with the entire Registry selected. This is the format that is normally used for backup purposes. The text option enables the Registry or an individual hive to be saved as a simple text file that can be viewed and edited using a word processor or text editor. Text files can not be imported though, and this is only intended as a means of viewing Registry files without using the Registry Editor. In theory, the Import feature enables all or part of the Registry to be restored from a backup file. In practice, importing Registry files tends to be problematic. Consequently, it is best to use the Restore and Backup facilities, which are more user friendly.

Editing data

The first problem when editing a Registry value is actually finding it. Even if you know what you are looking for and roughly where to find it, searching through the numerous entries in the Registry can still be very time consuming.

Fortunately, the Registry Checker has a Find facility that is similar to the Find Files and Folders facility of Windows Explorer. Selecting Find from the Edit menu brings up a Window like the one of Figure 3.32. Use

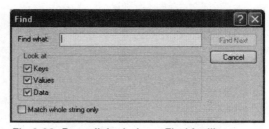

Fig.3.32 Regedit includes a Find facility

the textbox to enter the text you wish to search for, and use the radio buttons to select the fields of the Registry you wish to search.

You can also opt for a whole string search. In other words, a match will only be produced if the full string in the Registry matches the one you have entered. If this option is not selected, a match will be produced if the string you entered matches part of an entry in the Registry. The whole string option can help to keep the number of matches to more manageable proportions, but you have to know precisely what you are looking for.

Press the Find Next button to search for the string. If a match is found, it will be shown highlighted in the main window of the Registry Editor. If this one is not the entry you are looking for, call up the Find facility again and operate the Find Next button, or just select the Find Next option from the Edit menu. Keep doing this until the required entry is located or the whole of the Registry has been searched. Note that the My Computer entry should be selected prior to using the Find facility if you wish to search the entire registry. Select one hive key in order to search that hive for the specified string. This hive key and any sub-keys below it will be searched.

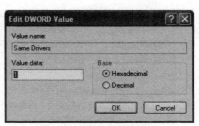

Fig.3.33 A typical window for editing data

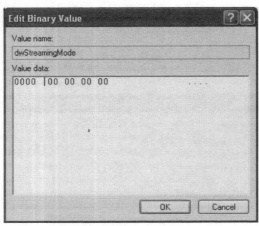

In order to edit a Registry entry double-click on its icon in the right-hand panel to bring up the editing window, as in Figure 3.33. The data can then be edited using the textbox. The edit window varies slightly in appearance depending on the type of data it contains. In this example it contains a double word, and the two radio buttons

Fig.3.34 Another version of the data editing window

enable the value to be given in hexadecimal or decimal. Figure 3.34 shows the editing window for a binary value. Left-click the OK button when you have finished, or the Cancel button if you change your mind.

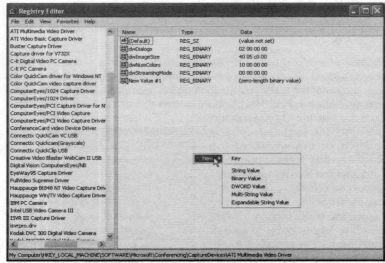

Fig.3.35 Adding a new entry to the Registry

It is also possible to right-click on an entry and then use the popup menu to delete or rename it. A Modify option is also available from this menu, and it brings up the appropriate edit window. In order to add a new entry, right-click in an empty part of the right-hand panel to bring up the menu shown in Figure 3.35. Then choose the required type of value (string, binary, etc.) from the submenu. The new entry will then appear in the right panel of the window, and it will be ready to have the name field edited. Then double-click on its icon and then edit its value in the normal way.

Clearly it is necessary to know exactly what you are doing before altering any registry entries. If you suspect an entry is giving problems it is not possible to remedy the problem by editing its data unless you know the correct data to use. Unless you have the necessary expertise it is better to alter the Registry only via indirect routes, such as installing or uninstalling software, using the Control Panel, etc.

Knowledge Base

In some circumstances there may be no option but to press on in an attempt to find a cure for the problem. With masses of important data on the hard disc and no means of backing it up, wiping the disc clean is not an option. The best course of action would be to have the computer fitted with some form of mass storage device so that the data could be backed up. Apart from leaving your reinstallation options open, this also guards against losing important data due to a hard disc failure. If you have a usable Internet connection and decide to press on rather than reinstall, it is worthwhile investigating the Microsoft Knowledge Base. There is actually a massive amount of help available at Microsoft's web site (www.microsoft.com), including articles on a large range of Microsoft products.

A good place to start is the Support section. This brings up a screen like the one in Figure 3.36, and this gives access to a FAQ section, a search facility, and newsgroups. Selecting the Search facility produces the page shown in Figure 3.37, which offers a selection of search tips. The search engine allows you to specify the product for which you require support, and the type of support required (article, driver file, etc.). You then put in some key words to help the search engine come up with something suitable. As with any search engine, the obvious search words do not always provide the best results. I found that "Windows XP Recovery Console" produced more helpful articles on boot problems than using "Windows XP boot failure", for example. Some of the numerous results

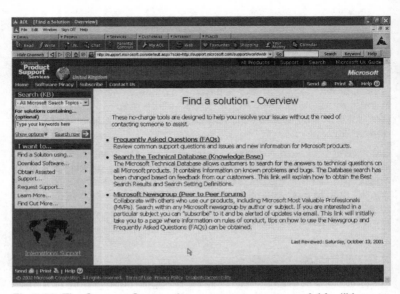

Fig.3.36 The Support Centre gives access to some useful facilities

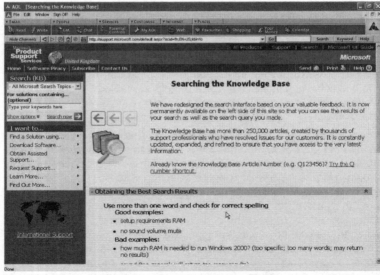

Fig.3.37 The Search facility should locate the required information

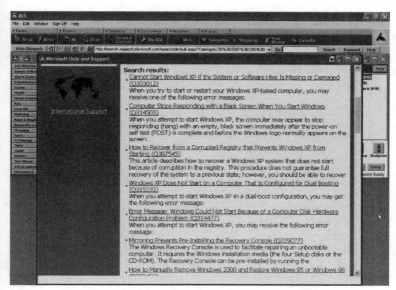

Fig.3.38 Some useful results provided by the Search facility

obtained from the "Windows XP Recovery Console" search are shown in Figure 3.38.

With perseverance, I would guess that practically any Windows problem could be solved using the information available from the Microsoft Knowledge Base. The only problem is that you will probably need a second PC to access the Internet while your faulty PC is being sorted out. Possibly, a friend can assist if you do not have a spare computer. Remember that much of the Windows XP related material on the web site is also included in the Help system, and is available provided the computer can at least be booted in Safe Mode. Select Help and Support from the Start menu to launch the Help system. This will produce a page like the one shown in Figure 3.39.

There is a search facility that helps the user to find information on specific topics. Type a search string into the textbox and then operate the green arrow button. A list of search results is then displayed in the left-hand panel of the window (Figure 3.40). Each result is a link, so left clicking on one of the entries takes you to the appropriate page in the Help system. The Help system is rather like an on-disc web site, and you navigate around it in normal browser fashion.

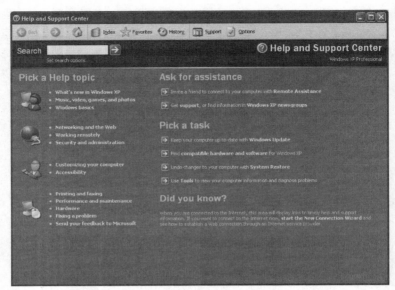

Fig.3.39 Do not overlook the built-in Help and Support Centre

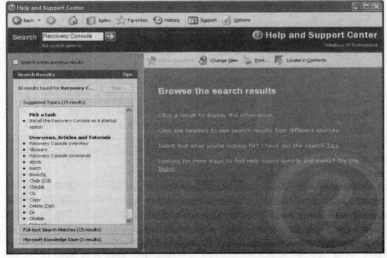

Fig.3.40 Search results produced by the built-in Help system

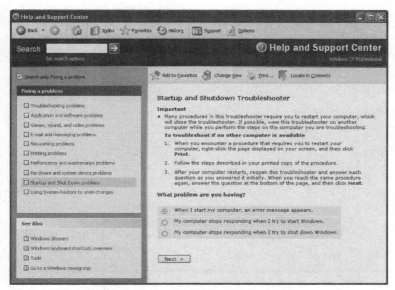

Fig.3.41 The Startup and Shutdown Troubleshooter

There is a Startup and Shutdown Troubleshooter that is similar to the same facility in Windows ME. This is accessed by first going to the Help and Support system, and then selecting the Fixing a problem link. Left-click the link for "Startup and Shut Down problems" in the left-hand section of the new page that appears. Then activate the "Startup and Shutdown Troubleshooter" link in the right-hand section of the window. This produces the initial page of the troubleshooter (Figure 3.41), which operates in standard Windows troubleshooter fashion. You make the suggested checks, answer the questions, and hope that eventually you find the cure for the problem.

System Restore

Windows XP has a System Restore facility that is essentially the same as the one introduced in Windows ME. This feature is given detailed coverage in chapter 5, and it will not be considered further here. However, it represents one of the main ways of restoring normal operation if Windows XP fails to boot or is unstable once it has been booted. Note though, that it is not relevant to a newly installed system as there will be no restoration point to return to.

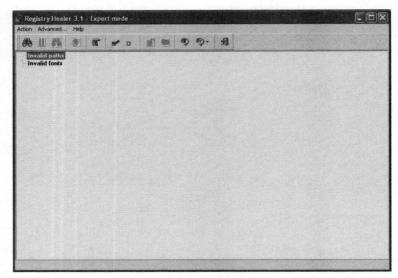

Fig.3.42 The initial screen of the Registry Healer program

Windows checkers

There is not exactly a world shortage of software to help fix Windows problems. The software on offer ranges from simple utilities that are designed to investigate and fix problems in one particular aspect of Windows, to large suites of software that cover just about everything. These larger software suites often have utilities that are designed to "tune" the system and maintain it in peak condition. Most utility suites include a Registry checker and repairer program, and these are also available as standalone programs.

Figure 3.42 shows the opening screen of Registry Healer, which is a standalone Registry scanner and repairer. This program can scan the Registry to search for various types of anomaly, and it then produces a list of results on the screen (Figure 3.43). It can then be used to correct the references that have been found by the scanning process.

Utility programs can be very useful, but they must be used with care. Things that seem to be errors can actually be correct, and "fixing" them can introduce rather than solve problems. Unless you know what you are doing it is best to restrict yourself to the non-expert modes where the program will take a softly - softly approach to things. This should ensure

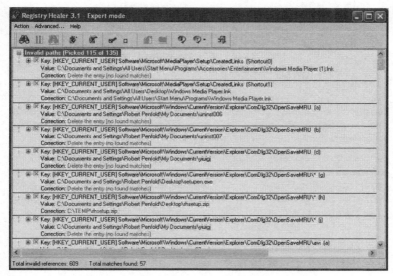

Fig.3.43 The results produced by scanning the Registry

that the program only improves the system set-up, and does not cause any damage. It is essential to use up to date utility software that is fully compatible with Windows XP. Any software released prior to the introduction of Windows XP is unlikely to have proper XP compatibility, and has the potential to do serious damage to a Windows XP installation.

Reinstallation

If the usual methods of fixing Windows fail to get results, realistically there are only two options available. One is to continue searching for the cause of the problem, running diagnostic software, checking through configuration files, checking the hardware and drivers, or anything else you can think of. Option two is to reinstall Windows. Initially reinstall it on top of the existing version, which will leave your applications software properly installed and with luck will cure the problem. If that fails, any important data must be backed up to another hard disc or other mass storage device. The hard disc can then be wiped clean and Windows plus all the applications software and data must be reinstalled "from scratch".

This may seem like a defeatist attitude, but searching for the cause of an obscure fault in Windows can be very time consuming. A straightforward reinstallation is almost certain to be quicker, and even reinstalling Windows "from scratch" could be a quicker route to success. It is also worth bearing in mind that reinstalling everything has the beneficial effect of removing the numerous unnecessary files that tend to start cluttering the hard disc as a Windows installation grows older. This will often produce a significant reduction in the time it takes for the system to boot, and for programs to load, and increase the general speed of operation when hard disc accesses are involved.

Where there is no easy solution to a Windows problem, professional PC maintenance engineers tend to opt for the reinstallation option sooner rather than later. For those with less experience of these things it will probably be more of a last resort than a routine method of fixing and streamlining a damaged Windows installation. However, having reinstalled everything you will probably be quite happy that you did.

Recurring problems

If you are very unlucky, having reinstalled everything "from scratch" the problem will return. It is likely that the problem will keep reappearing if you keep reinstalling Windows. Where the problem is in some way hardware related, perhaps only happening when the soundcard is used, the most likely explanation is that one of the drivers or the hardware itself is faulty. It is more likely to be a driver problem than a fault in the hardware, so check with the technical support department of the hardware manufacturer to see if a later version of the driver software is available. These days most manufacturers have the latest drivers available on their web sites, where there may also be some troubleshooting hints, so the relevant web site should be the first port of call.

If everything works fine at first, but things go seriously wrong after a while or steadily worsen, the most likely culprit is an applications program. Finding the program that is causing the problem can be quite time consuming. If one program consistently goes "walkabout" and all the others work perfectly, it is virtually certain that the troublesome program is responsible for its own downfall. It is possible for one program to interfere with the system and cause problems with just one other program, but this is quite rare. Normally this occurs because installing one program results in a DLL file for a second program being overwritten with an older version of the file. Provided the problem is fixed by reinstating the newer version of the file there should be no further difficulties.

If you simply keep reinstalling Windows and then install the applications in the same order, the problem will keep coming back. Installing the applications in reverse order should banish the problem, since the newer version of the DLL file will then replace the older version, rather than the other way round.

It is more common for the faulty software to damage the Windows installation, causing problems for itself and for other applications programs. The normal solution where recurring problems occur is to reinstall Windows plus one application. If that works all right for a while add a further application. If all is well add another application, and so on until a program is added and things start to go awry. It is then a reasonable assumption that the last program to be added is the one that is damaging the Windows installation.

Where to start

When a PC has problems booting into Windows XP there are clearly a number of approaches that can be used in an attempt to sort things out. So where do you start? Where the computer will not even boot into Windows XP in Safe Mode the options are relatively limited. If you have an emergency boot disc it might be possible to boot into Windows using this, and the installation is then usable. However, in order to fix the problem it might be better to go into the Recovery Console and use the Fixboot command to repair the boot files. The System File Checker program is another option. Where an error message reports a problem with a particular file, it might be possible to copy this from the Windows XP installation disc to the appropriate folder on the hard disc. From the Advanced Options menu you can try booting using the last settings that worked.

Fixing problems is generally easier if it is possible to boot into Safe Mode. The usual Windows facilities are then available if it is necessary to copy a file from the installation disc to the hard drive. Device Manager has some facilities unavailable in Safe Mode, but it is to a large extent usable. The built-in troubleshooting facilities are mostly operational in Safe Mode, and third party utilities should also work. Troublesome software and hardware can be installed or uninstalled, which will clear many boot-up problems. For inexperience users the best starting point is probably the built-in Startup Troubleshooter. This might not find awkward problems, but it should help to clear any simple startup problems.

It is best to resort to the System Restore facility where the problem proves to be less than straightforward to fix. By taking the computer back to an earlier configuration, most problems can be cured using this facility. The problem is likely to be a stubborn one if System Restore fails to find an answer. Reinstallation over the old system is well worth a try in these circumstances. Where that fails, the best option is probably to backup any unsaved data on the hard disc and then install Windows again from scratch.

Points to remember

If Windows fails to boot properly, do not be too eager to start fiddling with the system to find a cure. Try rebooting a few times to see if the problem clears itself.

If the computer fails during the POST (power-on self test) routine, it is not reaching the point where it starts to boot into Windows. The problem is then a hardware fault rather than something amiss with the Windows installation. There is probably a memory problem if the computer randomly boots or crashes at startup.

Where the boot process halts very early it is likely that the boot files on the hard disc have been damaged. They can be repaired using the Recovery Console and the FIXBOOT command (see chapter 2). The problem could also be a faulty hard disc, or the BIOS being configured incorrectly.

It will be possible to boot in Safe Mode unless the Windows installation is badly damaged. Some basic checks can then be made, such as checking the hard disc, etc. Safe Mode has some limitations, but it is generally much better in this respect that its Windows 9x equivalents.

Getting the computer to produce a boot log file can help to pinpoint the process that is causing the boot process to stall. However, boot logs can be very misleading and it is best not to jump to conclusions. Device Manager can be used to check whether the hardware and the hardware drivers are functioning correctly, but remember that some hardware is not installed or operational in Safe Mode.

If a hardware driver is suspected of causing problems, use Device Manager to remove the existing driver before reinstallation. Also, check the hardware manufacturer's web site for an up-dated driver.

Windows will often give an error message that gives some clue to the nature of the problem. Information on a specific error message can be found on the Microsoft web site.

If a program has recently been uninstalled, reinstalling it will probably reinstate the damaged or missing file.

Installing a program can also damage a file. This can result in a file being overwritten by an older version. Reinstalling Windows or one of the other application files will cure this problem. If the damaged file is on the Windows installation disc it can be copied from the disc using Windows Explorer or the Recovery Console.

Windows includes a Registry Editor program, but only use this utility if you know what you are doing.

Reinstalling Windows over the existing installation will cure boot problems in a fair proportion of cases, but not all of them. Reinstalling Windows from scratch will cure boot problems unless the problem is not really Windows related. Recurring problems are due to a hardware fault or a bug in an applications program.

There are numerous Windows checking programs available, and these will often help to sort out boot problems, and more minor annoyances. Many will also help to keep Windows working efficiently.

Much Windows XP troubleshooting information can be found at the Microsoft web site (www.microsoft.com), and some of this information is also included in the built-in Help system.

Windows XP has a very useful System Restore facility that will usually cure boot problems. It effectively moves the Windows installation back to a time when the computer functioned properly.

Data rescue

Learning the hard way

A hard disc failure is potentially a major disaster for all those who use the PC, but if you use PCs for some years it is a failure you are almost certain to experience. A complete failure of the disc means that all the data it contains is lost. There are companies that offer a data recovery services, but there is no guarantee that the contents of the disc will be recoverable, and the cost of a recovery service is too high for many users anyway. As a minimum, any important data files should be backed up onto floppy discs, CDRs, or any suitable media, so that they can be restored onto a new hard disc if the old unit fails.

Ideally, the entire contents of the hard disc drive should be backed up using a program that enables it to be properly restored onto a new hard disc. This is very much quicker and easier than having to reinstall and configure the operating system, and then reinstall all the applications programs and data. Also, any customisation of the operating system or other software will be automatically restored. If you have heavily customised software, after reinstallation it can take a great deal time to get it set up to your satisfaction.

Having a backup copy of the hard disc's contents is not only insurance against a loss of valuable data if a hardware failure occurs. It can greatly simplify things if there is a major problem with the operating system. Provided the PC was fully operational when the backup copy was made, resorting to the backup will provide a fully functioning PC again. Full backup software enables the system to be quickly restored to a previous and fully working configuration, but it in most cases it does so by installing the operating system from scratch and then reinstating program files, etc. Any data files produced since the backup was taken will therefore be lost.

A full backup is normally only undertaken every month or so, making it important to keep backup copies of data files as they are produced. A lot of data is otherwise left at risk, especially as the time for the next backup approaches. Provided data files are regularly saved to disc, there should be no difficulty in reinstating any missing data once a full backup has been restored. The Windows XP Backup utility installs the system from scratch and therefore loses any recently produced data. The System Restore facility operates in a different way, and it undoes changes to system and program files so that the system is effectively wound back to an earlier time. In this way the data files are left intact. Of course, System Restore is only usable if the file system is largely undamaged. Backup software is still usable even if the contents of the hard disc has been completely erased.

When a major problem with the operating system occurs and some form of restoration option is available, it is almost certainly best to resort to this method sooner rather than later. There is little point in spending large amounts of time trying to repair a damaged installation if it can be replaced with a backup copy quite quickly and easily. It is certainly worthwhile spending a small amount of time first to check for any minor problems that are easily sorted out. The backup method is "using a sledgehammer to crack a nut" if the problem is something minor that is easily corrected. If a search for any obvious problems proves to be in vain, it is time to resort to the backup software. The backup program's manual should give detailed instructions on maintaining an up-to-date backup and restoring the hard disc's contents.

The problem with the full backup method is that it takes a fair amount of time to maintain an up to date copy of the hard disc. Also, it is only feasible if your PC is equipped with some form of mass storage device that can be used for backup purposes, such as a CDR writer or a Zip drive. It could otherwise require well in excess of a thousand floppy discs to do a full backup of the hard drive! Even using some form of mass storage it can take a long while to backup the gigabytes of programs and data stored on many modern hard disc drives. The quickest and easiest way of providing a backup is to opt for a second hard disc drive. Due to the current low cost of hard discs, this could well be the cheapest method as well.

Split discs

Many PC users now split their large hard drives into two logical drives, which usually become drives C: and D: as far as the operating system is concerned. Drive C: is then used in the normal way and drive D: is reserved for backup purposes. This method is useless in the event that the hard drive develops a serious fault, because the main and backup drives are the two halves of one physical drive. If one becomes faulty it is unlikely that the other will be usable either. The point of this system is that the backup copy on drive D: is usable if there is a software problem rather than a fault in the hardware. Since most users have far more problems with the software than with hard disc faults, this method should get the user out of trouble more often than not.

Some users take a compromise approach and make a backup copy of the hard disc when it contains a newly installed operating system having all the hardware properly integrated into the operating system and fully operational. Ideally the disc should also have the applications programs installed, and any customisation completed. Any important data is backed up separately as it is generated. If the operating system becomes seriously damaged it is then easy to resort to the backup which should be reasonably compact, but gives you a basic system that is fully customised and ready to use. Any essential data can also be restored, but there is no need to restore any data files that are no longer needed on the hard disc.

Clean copy

An advantage of this method is that it returns the PC to a "clean" copy of the operating system. Over a period of time most modern operating systems seem to become slightly "gummed up" with numerous files that no longer serve any purpose, and things can generally slow down. By returning to a fresh copy of the operating system you will probably free up some hard disc space and things might run slightly faster. By not bothering to restore any unimportant data files you free up further hard disc space.

If you lack a proper backup copy of the hard disc and only have copies of the data files, all is not lost. In this situation you might prefer to put a fair amount of effort into fixing the damaged Windows installation rather than simply reinstalling everything. Even if you only use a few applications programs, reinstalling Windows and the applications software is likely to be pretty tedious and time consuming. If there are numerous programs to reinstall, the process is likely to be very tedious and time consuming.

Looking on the bright side, if everything does have to be restored from scratch you will have a "clean" copy of the operating system that should provide optimum performance. In fact many users habitually take the reinstallation route and consider any extra time and effort involved being well worthwhile.

The value of this approach depends on the amount of software you install and remove. It is probably doing things the hard way if you rarely or never make changes to the PC once it is set up to your satisfaction. It might be the only practical approach if you try every program you can lay your hands on.

I would not go as far as to advocate reinstalling everything at the first sign of trouble, but I would definitely advise against the opposite approach of always repairing the original set up regardless of how long it takes. Apart from the fact this could be a very time consuming approach, an installation that has been patched up on numerous occasions, and perhaps had a number of programs added, upgraded, and removed over a period of time, is unlikely to provide peak performance. In fact, I have encountered several installations of this type that took an eternity to go through the boot-up sequence, in one case taking almost 10 minutes to complete the process! Once booted, PCs of this type seem to give the hard disc drive a "hammering" at every opportunity. This is the most common symptom of a system that is operating well below par.

Apart from making the computer slow and irksome in use, this type of thing increases the wear on the hard disc drive and presumably shortens its operating life. It should be possible to discover the sources of the problem and improve results. There are Windows "cleaner" programs that can help to streamline a Windows installation and remove clutter from the hard disc. However, reinstalling everything "from scratch" is the solution favoured by most when this situation arises. This should always ensure optimum performance and might be quicker anyway.

Windows on Windows

On the face of it there is no need to wipe the hard disc clean and undertake a complete reinstallation from the beginning. Simply reinstalling Windows over the old installation should restore normality. As with so many things in computing it is a case of yes and no. Yes, in some cases simply going through the Windows set up routine will fix problems with the operating system and restore normal operation. Unfortunately, in other cases the problem will still exist once the reinstallation is complete. When Windows is installed on a hard disc, the Windows Setup program searches the disc for a previous installation and installed Windows application programs. Any installed software will be integrated with the new Windows installation, as may driver programs and other support files.

As a consequence, having reinstalled Windows it should not be necessary to reinstall the applications software as well. The down side is that any files giving problems with the old installation may be retained in the new one. Having reinstalled the operating system you could well find that it does not work any better than before. My experiences with Windows in general suggest that reinstalling Windows on top of the exiting installation probably has little more than a 50 percent chance of success. Possibly Windows XP will achieve a higher success rate. As reinstallation is a reasonably quick and easy process it is probably worthwhile giving it a try before resorting to an installation "from scratch", but do not be surprised if it does not have the desired effect.

Do not be tempted to try upgrading to a newer version of Windows by installing it on top of a non-working version. People sometimes try this, working on the basis that the new version will have little dependency on the old one, and the problem with the old version will be "blown away" by the new version. In practice there is little likelihood of this happening. The Windows Setup program may detect that there is a problem and refuse to go ahead with the upgrade. If it does proceed, the most likely outcome is that the reinstallation will go very wrong somewhere along the line, and that it will never be completed. If you do manage to get the new version installed, it will probably have more problems than the old one.

Preliminaries

If you do decide to go ahead with reinstallation "from scratch", it is essential to backup any important data files first. If you are using heavily customised applications programs it is also a good idea to make copies of the configuration files so that the customisation files are easily reinstated. In fact, any files that are unique to your particular installation should be backed-up, including things like speech profiles of voice recognition programs. Some of your applications programs may have facilities for saving and reinstating customisation files. In other cases simply overwriting the default files with your customised versions will probably have the desired effect. However, there is no guarantee that this will work.

It is worth emphasising that backing-up important files should not be left until the PC gives problems. If there is a serious fault in the hard disc it may be impossible to recover any files that have not been backed-up. Matters are less dire if the problem lies in the operating system rather than the disc itself, but it could still be difficult to make backup copies of important files. With the computer not booting into the operating system properly you are unlikely to have proper access to all the drives and applications programs. Provided Safe Mode is functioning properly you can boot into a version of Windows, but one where drives other than the hard and floppy discs will not be fully functioning. In most cases the CD-ROM drive or drives can be used for read operations, but writing to the CD writers is unlikely to be possible. This severely limits your backup options. There are ways of making a backup of a hard disc drive in an emergency, but this might involve buying some additional hardware. It is better to avoid getting into situations where drastic measures are needed in order to recover the situation.

Floppy discs

Floppy discs are suitable for backup purposes where only a limited amount of data is involved. The upper limit depends on how many floppy discs you are prepared to use, a factor that is probably a reflection of how desperate you are! Backing up 30 megabytes of data onto about 20 or so floppy discs will be quite time consuming, but is still well within the bounds of reason. Backing up several hundred megabytes onto dozens of floppy discs is not a very practical proposition, and the discs could well cost more than some more convenient backup systems! In terms of megabytes per pound, floppy discs are not very competitive these days.

Where floppy discs are suitable, there is a potential problem in that some of the files you wish to copy may be too big to fit on a single floppy disc. The capacity of a high-density 3.5-inch floppy disc is 1.44 megabytes when the standard PC disc format is used. Things like DTP and graphics files can be substantially larger than this. The normal copying facilities of Windows XP can not spread a large file across one or more discs. If you try to copy a file that is too large to fit onto the disc an error message to that effect will be produced. Fortunately, there are several Windows programs that can handle this problem. The later versions of the popular Winzip program for example, will compress and copy large files to several floppy discs if necessary. You can even copy a collection of files and save them as one large file spread across several discs.

Large scale

If floppy discs are not up to the task it is clearly necessary to resort to some form of mass storage device. It is highly unlikely that any installed device of this type will work in Safe Mode, apart from simple read-only CD-ROM drives. These are of no use in the current context. It might be possible to get non-standard PC drives (Zip, etc.) to operate in MS-DOS. Where this is possible, the manufacturer's literature should give instructions for making an MS-DOS boot disc. However, booting from an MS-DOS floppy disc will not enable the hard disc drive to be read if it uses the NTFS filing system. The hard disc drive should be readable provided it uses the FAT or FAT32 filing system.

Second disc

If you have large amounts of data to backup and no mass storage device, your choices are limited. One option is to simply keep trying to repair the Windows installation until you are successful. Any Windows installation should be repairable, and persistence should eventually pay off. You may get lucky and fix the problem fairly quickly, or a great deal of time could be involved in locating and removing the problem. The biggest drawback of this method is that you will still have no backup of the hard disc's contents, limiting your options if there are further problems with the Windows installation. Also, the contents of the disc will probably be lost forever if the drive becomes faulty.

Many users save data onto a hard disc thinking that their work is safe and secure, but this is definitely not the case. Having data on a hard disc is sometimes likened to hanging paper documents by a thin thread over an open fire. Modern hard drives are relatively reliable, but if used for long enough a hard disc drive will go wrong, and you will probably end up throwing away the drive together with all your hard work.

A better option is to add some form of mass storage device. An external (parallel port) Zip drive is not particularly expensive, and in an emergency it should work quite happily with the computer booted into MS-DOS. A few Zip discs can store several hundred megabytes of data, which should be sufficient to backup any important data files, configuration files, etc. However, as pointed out previously, the hard disc will not be accessible from MS-DOS if it uses the NTFS file system. Note that any form of USB or SCSI storage device is unlikely to work with Windows in Safe mode or with MS-DOS. This is simply because the interface will not be recognised in Safe Mode or in MS-DOS, rendering the drive "invisible" to the operating system.

My preferred option is to add another hard disc drive. These days this probably represents the cheapest means of adding large amounts of extra storage capacity to a PC, and a hard disc also has the advantage of being very fast. Read and write speeds are measured in megabytes per second, unlike some other storage systems where it is specified as so many megabytes per minute. A further advantage of the hard disc approach is that the disc should work properly with Windows booted in Safe Mode or the computer booted into MS-DOS. It should even work using the Windows XP booted into the command prompt version of Safe Mode or into the Recovery Console. A hard disc drive is one of the standard PC drives, and as such it does not require any special drivers for basic operation. This makes life easier at the best of times, but greatly eases things when the Windows installation is damaged.

Adding a drive

Fitting a second hard disc drive obviously requires the lid or side panel of the PC to be removed, followed by some delving around inside the computer. It is not one of the more difficult upgrades, but unless you are reasonably practical it would be advisable to have the upgrade done professionally. Most shops that sell hard disc drives also offer an upgrade service, but it will almost certainly cost substantially more to have the drive fitted for you. However, this extra cost is preferable to damaging the PC and having to pay a hefty repair bill. Assuming you feel confident enough to go ahead with the upgrade yourself, the first task is to open the PC to determine the current configuration.

With older PCs the top and two sides of the case are in one piece, and are released by removing four or six screws at the rear of the unit. Be careful, because there will probably be other screws here that hold other things in place, such as the power supply unit. With the right screws removed, the outer casing should pull away upwards and rearwards, but it will probably take a certain amount of force to pull it free. More modern cases have removable side panels, and with most types these are again held in place by four or six screws at the rear of the unit. Both panels must be removed in order to give full access to the drive bays. If your PC has one of the more unusual case styles it will be necessary to carefully examine the exterior in order to "crack" it.

A modern PC has the hard disc interface on the motherboard rather than provided by an expansion card. In fact, there are two hard disc interfaces on the motherboard, or possibly four on a modern PC. These are known as IDE interfaces, and this simply stands for integrated drive electronics. In other words, most of the electronics for the hard disc drive controller is built into the drive itself. At one time the IDE interfaces were strictly for hard disc drives, but in a modern PC they can be used for other types of drive. These multipurpose interfaces are more accurately called EIDE interfaces, which stands for enhanced integrated drive electronics. In practice they are still often referred to as just plain IDE interfaces. Many types of drive can be used with an EIDE interface, including CD-ROM, Zip, and LS120 drives.

In a typical PC the hard disc drive is connected to IDE port 1 and the CD-ROM drive is wired to IDE port 2. However, each IDE interface supports up to two devices, so the hard disc and CD-ROM drive could be connected to IDE port 1 via a single cable. A more common configuration with modern PCs is to have the hard disc on one IDE interface, with a CD-ROM or DVD drive and a CD writer on the other interface. Provided your PC has no more than three internal drives, excluding any floppy drives, it should certainly be able to support another hard drive.

If you look at the cabling inside the PC you should find some wide cables, know as "ribbon" cables, that connect the drives to the motherboard. With luck, at least one of these cables will have an unused connector that can be used with the new drive. Note that any spare connector on the drive that connects to the floppy disc drive is of no use with a hard disc drive. The floppy variety uses a completely different interface having a smaller connector. A suitable power supply lead and connector is also needed. The connectors come in two sizes, which are a larger one for 5.25-inch drives and a smaller one for

Fig.4.1 3.5-inch (left) and 5.25-inch (right) power connectors

the 3.5-inch variety (Figure 4.1). However, all the hard disc drives I have encountered use the larger connector regardless of whether they fit 3.5-inch or 5.25 in bays.

If you are out of luck, one or other of the required leads and connectors will not be present. If the hard disc and CD-ROM drive share an IDE interface, the other IDE interface will be available for the additional drive, but it will not be fitted with a cable. Another possibility is that the existing drives are connected to separate IDE interfaces using single cables rather than types having two connectors for drives. In either case a standard twin IDE data lead is needed in addition to the drive (Figure 4.2).

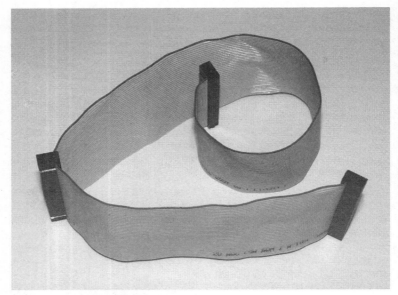

Fig.4.2 A standard twin IDE data lead

Bare drives

Hard drives are available in so called "bare" and "retail" or "boxed" versions. A bare drive may consist of nothing more than the drive itself. However, it will usually include an instruction manual and a set of fixing screws, but no data cable. Incidentally, if you find yourself with a hard drive but no matching manual, the web sites of most hard disc manufacturers include downloadable versions of the manuals for most of their hard disc units. Unless you are dealing with a very old or unusual drive, the information you require should be available on the manufacturer's web site.

The retail versions of hard drives normally include a cable in addition to a set of fixing screws and a more comprehensive manual. There may be other items such as a mounting cradle to permit a 3.5-inch drive to be used in a 5.25-inch drive bay. With modern drives there may well be two data cables included with the drive. One of these is a standard IDE cable that can be used with any IDE drive and any IDE interface. The other cable enables the drive to be used with a modern IDE interface that supports the UDMA66 and UDMA100 standards. UDMA66 and

UDMA100 have the potential of faster data transfers than older standards such as the UDMA33 variety, but they can only be used if they are supported by the motherboard, the drive itself, and the correct cable is used. The instruction manual for your PC should state whether or not it supports anything beyond UDMA33.

If in doubt, the safe option is to use a standard IDE cable. This may provide something less than the ultimate in performance, but the disc should still work very well. It should certainly work well enough for making a backup of the main drive. Some advise against using a UDMA33 device together with a UDMA66 or UDMA100 device and cable. It is generally considered safer to use a UDMA33 cable when using a UDMA66 or UDMA100 device on the same interface as a UDMA33 drive. In my experience a UDMA66/100 cable works just as well in this situation, but either way the fast drive will be reduced to UDMA33 operation.

Of course, it is perfectly all right to have UDMA33 devices on one IDE interface and UDMA66 or UDMA100 devices on the other. Rationalising things, this is probably the best solution. The new drive will presumably support UDMA66/100 operation, so you need to pair it with another UDMA66/100 drive in order to obtain optimum results. This normally means pairing it with the existing hard drive, because most CD-ROM drives only support UDMA33 operation. In theory there is some advantage in having devices on different IDE interfaces where it will be necessary to copy large amounts of data from one to the other. In practice this advantage might be outweighed if having the second drive on the other IDE interface downgrades it to UDMA33 operation. Anyway, in this situation I would pair the two hard drives on the first IDE interface.

If the PC only supports UDMA33 operation, the new drive will also operate in this mode whichever IDE interface it is connected to. Where there is a spare channel available on the second IDE interface, this is the best place to install the new drive. This places it on a different interface to the main hard drive, which might help to speed up data transfers between the two.

Static

If you buy virtually any computer add-on to fit inside a PC it will be supplied in packaging plastered with dire warnings about the dangers of static electricity. Some of these are a bit "over the top", and suggest that going anywhere near the device without the protection of expensive anti-static equipment will result in it being instantly zapped. In reality the risks of static induced damage occurring are probably quite small. On the other hand, computer add-ons have yet to fall in price so far that they are in the "two a penny" category, and the risk of damage occurring is a real one.

The likelihood of damage can be reduced to insignificant proportions by observing a few simple rules. Rule number one is to leave the device in its packaging until it is time to install it. The plastic bags, foam lined boxes, etc., used for computer bits and pieces are not just for physical protection. They are designed to keep static electricity at bay. In some cases the packaging is designed to insulate the contents from high voltages. In others it is designed to conduct electricity so that no significant charge can build up between any two points in the device being protected. Any charges of this type will be almost instantly short-circuited by the conductive packaging.

Rule number two is to make sure that you are not charged with a high static voltage that could damage the device when you remove it from the packing. When working on computers do not wear clothes that are known to be good generators of static electricity. Manmade fibres are the most prolific static generators, but most modern clothes are usually made from natural fibres or a mixture of manmade and natural fibres, so this is not the major problem that it was at one time.

To make quite sure that both yourself and the device being installed are charge free, hold the device in its packing in one hand, and touch something that is earthed with the other hand. Any charge in you or the device should then leak away to earth. The metal case of the computer is a convenient earth point. With the cover or side panels removed there should be plenty of bare metal to touch. Touching the paintwork will not provide reliable earthing since most paints are excellent electrical insulators. Note that the computer must be plugged into the mains supply, but it does not have to be switched on.

Rule number three is to keep the work area free of any large static charges. Any obvious sources of static charges should be removed from the vicinity of the computer. Television sets and computer monitors are good static generators, which means that the computer must be moved away from the monitor before you start work on it. This will normally be necessary anyway, because with the computer's base unit in its normal location it will probably be difficult to get proper access to the interior of the unit. It needs to be placed on a table where there is good access to the interior and plenty of light so that you can see what you are doing.

The table should preferably be one that it not precious, but if necessary the top can be protected with something like a generous quantity of old newspapers. It is a good idea to have the PC plugged into the mains supply but switched off at the mains socket. The earthed metal chassis of the computer will then tend to earth any static charges in its vicinity, preventing any dangerous charges from building up.

If you follow these simple rules it is very unlikely that the add-on device will be damaged by static charges. When dealing with hard disc drives it is as well to bear in mind that they are relatively delicate physically. Modern drives, although more intricate, are not as vulnerable as the early types. Even so, dropping a hard disc drive onto the floor is definitely not a good idea!

Jumpers

An IDE device has configuration jumpers that are used to set whether the unit will be used as the master or slave device on its IDE channel. Even if there is only one device on an IDE channel, that device must still be set as the master or slave unit. By convention, a single drive on an IDE channel is set as the master device. Therefore, if you are adding the new disc to an IDE channel that already has one device installed, the new drive must be set to operate as the slave device. If the new drive will be the sole device on its IDE channel, it must be set for master operation.

The rear of most CD-ROM drives and some IDE hard disc drives look something like Figure 4.3. The connector on the left is the power input and the one on the right is for the data cable. In between these are three

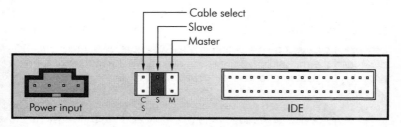

Fig.4.3 Typical layout for the rear of an IDE drive

pairs of terminals that can be bridged electrically by a tiny metal and plastic gadget called a jumper. A jumper can be seen in place in Figure 4.4. The "cable select" option is not used in a PC context, so only two pairs of contacts are relevant here. You simply place the jumper on the

Fig.4.4 A jumper fitted to a drive

master or slave contacts, depending on which option you require. The configuration jumper should be supplied with the drive incidentally, and is normally set at the master option by default on a hard disc drive.

With hard disc drives matters are not always as simple as the arrangement shown in Figure 4.3. There is often an additional set of terminals, and these are used where the drive will be used as the only device on an IDE channel. Using this setting will allow a lone drive to be correctly identified and used by the PC. If the drive has these additional terminals (or they are fitted in place of the cable select pins), you must use them for a sole IDE drive. It is very unlikely that the drive will be picked up properly by the BIOS if the normal master setting is used. Getting it wrong is not likely to produce any damage, but the drive will be unusable until the mistake has been corrected. The manual supplied with the drive should give details of the configuration settings available.

If the new drive is used as the slave device on the primary IDE channel, the other hard drive will presumably be the master device on this channel. The existing drive will need its configuration setting altered if it is set to operate as the sole IDE device on its channel. The manual supplied with the PC should give details of the configuration settings. Alternatively, it should be possible to identify the drive from its markings, and it will almost certainly be possible to find its instruction manual on the Internet.

If there is no device on the secondary IDE channel, or only a single CD-ROM, and the motherboard only supports UDMA33 operation, it would probably be best to add the new drive on this channel. If a CD-ROM is present on this channel, adding the new drive as the secondary slave device is unlikely to require any configuration changes to the CD-ROM drive. If no device is already present, simply add the new drive as the master device or sole device, as appropriate. As pointed out previously, in theory data exchanges between the two hard discs will be quicker if they are on different IDE channels. Where possible, it is therefore better to arrange things this way when using UDMA33 IDE ports.

It is definitely a good idea to check the configuration setting of the new drive, and where necessary alter it, prior to fitting the drive in the case. Once the drive is fitted inside the case it can be difficult to get at the jumper and terminals, and it can be very difficult indeed to see what you are doing when adjusting the jumper. Note that you do not have to look at the jumpers on the existing drives to determine their master/slave settings. The BIOS usually shows which drive is present on each IDE channel during the startup routine.

Getting physical

It is not essential to install the new hard drive in the computer as a fixture. You may prefer to simply connect the new drive to the data and power cables, do the backup, reinstallation and restoration, and then disconnect the drive again. It can then be stored safely away somewhere in case it is needed at some later date. With the drive in storage rather than in use it should not wear out, and should be ready for use if it is needed a few years "down the line". I used this method successfully with a couple of PCs for many years, although not strictly out of choice. If your PC has one of the minimalist cases you may find that there are no spare bays for another hard disc drive.

Note that it is possible to use a 3.5-inch drive in a 5.25-inch drive bay using an adapter. This is just a metal cradle into which the drive is bolted, and the whole assembly then fits into the drive bay just like a 5.25-inch drive. This adapter should be available from any large computer store. As pointed out previously, it is sometimes (but not always) included with boxed retail versions of hard disc drives.

When temporarily connecting a drive it is essential to make sure that no exposed connections on the unit come into electrical contact with the metal case, expansion cards, etc. Some drives are fully enclosed, but most have the underside of the circuit board exposed (Figure 4.5). Often the easiest way of keeping the drive safe is to place it on top of the computer with some newspaper to insulate the drive from the case. With a PC that has some form of tower case it is usually easier to work on the unit if it is placed on its side. The drive can then be placed on the side of the drive cage, again with newspaper being used to provide insulation.

Probably most users will wish to use the additional disc as a permanent feature. This is essential if you wish to use it to make frequent backups or you will be making backup copies of data files as they are generated. If you are using a drive bay that has no front opening, the new drive must be slid in from the rear. Any expansion cards that get in the way must be removed temporarily. Remove the screws that fix the cards to the rear of the chassis and it should then be possible to pull the cards free. The

Fig.4.5 The connections on the underside of the drive must not be allowed to come into contact with the chassis, etc.

sockets on the drive are at the rear, so the other end is pushed into the rear of the drive bay. The manufacturer's name, etc., are marked on the top plate of the drive, so this side should be facing upward. In most cases the drive can be fully pushed into the bay, but it is sometimes necessary to ease it back slightly to get the mounting holes in the drive and the bay to match up properly.

In days gone by it was necessary to use plastic guide rails to mount the drives in the case, but most PCs made within the last eight years or more have drive bays that take the drives without the need for these rails. There are some exceptions, and these use an updated version of the guide rail system. With the old system there were two guide rails, and one was bolted on each side of the drive. The drive was then slid into place and the rails were bolted to the chassis. The new system has one guide rail per drive, and it usually just clips into place. One side of the drive is bolted to the chassis in the normal way, while the other simply clips into place. The point of this is that there is often limited access to one side of the drive bay. Using the clip-on rail on the appropriate side of the drive avoids the difficulty of fitting the mounting bolts on the awkward side.   Your PC should have been supplied with one or two spare rails if it uses this type of drive mounting system

Four mounting bolts are normally supplied with the drive, and with the standard method of mounting these are used to secure the drive to the bay. If no fixing screws were supplied with the drive, the PC may have been supplied with some odds and ends of hardware. If so, there will probably be some suitable screws in amongst these. Failing that, you will have to by some metric M3 screws about 6 millimetres long. Note that the mounting screws must be quite short, and should not protrude more than a few millimetres into the drive. Longer mounting bolts could easily damage something inside the drive.

With a so-called "external" drive bay, it might be easier to insert the drive from the front. Where the interior of the computer is very crowded this can avoid having to remove expansion cards to get the drive in place. An external bay is really intended for use with a floppy drive, CD-ROM drive, or some other type where access is needed to the drive for changing discs. However, an external bay is perfectly suitable for a wholly internal drive such as a hard disc unit. The plastic cover at the very front of the bay can be carefully prised out using a flat bladed screwdriver, and it might then be possible to slide the drive in through the front of the case. There will probably be a metal plate behind the plastic cover though. It may be possible to remove this by first removing two or three fixing screws, but in most cases the plate has to be repeatedly twisted backwards and forwards until the thin pieces of metal holding it in place fatigue and break. With the drive in place, the plastic cover plate can be clipped back into position.

Cabling

The ribbon cable used to provide the data connection has three identical connectors. There is no specific connector for the motherboard and each drive, but because the cable is quite short it will probably have to connect everything together in a particular way in order to reach everything. It should not take too long to fathom out the best way of using the cable. Things are much easier when the new hard drive is the sole device on an IDE channel. The cable should then connect the motherboard to the drive without difficulty.

The connectors must be fitted to the motherboard and drives the correct way round. In theory the connectors are polarised and can only be fitted the right way round. There is a protrusion on the lead's connectors and

Fig.4.6 Two polarised IDE connectors on a motherboard

a matching groove in the connectors on the motherboard and drives. Figure 4.6 shows the polarising keys in the two IDE connectors on a motherboard.

Unfortunately, some connectors, and mainly those on motherboards, are sometimes a bit too minimalist and are not properly polarised. In addition, some IDE connectors lack the polarising key. A search through the appropriate instruction manuals should show which is pin 1 on each connector. This information is often marked on the motherboard and the drives themselves. To make things easier, the ribbon cable has one red lead while the other 39 are grey. The convention is for the red lead to carry the pin 1 connection. Provided this lead is adjacent to pin 1 on the connector for the motherboard and both drives, everything will be connected together properly.

A spare power cable is needed for the new drive, and if there is a spare drive bay there should really be a spare power lead as well. However, it might be fitted with the smaller connector for 3.5-inch floppy drives, whereas it is the larger power connector that is required for hard disc drives, whether they are of the 3.5-inch or 5.25-inch variety. A large computer store should be able to provide a 3.5 to 5.25-inch power connector adapter. If there is no spare power cable, a splitter adapter is available. This provides two power connectors from a single power lead. Remove the power lead from the existing hard disc drive and connect it to the splitter. The two remaining connectors of the splitter are then connected to the hard disc drives. The power connectors are fully polarised and can only be connected the right way around. They are also quite stiff, and often need a certain amount of force in order to get them properly connected or disconnected again.

BIOS Setup

Having physically installed the hard disc it will be necessary to go into the BIOS Setup program and set the appropriate parameters for the new disc. The BIOS is something that most PC users never need to get involved with, but for anyone undertaking PC upgrading it is likely that some involvement will be needed from time to time. It is certainly something that can not be avoided if you add a second hard disc drive. In days gone by it was necessary to have a utility program to make changes to the BIOS settings, but this program is built into a modern PC BIOS.

A modern BIOS Setup program enables dozens of parameters to be controlled, many of which are highly technical. This tends to make the BIOS intimidating for newcomers and even to those who have some experience of dealing with PC technicalities. However, most of the BIOS settings are not the type of thing the user will need to bother with, and very few are relevant to the hard disc drives.

BIOS basics

Before looking at the BIOS Setup program it would perhaps be as well to consider the function of the BIOS. BIOS is a acronym and it stands for basic input/output system. Its primary function is to help the operating system handle the input and output devices, such as the drives, and ports, and also the memory circuits. It is a program that is stored in a ROM on the motherboard. These days the chip is usually quite small and sports a holographic label to prove that it is the genuine article (Figure 4.7). Because the BIOS

Fig.4.7 A modern BIOS chip. This contains the Setup program as well as the BIOS

program is in a ROM on the motherboard it can be run immediately at start-up without the need for any form of booting process. It is the BIOS that provides the test procedures when a PC is switched on, and the BIOS also starts the boot process.

The BIOS can provide software routines that help the operating system to utilise the hardware effectively, and it can also store information about the hardware for use by the operating system, and possibly other software. It is this second role that makes it necessary to have the Setup program. The BIOS can actually detect much of the system hardware and store the relevant technical information in memory. Also, a modern BIOS is customised to suit the particular hardware it is dealing with, and the defaults should be sensible ones for the hardware on the motherboard. However, some parameters have to be set manually, such as the time and date, and the user may wish to override some of the default settings.

The Setup program enables the user to control the settings that the BIOS stores away in its CMOS memory. A backup battery powers this memory when the PC is switched off, so its contents are available each time the PC is turned on. Once the correct parameters have been set it should not be necessary to change them unless the hardware is altered, such as a new hard disc drive being added or the existing hard disc being upgraded. In practice, the BIOS settings can sometimes be scrambled by a software or hardware glitch, although this is not a common problem with modern PCs.

Entry

In the past, there has been several common means of getting into the BIOS Setup program, but with modern motherboards there is only one method in common use. This is to press the Delete key at the appropriate point during the initial testing phase just after switch-on. The BIOS will display a message, usually in the bottom left-hand corner of the screen, telling you to press the "Del" key to enter the Setup program. The instruction manual should provide details if the motherboard you are using has a different method of entering the Setup program. The most common alternative is to press the "Escape" key rather than the "Del" key, but numerous alternatives have been used over the years, and no doubt some of these are still in use.

Every PC should be supplied with a manual that has a section dealing with the BIOS. Actually a lot of PCs are supplied with a very simple "Getting Started" style manual, but this is usually augmented by the manufacturers' manuals for the main components. It is then the motherboard manual that will deal with the BIOS. It is worth looking through the BIOS section of the manual to before you actually go into the BIOS program. This will give you an idea of how things work, but do not bother too much about the more obscure settings. In the current context it is only some of the Standard CMOS settings that are of interest.

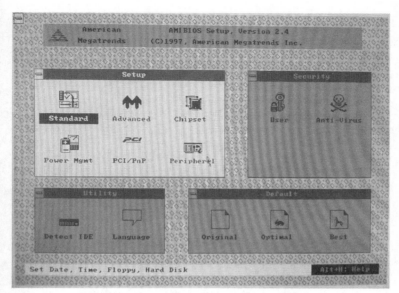

Fig.4.8 The initial screen of an AMI BIOS Setup program

Do not expect the manual to give detailed explanations of the various settings. Most motherboard instruction manuals assume the user is familiar with all the BIOS features, and there will be few detailed explanations. In fact, there will probably just be a list of the available options and no real explanations at all. This does not really matter, and you really only need to know how to get into the BIOS, make a few changes, save the changes, and exit the program.

There are several BIOS manufacturers and their BIOS Setup programs each work in a slightly different fashion. The Award BIOS and AMI BIOS are two common examples, and although they control the same basic functions, they are organised in somewhat different ways. A modern AMI BIOS has a Setup program that will detect any reasonably standard mouse connected to the PC, and offers a simple form of WIMP environment (Figure 4.8). It can still be controlled via the keyboard if preferred, or if the BIOS does not operate with the mouse you are using. The Award BIOS is probably the most common (Figure 4.9), and as far as I am aware it only uses keyboard control.

Apart from variations in the BIOS due to different manufacturers, the BIOS will vary slightly from one motherboard to another. This is simply

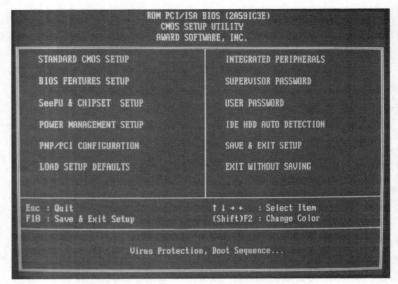

Fig.4.9 The initial screen of an Award BIOS Setup program

due to the fact that features available on one motherboard may be absent
or different on another motherboard. Also, the world of PCs in general is
developing at an amazing rate, and this is reflected in frequent BIOS
updates. Fortunately, the Standard CMOS section has not changed much
over the years, so it should not differ significantly from the one described
here unless you are dealing with a computer than falls into the "antique"
category.

Standard CMOS

There are so many parameters that can be controlled via the BIOS Setup
program that they are normally divided into half a dozen or more groups.
The most important of these is the "Standard CMOS Setup" (Figure 4.10),
which is basically the same as the BIOS Setup in the original AT style
PCs. The first parameters in the list are the time and date. These can
usually be set via an operating system utility these days, but you can still
alter them via the Setup program if you prefer. There are on-screen
instructions that tell you how to alter and select options. One slight oddity

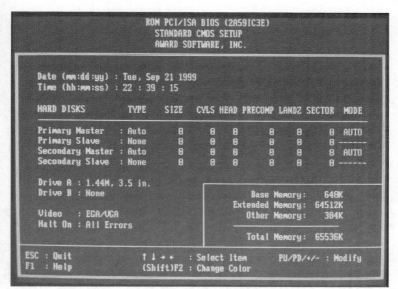

Fig.4.10 A typical Standard CMOS Setup screen

to watch out for is that you often have to use the Page Up key to decrement values, and the Page Down key to increment them.

With virtually any modern BIOS a help screen can be brought up by pressing F1, and this will usually be context sensitive (Figure 4.11). In other words, if the cursor is in the section that deals with the hard drives, the help screen produced by pressing F1 will tell you about the hard disc parameters. It would be unreasonable to expect long explanations from a simple on-line help system, and a couple of brief and to the point sentences are all that will normally be provided.

Drive settings

The next section is the one we need, and it is used to set the operating parameters for the devices on the IDE ports. The hard disc is normally the master device on the primary IDE channel (IDE1), and the CD-ROM is usually the master device on the secondary IDE channel (IDE2). However, to avoid the need for a second data cable the CD-ROM drive is sometimes the slave device on the primary IDE interface. You might

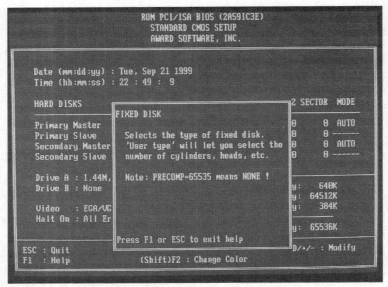

Fig.4.11 Most Setup programs provide context sensitive help

have fitted the new drive as any of the four available devices apart from the primary device on IDE1, which will be the original hard disc drive. If in doubt, this table should help you decide which device it is:

IDE channel	If the new drive is...
IDE1 secondary	on the same cable as the original hard drive
IDE2 primary	the sole device on the opposite channel to the original hard disc
IDE2 secondary	on the same cable as the CD-ROM drive (or other device such as a CD writer)

Having decided how the new drive fits into the overall scheme of things you can set the appropriate parameters. The drive should really be supplied with a manual that provides the correct BIOS settings, but it is usually possible to get by without it. One of the parameters is the hard disc's type number. In the early days there were about 40 standard types of hard disc drive, and it was just a matter of selecting the appropriate type number for the drive in use. The BIOS would then supply the appropriate parameters for that drive.

This system was unable to cope with the ever increasing range of drives available, and something more flexible therefore had to be devised. The original 40 plus preset drive settings are normally still available from a modern BIOS, but there is an additional option that enables the drive parameters to be specified by the user. This is the method used with all modern PCs and their high capacity hard disc drives, so choose the Custom setting and ignore the drive numbers.

The drive table parameters basically just tell the operating system the size of drive, and the way that the disc is organised. Although we refer to a hard disc as a singular disc, most of these units use both sides of two or more discs. Each side of the disc is divided into cylinders (tracks), and each cylinder is subdivided into several sectors. There are usually other parameters that enable the operating system to use the disc quickly and efficiently. You do not really need to understand these parameters, and just have to make sure that the correct figures are placed into the drive table. As pointed out previously, the manual for the hard drive should provide the correct figures for the BIOS. If you do not have the manual, it can probably be downloaded from the disc manufacturer's web site.

If you do not have the manual or prefer to take an easier option, a modern BIOS makes life easy for you by offering an "Auto" option. If this is selected, the BIOS examines the hardware during the start-up routine and enters the correct figures automatically. This usually works very well, but with some drives it can take a while, which extends the boot-up time. If the PC has been set up with this option enabled, the drive table will be blank.

There is an alternative method of automatic detection that avoids the boot-up delay, and any reasonably modern BIOS should have this facility. If you go back to the initial menu you will find a section called something like "IDE HDD Auto Detection" (Figure 4.12), and this offers a similar auto-detection facility. When this option is selected the Setup program examines the hardware on each IDE channel, and offers suggested settings for each of the four possible IDE devices. If you accept the suggested settings for the hard disc drive (or drives) they will be entered into the CMOS RAM. There may actually be several alternatives offered per IDE device, but the default suggestion is almost invariably the correct one. If you do not know the correct settings for a drive, this facility should find them for you.

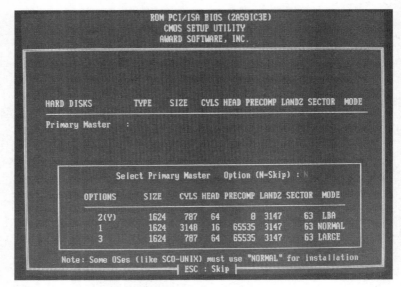

Fig.4.12 An IDE auto-detection screen

It is perhaps worth mentioning that with an IDE drive the figures in the drive table do not usually have to match the drive's physical characteristics. Indeed, they rarely if ever do so. The electronics in the drive enable it to mimic any valid physical arrangement that does not exceed the capacity of the drive. In practice it is advisable to use the figures recommended by the drive manufacturer, as these are tried and tested, and should guarantee perfect results. Other figures can sometimes give odd problems such as unreliable booting, although they are within the acceptable limits.

The last parameter for each IDE drive is usually something like Auto, Normal, LBA (large block addressing), and Large. Normal is for drives under 528MB, while LBA and Large are alternative modes for drives having a capacity of more than 528MB. Modern drives have capacities of well in excess of 528MB, and mostly require the LBA mode. The manual for the hard drive should give the correct setting, but everything should work fine with "Auto" selected.

It is increasingly common for modern motherboards to have four rather than two IDE interfaces. With a motherboard of this type it will usually be possible for the added hard disc drive to have its own IDE interface even if the PC is already fitted with something like one hard disc drive, a CD-ROM drive and a CD writer. Finding a spare IDE channel for the new drive should be that much easier, but in other respects things are essentially the same as when dealing with a twin IDE port motherboard. Motherboards that have more than two IDE ports usually have some form of RAID controller, and these provide clever facilities such as the ability to automatically backup data written to one drive on another drive. It is clearly worthwhile investigating any facilities of this type, which could clearly be more than a little useful in the current context.

Drive letters

Some users get confused because they think a hard drive that will be have more than one partition should have separate entries in the BIOS for each partition. This is not the case, and as far as the BIOS is concerned each physical hard disc is a single drive, and it has just one entry in the CMOS RAM table. The partitioning of hard discs is handled by the operating system, and so is the assignment of drive letters. The BIOS is only concerned with the physical characteristics of the drives, and not how data will be arranged and stored on the discs. There is usually no point in using more than one partition if you are adding a drive for backup purposes. The only, and fairly obvious exception, is where the drive you are backing up has been partitioned to operate as two or more logical drives. It is then advisable to have the partitioning of the backup drive match that of the main drive as closely as possible.

The other Standard CMOS settings are concerned with the floppy discs and the default display type, and should simply be left as they are. The same is true of the settings in the other pages of the BIOS Setup program. Do not be tempted to start playing around with these unless you know exactly what you are doing. Entering silly settings is unlikely to damage anything, but could well prevent the PC from operating properly. The BIOS will probably have options that enable the previous settings to be reinstated, or default settings to be used. These can be useful if you should accidentally scramble a few parameters.

Note though, that no settings are actually altered unless and until you select the Save Parameters and Exit option, and then answer Yes when asked to confirm this action. This is clearly the route you should take if everything has gone according to plan. Take the Exit Without Saving option if things have not gone well. Simply switching off the PC or pressing the reset button should have the same effect.

Strategies

With the early PC hard disc drives it was necessary to do low level formatting of the drive before it could be partitioned and the high level formatting could be undertaken. Modern hard drives are supplied with the low level formatting already done. If there is a low level formatting option in the BIOS Setup program, never use it on an IDE hard disc drive. Do not use any similar facility in any utility suites that you might have.

No low level formatting is required, but with operating systems such as Windows 9x and Windows XP, the hard disc drive must be partitioned and high-level formatted before it can be used.

The best way to proceed with the data recovery depends on the condition of the Windows XP installation. Your options are very limited if it is not even possible to boot in Safe Mode. Probably the only way of tackling the problem is to have the new drive set as the master on the primary IDE channel and the original hard disc on any available IDE channel. Windows XP is then installed from scratch onto the new drive. It should then be possible to boot into the new installation and copy the files you need from the original hard disc. Any high capacity backup devices fitted to the computer should work properly with the new installation in place. It is then possible to copy the files to the new hard disc or the backup devices.

Where it is possible to boot into Windows in Safe Mode an alternative strategy is available. The existing hard disc drive can be left as the boot drive and the second hard disc is then placed on any available IDE channel. With the computer booted in Safe Mode the required files on the main hard drive can then be copied to the second drive. Windows XP can be installed from scratch onto the main drive, which will result in all the files on the main drive being erased. The rescued files on the second drive can then be copied back to the main drive.

This is the best method to use if you do not wish to use the new drive as the main one. For example, if you obtain a cheap backup drive that has a much lower capacity than the main one, you will probably not wish to use the new drive as the main one. The second hard drive can be removed once the file recovery has been completed, but it is probably better to leave it in place as a backup drive for important files.

Patitioning

The new drive can be partitioned from within Windows XP and then formatted using the FAT32 or NTFS file system. If you wish to use the FAT32 file system for some reason, Microsoft recommend partitioning and formatting drives larger than 32 gigabytes using Windows 9x rather than Windows XP. This is simply because Windows XP is not fully equipped to deal with the partitioning and formatting of large discs using this format. Partitioning and formatting using Windows 9x and XP will be described here, starting with Windows 9x.

In order to partition and format the disc using Windows 9x it is not necessary to install Windows 9x onto the drive. All that is needed is a Startup disc, and one of these is normally produced as part of the Windows 9x installation process. If you do not have a Startup disc, one can be made using a system that runs Windows 9x. Start by going into the Windows Control Panel, and one route to this is to operate the Start button, and then select Settings and Control Panel. Once in the control panel double-click on the Add/Remove Programs icon, select Startup Disk, and finally operate the Create Disk button. Then follow the onscreen prompts. A blank 1.44 megabyte floppy disc is required.

Note that you will be asked to insert the Windows 95/98/ME CD-ROM into the CD-ROM drive, because some of the files required are not normally stored on the hard disc. The method of making the disc is exactly the same for all three operating systems (95, 98, and ME) incidentally.

Having obtained the Startup disc, it should be used to boot the computer into the Windows 9x version of MS-DOS. It is probable that the BIOS will already be set to boot from the floppy disc drive, but if necessary you must use the BIOS Setup program to set the floppy drive as a boot device. There will be a page in the BIOS called something like BIOS Features Setup (Figure 4.13), and this should enable various boot sequences to be chosen. Choose one that has the floppy disc (drive A:) as the first boot device, and hard drive C: as the second. Any subsequent boot options are irrelevant, since the PC will always boot from one or other of the first two options.

With the computer booted-up and running MS-DOS or the Windows 95/98/ME equivalent of MS-DOS, the new hard drive will not be accessible. Until it has been partitioned it will be largely "invisible" to the operating system. Note that a drive using the NTFS format will also be largely "invisible" to the system, so make sure that you process the right disc

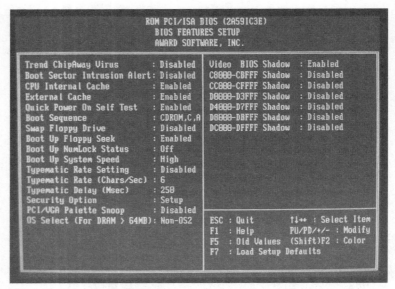

ROM PCI/ISA BIOS (2A591C3E)
BIOS FEATURES SETUP
AWARD SOFTWARE, INC.

Trend ChipAway Virus : Disabled	Video BIOS Shadow : Enabled
Boot Sector Intrusion Alert: Disabled	C8000-CBFFF Shadow : Disabled
CPU Internal Cache : Enabled	CC000-CFFFF Shadow : Disabled
External Cache : Enabled	D0000-D3FFF Shadow : Disabled
Quick Power On Self Test : Enabled	D4000-D7FFF Shadow : Disabled
Boot Sequence : CDROM,C,A	D8000-DBFFF Shadow : Disabled
Swap Floppy Drive : Disabled	DC000-DFFFF Shadow : Disabled
Boot Up Floppy Seek : Enabled	
Boot Up NumLock Status : Off	
Boot Up System Speed : High	
Typematic Rate Setting : Disabled	
Typematic Rate (Chars/Sec) : 6	
Typematic Delay (Msec) : 250	
Security Option : Setup	
PCI/VGA Palette Snoop : Disabled	
OS Select (For DRAM > 64MB): Non-OS2	ESC : Quit ↑↓→ : Select Item
	F1 : Help PU/PD/+/- : Modify
	F5 : Old Values (Shift)F2 : Color
	F7 : Load Setup Defaults

Fig.4.13 An example BIOS Features Setup screen. Amongst other things, this is used to set the required boot option

drive. Once the new drive is partitioned the operating system will be more willing to admit to its existence, but it will still be of no use until high-level formatting has been performed using the MS-DOS FORMAT program. However, you must first prepare the disc using the FDISK partitioning program. The Windows Startup disc contains copies of both FDISK and FORMAT, which are automatically placed on the disc for you when the Startup disc is created.

FDISK

FDISK is used to create one or more DOS partitions, and with discs of 2.1 gigabytes or less you may wish to have the whole of the disc as a single partition. Assuming the original hard disc has one partition, the new hard disc drive then becomes drive D:. By creating further partitions it can also operate as drive E:, drive F:, etc. The primary partition is normally the boot disc, and this is where the operating system would be installed. Obviously this does not apply to a second hard drive, and the primary partition is simply the first partition on the disc.

The MS/DOS and Windows 95 file systems set the 2.1-gigabyte partition limit. There is also an 8.4-gigabyte limit on the physical size of the drive. With Windows 98 or ME and any reasonably modern BIOS these limits do not apply, but you must use the FAT32 file system. To do this simply answer yes when FDISK is first run, and you are asked if you require support for large hard disc drives. Even if you do not wish to have a large disc organised as one large partition, it is still best to opt for large hard disc support. FAT32 utilises the available disc space more efficiently and reduces wastage. Note that if you only require a single partition you must still use the FDISK program to set up this single partition, and that the FORMAT program will not work on the hard drive until FDISK has created a DOS partition.

Some hard discs are supplied complete with partitioning software that will also format the disc and add the system files, which will be copied from the boot disc. Where a utility program of this type is available it might be better to use it instead of the FDISK and FORMAT programs. These MS-DOS programs are fairly straightforward in use, but using the software supplied with the drive will almost certainly be even easier. The only problem is that the software might be intended for use with drive C:, and might give problems if you try to use it with drive D:. The instructions supplied with the software should make it clear whether the software is suitable for use with a second hard disc drive. If the program insists on placing the system files on drive D:, this is not really a major problem. The system files will waste a small amount of disc space, but should not give any problems when the system is booted provided the boot options are set correctly in the BIOS. If in doubt, simply use FDISK and FORMAT.

Using FDISK

Once you are in FDISK there is a menu offering these four choices (see also Figure 4.14):

1. Create DOS partition or logical DOS drive

2. Set the active partition

3. Delete partition or logical DOS drive

4. Display partition information

5 Change current fixed drive

Normally the first thing we need to do is create a DOS partition using option one, which is the default. However, in this case we are dealing with an additional hard drive, and we must first make sure that it is the

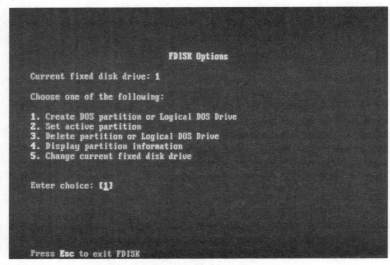

Fig.4.14 The main menu of the FDISK program

one FDISK is dealing with. It is very important that you do not accidentally use FDISK with the wrong drive, since to do so would almost certainly remove all the data from the disc you are trying to backup! Select option 5, which should bring up a screen like that in Figure 4.15. The original hard disc unit is drive 1 and the new hard disc is drive 2. In this example drive 1 (C:) is the original drive of about 10 gigabytes in capacity, and drive 2 is the additional rescue drive having a capacity of about 2.4 gigabytes. Drive 2 will eventually be drive D:, but at this stage it has not yet been assigned a drive letter. If the current disc is drive 1, enter 2 for this parameter and press the Enter key to go back to the main screen.

Once drive 2 has been set as the current drive it can be partitioned, and option 1 can be selected. This takes you into a further menu offering these three options (Figure 4.16):

1. Create primary DOS partition

2. Create extended DOS partition

3. Create logical DOS drive(s) in the extended DOS partition

It is a primary DOS partition that is required, so select option one, which should again be the default. After the disc has been given a quick test you will be asked if you wish to use the maximum space for the partition.

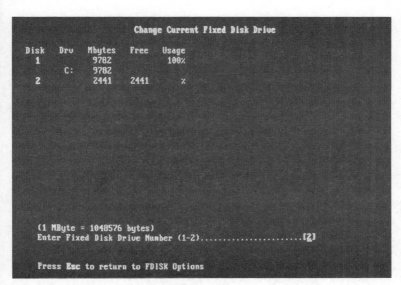

Fig.4.15 The partition information screen

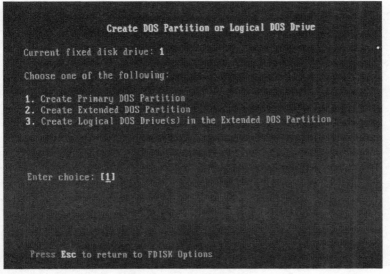

Fig.4.16 Creating a partition on a new hard disc

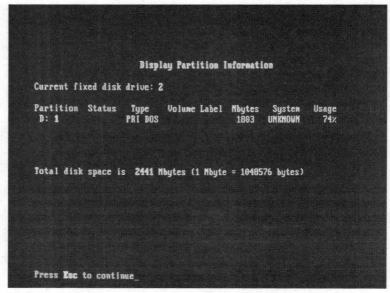

Display Partition Information

Current fixed disk drive: 2

Partition Status Type   Volume Label Mbytes System   Usage
D: 1   PRI DOS   1803   UNKNOWN 74%

Total disk space is 2441 Mbytes (1 Mbyte = 1048576 bytes)

Press Esc to continue_

Fig.4.17 Checking that the new partition has been created

If you answer yes, the whole disc, or as much of it as FDISK can handle, will be used for the partition. If you answer no, you will then have to specify the size of the primary partition in megabytes. After a further quick check of the disc the new partition will be created. Having created the partition, press the Escape key to return to the original menu. It is a good idea to select option four to check that the partition has been created successfully (Figure 4.17).

If a further partition is required select option one, and then option two, which is "Create extended DOS partition" (Figure 4.18). Enter the size of the partition you require and press the Return key to create the partition. Then press the Escape key, which will bring up a message saying "No logical drives defined" (Figure 4.19). In other words, you have created a partition, but as yet it does not have a drive letter. Assuming you require all the space in the partition to be one logical drive, simply press the Return key. This will make the partition drive E:, and a screen giving this information will appear (Figure 4.20). Press the Escape key to return to the main menu, and use option four to check that the partition has been created successfully.

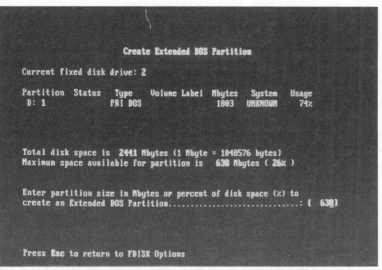

Fig.4.18 Provided there is some spare capacity, one or more additional partitions can be added

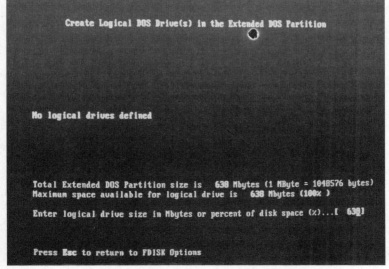

Fig.4.19 An extended partition must be given a drive letter

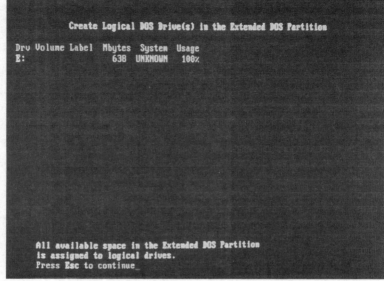

Fig.4.20 If all goes well, a screen showing the drive letter of the new
partition will appear

It has been assumed here that the original hard disc has a single FAT32
partition. If it has more than one partition these will be drives C:, D:, etc.,
and the drive letter or letters for the additional drive will be moved up
accordingly. For example, if the original disc is used as drives C: And
D:, partitions of the new drive would become drives E:, F:, etc. These
MS-DOS drive letters are not really of much importance once Windows
XP is in use, since it will assign its own drive letters.

Formatting

Having created the partitions you require, the "FORMAT" command can
then be run. First you will have to press the Escape key twice to exit
FDISK, and then the computer must be rebooted so that the new partition
information takes effect. Make sure you format the correct disc, because
formatting a disc that is already in use will destroy any data it contains.
To format drive D: use this command:

format D:

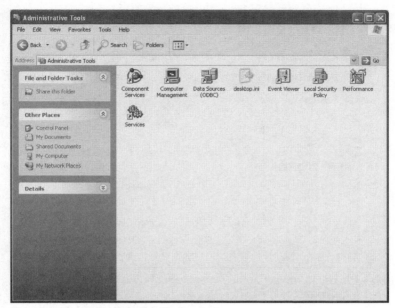

Fig.4.21 The Administrative Tools window

This will bring up a warning to the effect that all data in drive D: will be lost if you proceed with the format. As yet there is no data to lose, so answer yes to proceed with the formatting. It might take several minutes to complete the task, since there are a large number of tracks to be processed and checked. If the hard disc has more than one partition and is operating as drive D:, drive E:, etc., each partition must formatted using a separate "FORMAT" command. To format drive F: for example, this command would be used:

format F:

The new hard disc drive should then be fully operational, and it should appear in My Computer, etc., if you boot the computer in Safe Mode. The files you wish to rescue can then be copied to the new drive using Windows Explorer with Copy and Paste facilities. Windows XP is then installed from scratch onto the original hard disc and the rescued files can then be copied back to this drive.

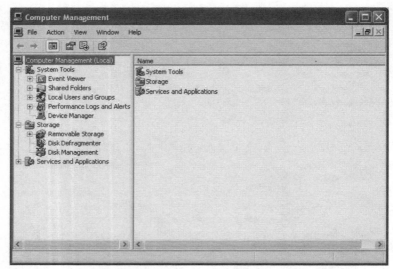

Fig.4.22 The Computer Management window gives access to several utilities

Computer Management

Partitioning and formatting from within Windows XP is achieved with the aid of the Computer Management utility. This can be run by going to the Windows Control Panel and double clicking the Administrative Tools icon. This produces a window like the one of Figure 4.21, and double clicking the Computer Management icon produces the new window of Figure 4.22. Several utilities are available from the Computer Management window, but the one required in this case is Disk Management. Left clicking this entry in the left-hand panel changes the window to look something like Figure 4.23.

Details of the boot drive are given at the top of the right-hand panel. The bottom section gives details of both drives, and the new backup drive is Disk 1. This is described as "Unallocated", which means that it is not partitioned or formatted at this stage. The black line to the right of the Disk 1 label and icon also indicates that it is not partitioned. To partition the disc, right-click on the black line and then select the New Partition option from the popup menu. This launches the New Partition Wizard (Figure 4.24). Windows XP can use two types of disc, which are the basic and dynamic varieties. The New Partition Wizard only handles

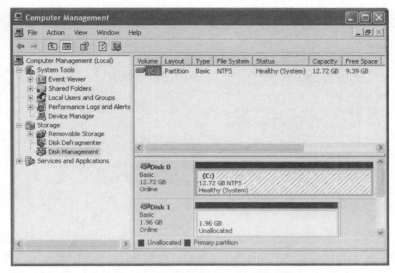

Fig.4.23 The window with the Disk Management utility selected

basic discs, and these use conventional partitions that are essentially the same as those used by MS-DOS and earlier versions of Windows. For simple backup purposes a basic disc is perfectly adequate.

Operate the Next button to move on with the partitioning, and a window like the one in Figure 4.25 should appear. Either an extended or a primary partition can be selected using the radio buttons, and in this case it is a primary partition that is needed. The size of the partition is selected at the next window (Figure

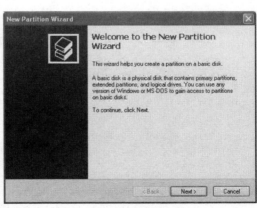

Fig.4.24 The opening screen of the Partition Wizard

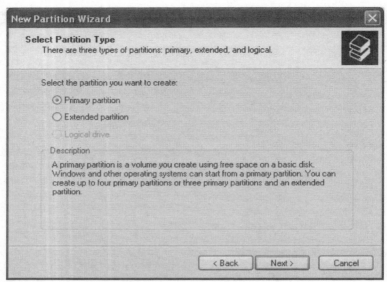

Fig.4.25 Use this window to select the partition type

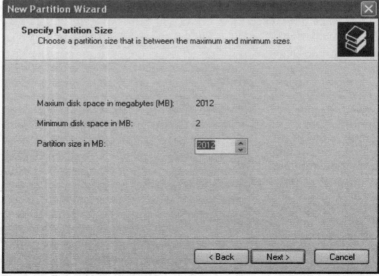

Fig.4.26 This window is used to set the partition size (in megabytes)

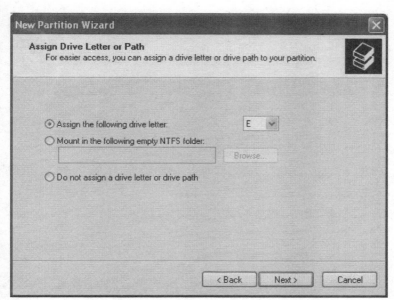

Fig.4.27 Here a drive letter is assigned to the new partition

4.26), and the maximum and minimum usable sizes are indicated. All the available disc space will be used by default, but a different size can be used by typing a value (in megabytes) into the textbox. Operating the Next button brings up the window of Figure 4.27 where a drive letter is assigned to the new partition. Unless there is a good reason to do otherwise, simply accept the default drive letter.

At the next window (Figure 4.28) you have the choice of formatting the new partition or leaving it unformatted. Since the partition will not be usable until it is formatted, accept the formatting option. One of the menus offers a choice of FAT, FAT32, or NTFS formatting. Settle for the default option of NTFS formatting unless you need compatibility with another Windows operating system. Also settle for the default allocation unit size, which will be one that is appropriate for the partition size. A different name for the drive, such as "Backup", can be entered into the textbox if desired. Tick the appropriate checkbox if the capacity of the disc is barely adequate to backup your files, and you wish to enable file and folder compression.

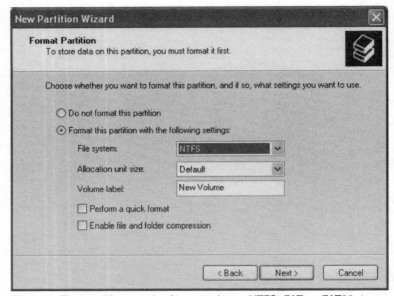

Fig.4.28 The partition can be formatted as a NTFS, FAT, or FAT32 type

Left-click the Next button when you are satisfied with the settings. The next window (Figure 4.29) lists all the parameters that have been selected, and provides an opportunity to change your mind or correct mistakes. If necessary, use the Back button to return to earlier windows and change some of the settings. Operate the Finish button if all the settings are correct. The partition will then be created, and it will appear as a blue line in the Disk Management window. It will then be formatted, and this may take half an hour or more for a large partition. The area below the blue line indicates how far the formatting process has progressed.

Eventually the formatting will be completed, and the Disk Management window will show the new disc as containing a primary partition using the appropriate file system (Figure 4.30). Once the formatting has been completed, files on the main drive can be copied to the new partition using the Cut and Paste facilities of Windows Explorer.

If space has been left for a further partition on the disc, right click on the black section of the line that represents the vacant disc space. Then select the New Partition option from the popup menu, and go through the whole partitioning and formatting process again. A maximum of four primary partitions can be used on each physical disc.

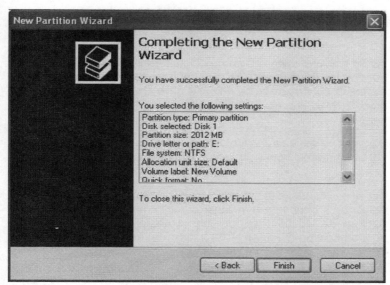

Fig.4.29 *This window lists all the parameters that have been selected*

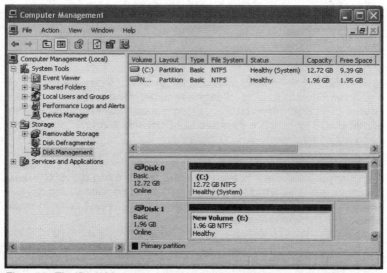

Fig.4.30 *The Disk Management window shows the new partition*

Points to remember

Do not wait until things go wrong before backing up data. It should be possible to rescue your data if the operating system becomes seriously damaged, but it might be expensive to have it rescued from a faulty hard drive.

Data rescue services are available, but there is no guarantee that data will be retrievable from a damaged hard drive.

Not all backup devices will work with Windows in Safe Mode or in MS-DOS. Lack of operation in either of these modes does not render a backup device useless, but life is easier when using a more accommodating drive. An NTFS partition is "invisible" to the system if the computer is booted into MS-DOS.

If you find yourself with a Windows installation that seems to be impossible to repair, and no usable device to backup masses of important data, there are three options. Carry on trying to repair Windows for as long as it takes, abandon your data and reinstall Windows from scratch, or add a suitable backup device so that the data can be rescued prior to reinstalling Windows.

Another hard drive is the most practical option when disaster has struck and an emergency backup of data is required. These days a hard disc drive is a relatively cheap backup option that will work in both Safe Mode and MS/DOS since it is a standard MS-DOS and Windows drive. Hard discs are also relatively fast in operation.

A modern PC can have at least four IDE drives (hard discs, CD-ROM drives, etc.) and will usually be able to accept an additional hard drive. If necessary, you can temporarily disconnect a CD-ROM drive to make way for the backup drive.

If the PC will not even boot into Safe Mode, probably the best rescue method is to add a new hard drive as disc C: and have the original hard disc as drive D:. In other words, set the new drive as the primary master and the original drive as the primary slave. Install Windows XP onto the new drive and then copy your data from the old drive.

A hard disc drive has to be partitioned and then high-level formatted before it is ready for use. This can be done using a Windows 9x Startup disc and the FDISK and FORMAT commands if a FAT32 disc is required. This is the best method for discs having a capacity of 32 megabytes or more. FDISK must be used even if the disc will be organised as one large partition. No low-level formatting is required with a modern hard disc drive, since this formatting is done at the factory.

The Windows XP Disk Management utility can be used to create partitions and format them using the FAT, FAT32, and NTFS file systems. However, this utility is only available if the computer can be booted into Windows XP, either normally or in Safe Mode.

Proper backup software can be used to backup your data, but Windows Explorer enables data to be easily copied from one drive to another. Complete directory structures can be copied using the Copy and Paste facilities and the usual dragging techniques.

4   Data rescue

Backup and restore

Backup?

Using the methods outlined in the previous chapter it is possible to recover data from the hard disc when there is a serious problem with the operating system. Using a data recovery service it might even be possible to recover data from a faulty hard disc, albeit at a price. It is definitely advisable to avoid putting yourself into a situation where emergency measures have to be taken in order to avoid the loss of vital data, and this means backing up any important data. Of course, it you use a PC purely for pleasure and do not have any important data to back up, there will probably be little point in going to the trouble of backing up the hard disc. In the event of a serious problem everything can be reinstalled and there is no important data to lose.

These days most computer users are not dabblers, and their PCs are put to good uses. This means that important data is usually generated, and generated in large quantities. Whether it is family photographs from a digital camera, the company accounts, or your latest novel, most PCs contain data that is precious to the users. It makes sense to produce backup copies of this data, even if it does involve a certain amount of time and expense.

Better save than sorry

If you are going to do the sensible thing and backup important data it is not essential to use any backup software. Having stored a file onto the hard disc using the Save function of the application software you can simply select Save As and store it again on another drive, such as a ZIP drive or CD writer. This method enables data files to be restored to the hard disc using Windows Explorer if a major failure of some kind should occur, but it does not allow the operating system to be restored. Neither will it restore any of your applications software or any customisation of that software. If the hard disc has to be replaced or the operating system becomes seriously damaged, the operating system has to be reinstalled, the applications programs are then installed again, and finally the data files are restored.

This is not a particularly quick or neat way of doing things, but for most users it will get the PC fully operational again in a reasonable amount of time. It has the advantage that it requires a minimal amount of time to maintain the backup copies, since only data files are being copied. As pointed out in previous chapters, it also gives you a "clean" copy of Windows that should operate quickly and efficiently. There are actually backup programs that will automatically make copies of data files, but these are probably only a worthwhile proposition if you are producing large numbers of data files.

If you use applications that only generate small amounts of data, an ordinary floppy disc drive is adequate for making backup copies as you generate them. Unfortunately, modern applications programs tend to generate large amounts of data. With a relatively simple application such as word processing the amounts of data generated might be reasonably small, but software such as graphics and desktop publishing programs usually produce large amounts of data. The folder used to store the files for this book will probably contain something like 500 megabytes of data by the time the book is finished. Backing up data requires some form of mass storage device when large files or large amounts of small files are involved.

Backup software

For anything beyond backing up data files it is best to resort to some sort of backup program. With these it is possible to save selected directories or directory structures, or the entire contents of the hard disc drive. I think I am correct in stating that every version of Windows is supplied complete with a backup program that has the imaginative name of Backup. Although basic compared to some programs of this type it does the job well enough for most users. Its lack of popularity possibly stems from the fact that the equivalent facility in Windows 3.1 was something less than user friendly, causing many users to look elsewhere for a backup utility.

Perhaps the problem is simply that the Backup program is a part of Windows that has often been easy to overlook. Anyway, the Windows

Fig.5.1 The initial window of the Backup or Restore Wizard

XP version is more user friendly and powerful than previous versions, and it is definitely there if you seek it out. With the Professional version of Windows XP it is installed by default, but with the Home Edition it will probably have to be installed from the Valueadd\Msft\Ntbackup folder on the installation CD-ROM.

Backup Wizard

Once installed, the Backup program is run by selecting All Programs from the Start menu, followed by Accessories, System Tools, and then Backup. By default the Backup Wizard (Figure 5.1) runs when this program is launched, and initially it is probably best to use the wizard. Operate the Next button to move on to the first stage of using the Backup Wizard (Figure 5.2). Here you have the choice of backing up or restoring data, but it is obviously necessary to produce a backup disc before anything can be restored. Therefore, initially the Backup radio button has to be selected.

5 Backup and restore

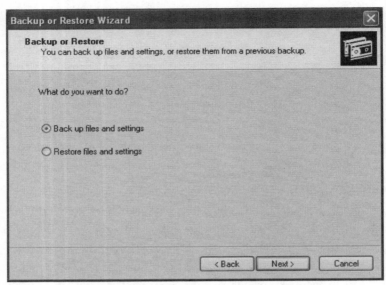

Fig.5.2 This window provides Backup and Restore options

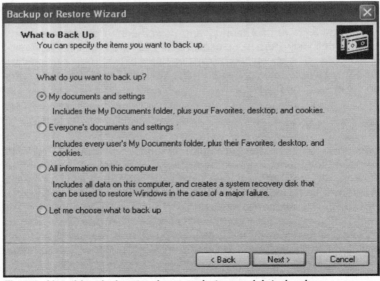

Fig.5.3 Use this window to choose what you wish to backup

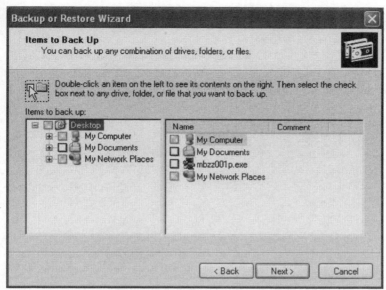

Fig.5.4 With the aid of this file browser you can select the files or folders you would like to backup

The next window (Figure 5.3) is used to select the data to be backed up. The top option produces a backup of the My Documents folder plus some system settings and cookies. The second option is similar, but it provides a backup of the documents and settings for all users. Using the fourth option produces a file browser (Figure 5.4) so that the user can select the files and folders that will be backed up. The third option is the one that is of most use if the system becomes seriously damaged or the hard disc becomes unusable. It permits the whole system to be backed up, and it also produces a recovery disc that enables it to be easily restored again. In fact the restoration process is almost totally automated. It is the third option that will be considered here.

The next window (Figure 5.5) enables the backup drive to be selected, and a variety of drive types is supported. These include Zip discs, local hard drives, and some tape backup systems. Unfortunately, CD writers are not supported. Sometimes there are ways of working around this limitation, but it is probably best to opt for a third party backup program if you wish to use CD-R or CD-RW discs to hold the backup files. Use the menu or the Browse option to select the correct drive. If you select a device that is not supported by the Backup program, an error message

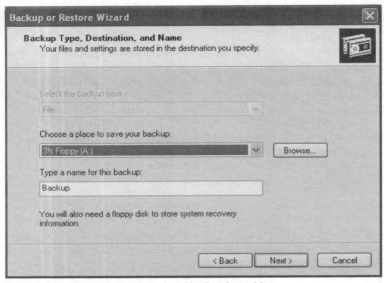

Fig.5.5 Use this window to select the backup drive

Fig.5.6 The selected options are shown before the backup is started

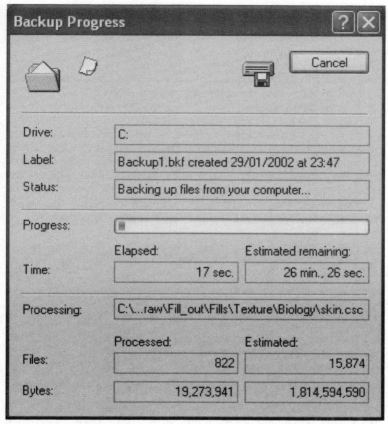

Fig.5.7 This window shows how the backup process is progressing

will be produced when Windows tries to create the file. This will simply state the backup file could not be produced.

By default, the backup file is called "Backup" but the name in the textbox can be changed to any valid filename. Operating the Next button moves things on to a window like the one in Figure 5.6. This shows the options that have been selected, and provides an opportunity to change your mind or correct mistakes. Use the Back button if it is necessary to return to earlier windows to make changes, or operate the Finish button to go ahead and make the backup file.

5　Backup and restore

*Fig.5.8 The floppy disc is inserted into drive A: when this
message appears*

A window like the one shown in Figure 5.7 will appear, and this shows
the progress made by the Backup program. It provides an estimate for
the time remaining until the task is completed, and this will vary massively
depending on the amount of data to be saved and the speed of the
backup device. With many gigabytes of data to backup it is definitely a
good idea to use a fast backup device such as a second hard disc drive.
With a slow backup device the process can take many hours.

*Fig.5.9 This message appears once the backup file has been
completed*

Where appropriate, you will be prompted when a disc change is
necessary. With multiple disc backups, always label all the discs clearly.
You will then be able supply the right disc each time when restoring the
backup copy. Do not worry if the size of the backup file is substantially
less than the total amount of data on the hard disc. The backup file is
probably compressed, or perhaps no backup copies are made of
standard files that are available from the Windows XP installation disc.
Anyway, it is quite normal for the backup file to be significantly smaller
than the source.

The message shown in Figure 5.8 will appear towards the end of the
backup process. The floppy disc is needed to make an automatic
recovery disc. This disc is needed in order to restore the system from
the backup disc, and the backup is of relatively little value without the
recovery disc. Insert a 1.44-megabyte floppy disc into drive A: and

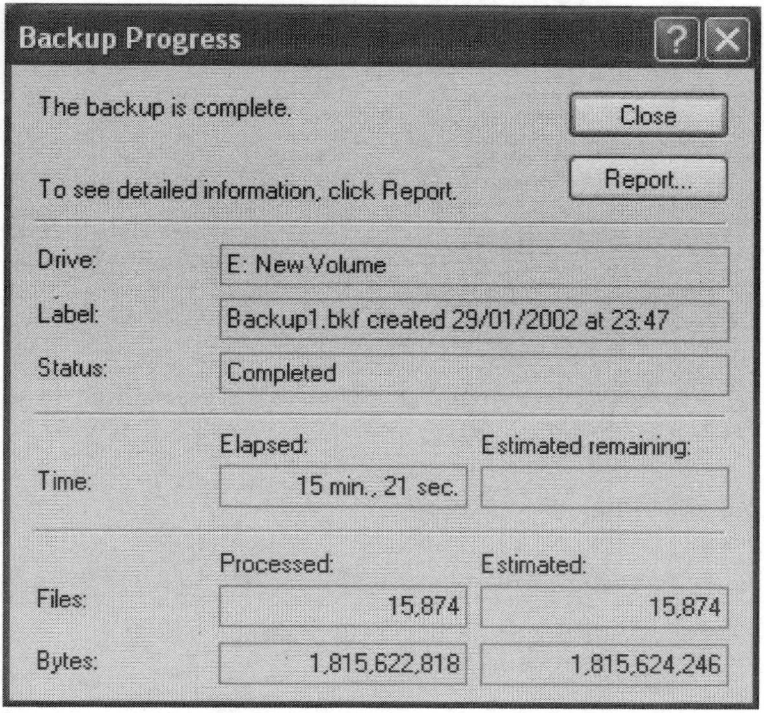

Fig.5.10 The Backup Progress window provides some statistics

operate the OK button. The message of Figure 5.9 appears once the recovery disc has been completed. Label the disc as indicated in the message and store it safely. The automatic recovery process is not possible without this disc. Finally, you are returned to the Backup Progress window (Figure 5.10), which should indicate that the backup has been completed successfully.

Restoring

There is little point in having a means of restoring the backup that requires the computer to boot normally into Windows XP, since this will often be impossible when the restoration feature is needed. The Windows XP method of restoring a full system backup is more straightforward than the Windows 9x equivalent. In fact the Windows XP method makes the

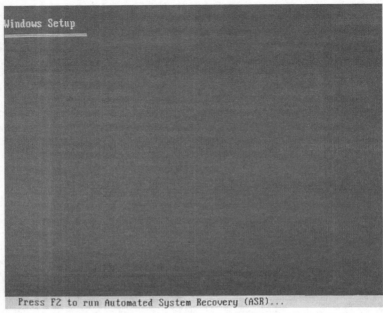

Windows Setup

Press F2 to run Automated System Recovery (ASR)...

Fig.5.11 Press the F2 key as soon as this message appears at the bottom of the screen

process about as simple as it is ever likely to be. It is termed the Automated System Recovery, and it certainly lives up the automated part of its name.

The first task is to boot from the Windows XP installation CD-ROM, and the BIOS must be set to boot from the CD-ROM drive before it tries to boot from the hard disc drive. If the boot sequence is the other way around, the computer will probably start to boot from the hard drive and the CD-ROM drive will be ignored. With the installation disc in a CD-ROM drive and the correct BIOS settings, a message saying "Press any key to boot from CD-ROM" will appear for a few seconds at the beginning of the boot process. Press any key while this message is displayed or the computer will revert to booting from the hard disc drive.

Messages appear along the bottom of the screen when the computer starts booting from the CD-ROM. Look for the one that says "Press F2 to run Automated System Recovery (ASR)", as in Figure 5.11. This message only appears briefly, so press F2 as soon as it appears. After some disc

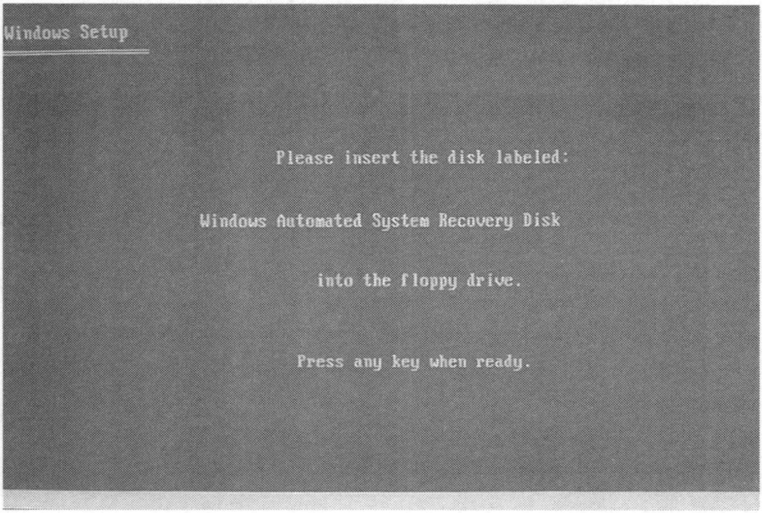

Windows Setup

Please insert the disk labeled:

Windows Automated System Recovery Disk

into the floppy drive.

Press any key when ready.

Fig.5.12 Insert the backup disc into drive A: when this prompt appears

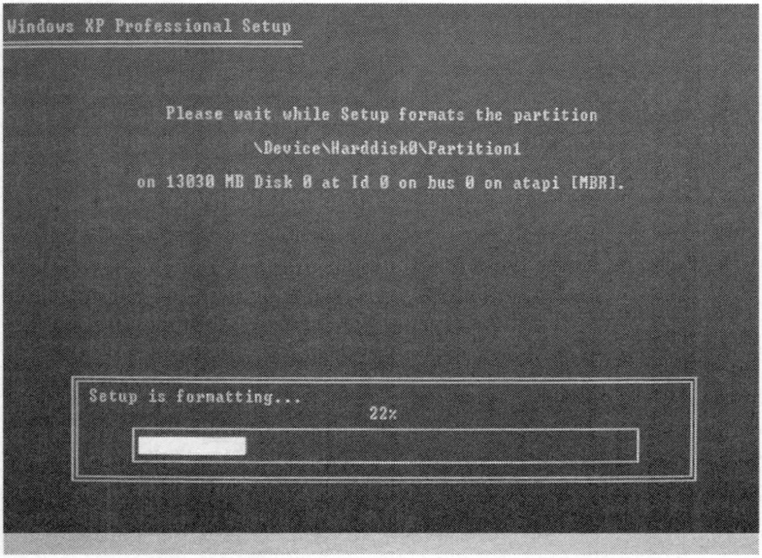

Windows XP Professional Setup

Please wait while Setup formats the partition
\Device\Harddisk0\Partition1
on 13030 MB Disk 0 at Id 0 on bus 0 on atapi [MBR].

Setup is formatting...   22%

Fig.5.13 Formatting erases all data stored in the disc partition

Fig.5.14 The Setup program briefly examines the disc drives

Fig.5.15 It takes a few minutes for the installation files to be copied

activity the message of Figure 5.12 will appear, and the floppy disc produced when backup was made must be placed in drive A:. Then press any key to continue. The restoration process requires little intervention from the user, but it is as well to keep an eye on things in case something goes

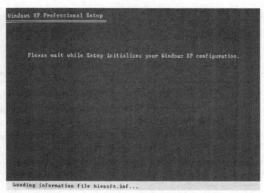

Fig.5.16 More files are loaded

wrong. First the partition used by the system is formatted, which effectively wipes all data from the partition. If there is any data on the disc that has not been backed up, it is lost forever at this stage. The formatting will take several minutes, and an onscreen "fuel gauge" shows how far the formatting has progressed (Figure 5.13).

A similar gauge is used at the next screen (Figure 5.14), where the program examines the disc drives. This is usually much quicker than formatting the restoration partition, and this screen may only appear for a second or two. A further gauge appears on the next screen (Figure 5.15), and here the program copies some files to the hard disc. Next the program loads some more files (Figure 5.16). The computer is then rebooted, and it will reboot after several seconds even if you do not press Return to restart the computer (Figure 5.17).

Fig.5.17 The computer will reboot automatically if the Return key is not operated

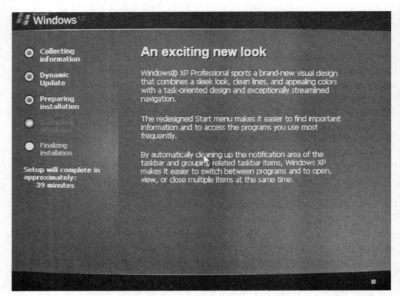

Fig.5.18 Installation starts in earnest once the computer has rebooted

Note that the Automated System Recovery disc in drive A: must be removed at this stage. The computer might try to boot from this disc if it is left in the drive, and this would probably prevent the computer from rebooting properly. If the reboot should stall because the disc is left in drive A:, removing it and pressing any key should get things underway again.

Windows is installed on the appropriate partition after the computer has rebooted, and a screen like the one in Figure 5.18 shows how the installation is progressing. Once Windows has been installed, the Automated System Recovery Wizard runs (Figure 5.19). This does not require any input from the user though, and you can just sit back and watch while your files are restored to the hard disc (Figure 5.20). Once this has been completed, the usual login screen (Figure 5.21) appears. You login using your normal password, and the computer then goes into Windows XP (Figure 5.22). This should look the same and have the same settings that were in force when the backup was made. Any programs, data, etc., on the partition that was backed up should be included in the restored installation.

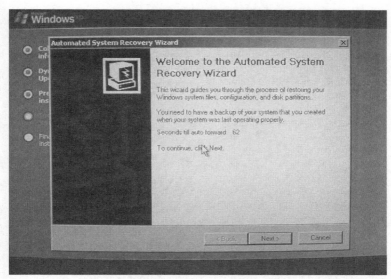

Fig.5.19 The Automated System Recover Wizard runs once Windows XP has been reinstalled

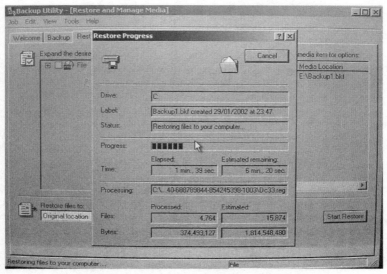

Fig.5.20 The Restore program copies files to the hard disc

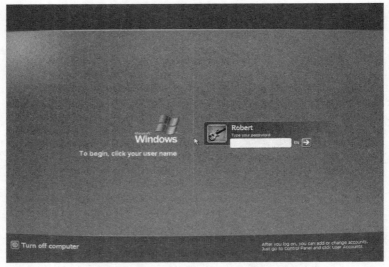

Fig.5.21 Login normally once the files have been restored

Fig.5.22 Windows XP should now look and work as before

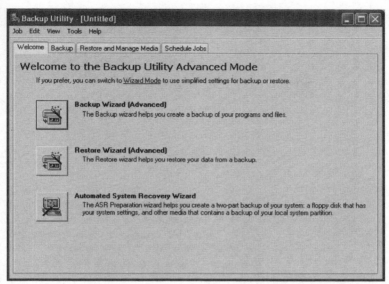

Fig.5.23 Three options are offered when Advanced Mode is selected

In practice there might be one or two minor differences to the system. In particular, any passwords or other data hidden on the disc in "invisible" files will not have been placed on the backup disc. Files of this type are very secure, but they are "invisible" to the Backup program. It is therefore unable to save them in the backup file. This should not be of any major consequence, because the relevant applications can be run, and the passwords (or whatever) can be stored on the hard disc again. Of course, any data files produced after the backup was made will not be automatically restored to the hard disc. They must be restored manually, and it is essential to make sure that any recent data files are backed up before you start the restoration process.

Advanced Mode

Use of the Backup Wizard is not mandatory, and the Backup program can be controlled directly by the user. Start running the program in the usual way, but left-click on the "Advanced mode" link. This produces a window like the one in Figure 5.23, and two of the buttons give access to more advanced versions of the Backup and Restore wizards. The third

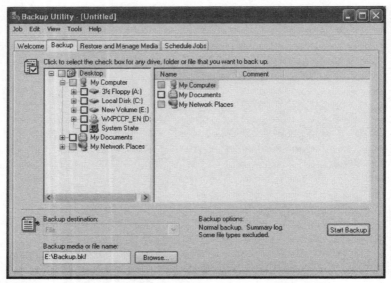

Fig.5.24 The Backup program enables the source files to be selected easily

button provides another route to the Automated System Recovery Wizard. The tabs near the top of the window provide manual operation of the Backup and Restore programs, and to scheduled backups.

Figure 5.24 shows the window for the Backup program. The files and folders to be backed up are selected in the upper section of the window, while the backup drive and filename are entered in the textbox near the bottom left-hand corner of the window. The usual Browse facility is available here. Once everything has been set up correctly, the Start Backup button is operated. The Restore program's window is shown in Figure 5.25. The upper section of the window is used to locate and select the backup file, and the lower section is used to select the destination of the restored backup. This will usually be the original location, but it can be restored to an alternative location. Once everything has been set correctly, the Start Restore button is operated.

The Backup and Restore programs are not difficult to use, and are certainly more user friendly than the equivalent functions in some previous versions of Windows. However, except where some very simple backup and restore operation is required, it is probably best to use the wizards.

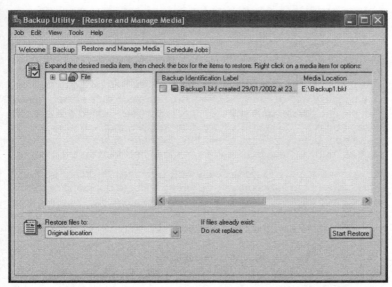

Fig.5.25 The Restore program enables the backup file and destination to be selected

These should ensure that you do not overlook anything, and that backup files can always be successfully restored. The Automated System Restore facility is an invaluable facility, and one that it is well worth using. In the past it has been slow, difficult, and expensive to implement this type of backup system. With this facility and an inexpensive hard disc added to the PC, the entire system can be backed up quite rapidly and restored again with ease.

System Restore

As pointed out previously, Windows XP has a very useful facility called System Restore. It has to be emphasised that this is not a conventional backup/restore program, and it can not be used to make a set of backup discs for use in the event of a hard disc failure. System Restore uses the hard disc to store the backup files, and if the hard disc fails, the backup files are inaccessible. It only makes backup copies of system and program files that are deleted or changed, and no backup copies are made of most files.

System Restore is designed specifically to deal with problems in the operating system. The normal Backup and Restore programs are used to deal with hard disc failures. The purpose of System Restore is to take the system back to a previous configuration that worked. If there is a problem with the current configuration, taking the system back to a previous state should cure the problem. System or program files that have been deleted or changed since the restoration date are returned to their previous state, and any files that have been added are deleted. Strictly speaking, System Restore is a program that will work around operating system problems rather than fix them. It will often provide a quick fix, but you have to be careful not to reintroduce the problem.

The general idea is to periodically add new restore points so that if something should subsequently go wrong with the operating system, it can be taken back to a recent restore point. Incidentally, Windows adds restoration points periodically, so it is not essential to routinely add your own. The main reason for adding your own restoration points is when there is increased likelihood of problems occurring. The most common example of this is adding a restore point prior to installing new software.

If anything should go horribly wrong during the installation process, going back to the restoration point should remove the rogue program and fix the problem with the operating system. You can then contact the software publisher to find a cure to the problem, and in the mean time your PC should still be functioning properly. It is also worth adding a restoration point prior to adding or removing new hardware. This provides a way back to normality if adding or removing the device drivers has dire consequences for the Windows installation.

When going back to a restoration point the program should remove any recently added programs, but it should leave recently produced data files intact. Of course, with any valuable data that has not been backed up already, it would be prudent to make backup copies before using System Restore, just in case things do not go according to plan. The program does itself does provide a way around this sort of problem in that it does permit a restoration to be undone. If a valuable data file should vanish "into thin air" it should be possible to return the PC to its original configuration, backup the restored data, and then go back to the restoration point again. System Restore only backs up and restores system and program files, so it is unlikely to be responsible for data files going "absent without leave".

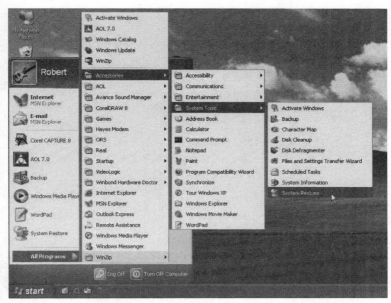

*Fig.5.26   The System Restore facility is buried deep in the Start
         menu system*

In use

The System Restore program is buried deep in the menu structure (Figure
5.26), but it can be started by going to the Start menu and then selecting
All Programs, Accessories, System Tools, and System Restore.   The
program is controlled via a Wizard, so when it is run you get the screen
of Figure 5.27 and not a conventional Windows style interface. The radio
buttons give three options, which are to go back to a restoration point,
create a new one, or undo the last restoration. When the program is run
for the first time there is no restoration to undo, so this option will not be
present. Hence only two radio buttons are shown in Figure 5.27.

As pointed out previously, the system will automatically create restoration
points from time to time, but you will probably wish to create your own
before doing anything that will make large changes to the system. Start
by selecting the "Create a restore point" option and then operate the
Next button. The next screen (Figure 5.28) asks the user to provide a
name for the restore point, and it is helpful if the name is something

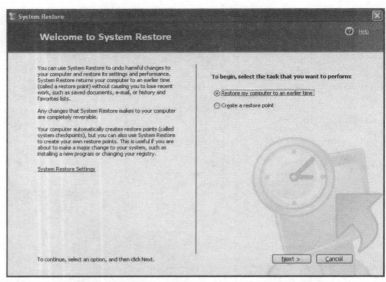

Fig.5.27 The System Restore facility is controlled via a wizard

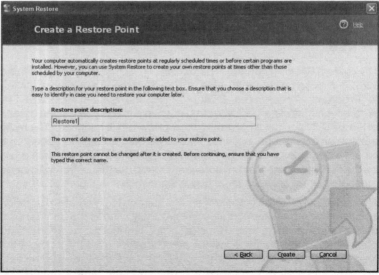

Fig.5.28 First the restore point has to be named

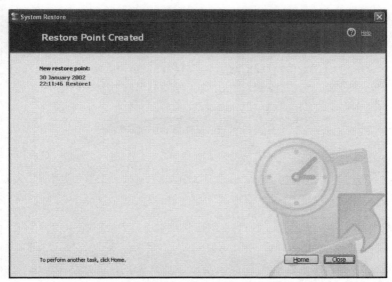

Fig.5.29 After a delay of at least a few seconds, this screen confirms that the restoration point has been created

meaningful. If the restore point is added prior to installing a word processor, it could be called "preword" for example. There is no need to include a date, as the program automatically records the date and time for you. There will be a delay of at least several seconds when the Next button is pressed, and then a screen like the one shown in Figure 5.29 will appear. This confirms that the restore point has been created, and it shows the name, date and time for the restore point.

It takes me back

To go back to a restoration point, run the program as before, and select the Return my computer to an earlier time option. Operate the Next button, and after a short delay a screen like the one of Figure 5.30 will appear. If there are a number of restore points available you can use the arrow heads in the calendar to find the one you require. The dates on the calendar in larger text are the ones that have restore points. Left clicking on one of these will show the available points in the screen area just to the right of the calendar. Left-click on the required restore point and then operate the Next button.

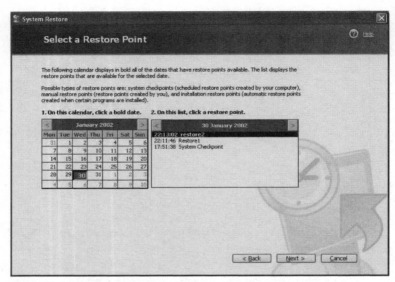

Fig.5.30 Use this window to select a restoration date and point

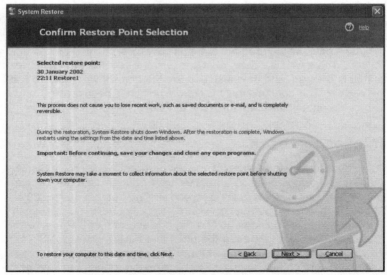

Fig.5.31 Heed the warnings before going ahead with the restoration

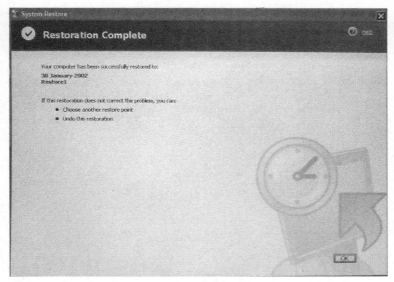

Fig.5.32 This window appears when the restoration has been completed successfully

This brings up a screen like Figure 5.31, complete with some warning messages. Where appropriate, save your data and close any programs that are running before proceeding. If you are satisfied that the correct restore point has been selected and that everything is ready, operate the Next button and the program will begin the restoration process. The computer will logoff from Windows XP, and then a small window will show how far the restoration process has progressed. The computer will automatically reboot once the process has been completed.

Login in again in the normal way, and after a short delay and some disc activity the usual Windows startup screen will appear, but at this stage it will not contain any icons. There should be a window like the one shown in Figure 5.32, confirming that the system has been successfully returned to the specified restore point. It also indicates the options if the PC fails to operate properly using this restore point. Left-click the OK button to finish the boot process, and the computer should then have shifted back in time to the appropriate restoration point.

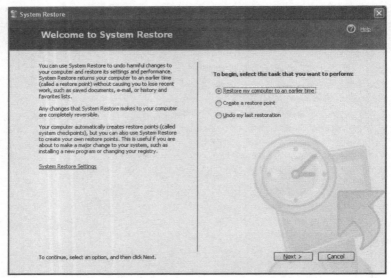

Fig.5.33 The opening screen now has three radio buttons

Undo

It is possible to undo a restoration once the System Restore facility has been used. Running the System Restore program produces an opening Window that has three radio buttons (Figure 5.33). Operate the button labelled "Undo my last restoration" and then left-click the OK button. This brings up the warning screen of Figure 5.34. If everything is ready to proceed, operate the Next button. Undoing a restoration follows along the same lines as returning to a restoration point. After logging out, rebooting, and logging in again, a message like the one in Figure 5.35 will appear on the screen. Operate the OK button, and the system should be returned to its original state.

Windows XP is still relatively new at the time of writing this, but the System Restore utility should be a very worthwhile facility. The similar feature in Windows ME can be very useful as a quick solution to a system that refuses to operate properly. It is not infallible though, and some problems can prevent the System Restore from returning the computer to an earlier configuration. In addition, there is no guarantee that returning to a restore point will cure every problem. It is probably not a good idea to use the

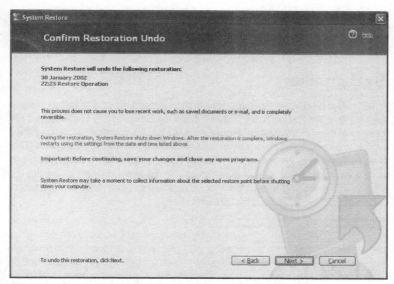

Fig.5.34 *Operate the Next button if you are ready to proceed*

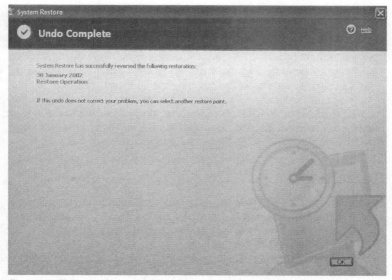

Fig.5.35 *This window appears once the restoration has been undone*

System Restore program as a first resort if there is a problem with the operating system, but it is certainly worth a try where the problem has no simple solution. It will often have the desired effect.

System files

If Windows becomes troublesome due to a missing or damaged system file, life is a lot easier if you have a backup copy of the file in question. One of the main causes of problems are DLL (dynamic link library) files, which are used extensively by Windows and applications programs. DLL files provide program code for frequently performed functions, such as displaying menus and dialogue boxes. Some are supplied as part of the Windows operating system, while others are loaded onto the hard disc when applications programs are installed.

Reinstalling a standard DLL file from the Windows installation disc should not be difficult, but one installed by an application program could be more difficult to replace. Firstly, you might not know which program supplied the file. The second problem is that searching the relevant CD-ROM for the file might not be successful. Files are often stored on installation discs in some form of compressed or archived form, making it difficult to locate and extract the one you require.

The DLL files are likely to be liberally spread across the hard disc, but using Windows Explorer it is easy to locate all of these files and copy them to a mass storage device such as a CD writer. The amount of storage space required will vary considerably from one Windows installation to another, and the more applications that are installed the more DLL files there will be. Backing up the DLL files on one of my PCs required some 500 megabytes or so of storage space, which is probably quite typical. Since the DLL backup is intended for use when the system becomes damaged, rather than for use in the event of a hard disc failure, many users simply copy the files to a folder on the hard disc.

Searching

In order to copy the DLL files, launch Windows Explorer and then operate the large Search button near the top of the window. Then left-click the All files and folders link in the left-hand section of the main window. Enter "*.dll" as the filename in the text box for all or part of the filename. The "*" character in the filename tells the search program to accept anything as the main part of the filename. Any file that has a "dll" extension will

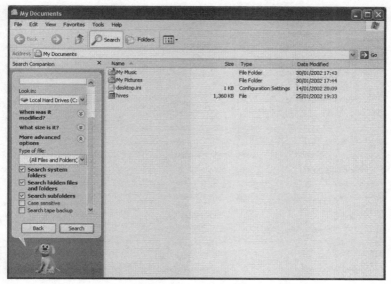

Fig.5.36 Setting the correct search parameters

therefore produce a match. Make sure that the local drives (the hard discs) are selected in the pop-down menu. In other respects the default settings should suffice, but it is as well to check the advanced settings by left clicking the appropriate button. The program must be set to search system folders, subfolders, and for hidden files. You should now have something like Figure 5.36.

When you operate the Search button, the program will search the hard disc drive or drives for any file that has "dll" as the extension. As it will thoroughly search all the folders on all the hard disc drives it should find every DLL file in use by the system. You should end up with something like Figure 5.37, with a large number of DLL files listed in the right-hand section of the window.

I am not exaggerating when I say that there will probably be a few thousand files listed! In this example the PC has a typical hardware specification and only a few applications loaded. The search still found some 3,761 files having a "dll" extension! Despite the large number of files, copying them is very easy. Highlight all the files by going to the Edit menu and choosing the Select All option. Then go to the Edit menu

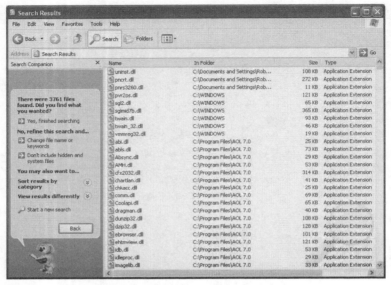

Fig.5.37 A huge number of DLL files will be found

again and select Copy. The DLL files can then be Pasted to backup folder on the hard drive, a CD-R, or whatever, using Windows Explorer.

If the files are to be stored on something like Zip discs that can not store all the files on a single disc, the copying process becomes more difficult. Batches of files must be highlighted manually and copied to the backup discs, being careful not to have any batch larger than the storage capacity of the disc. It is possible that during the copying process you will be asked whether or not to overwrite a file that has already been copied, with another file of the same name. The rule here is to not replace a newer file with an older version, so check the dates of the two files and proceed accordingly.

Obviously it could be very time consuming to manually search the backup disc or discs for a specific DLL file that you need. The quick way is the use the Search Files or Folders facility of Windows Explorer. This can search through thousands of files and locate the one you require in a few seconds. Having found the required file, the Copy and Paste facilities of Windows Explorer can be used to copy it to the appropriate folder on the hard disc.

Points to remember

Backing up data and (or) system information to another drive is the only way to guard against a hard disc failure. Backing up system information to the main hard drive is sufficient to guard against problems with the operating system.

Floppy discs are inadequate to cope with the large amounts of data produced by many modern applications. A CD writer, Zip drive, additional hard disc, or some other form of mass storage device is required. A mass storage device is also required in order to make a full backup of the main hard disc drive. Note that some backup programs (including the Windows XP Backup program) are not compatible with CD writers.

It is only necessary to save important data and configuration files, but it is much quicker to get things back to normal if you make a full backup of the hard drive.

Plenty of third party backup software is available, but the Windows XP Backup utility is adequate for most purposes. Combined with an additional hard disc drive, this provides a fast and cost effective method of providing a full system backup.

The Windows Backup program can be used to backup selected files, or a full backup of the hard disc can be provided. Regularly backing up the full contents of a hard disc is relatively time consuming, but restoring a full backup is the quickest way to get the computer into full working order again if a major problem occurs.

The Windows XP Backup program can be used without wizards, but for most purposes the wizards provide the easiest and most reliable means of handling backup and restore operations.

Windows XP has a System Restore program that can be used to take the system back to the way it was at some previous time. Using System Restore to take the system back a day or two will usually remedy boot problems, etc. Any data files generated since the restoration point will not be erased.

5   Backup and restore

It is worthwhile making a backup copy of all the DLL files on the hard disc. In the event of a DLL file becoming deleted or overwritten by an older version, the original is then easily found and reinstated. It is not necessary to have a backup device for the DLL files. Storing them in a folder on the hard disc is perfectly all right.

Reinstallation

Clean sweep

Things have gone badly, attempts to fix the Windows installation have failed, System Restore does not get things working again, and there is no backup of the complete system. You therefore decide it is time to install Windows XP from scratch. Alternatively, the system may be working, but with numerous programs having been installed and uninstalled, it is running in a very hesitant fashion. Either way, having decided to install Windows and your applications from scratch, and having also done any necessary backing up of data files, etc., how do you start the reinstallation process?

Before you start, it is worthwhile considering the alternative option. Unless you have definitely decided that it is time to "sweep away the cobwebs" and start from scratch, I would certainly recommend trying to fix Windows by reinstalling it on top of the broken version. If this fails to cure the problem, then it is time to install Windows from scratch. The advantage of reinstallation on top of the old Windows installation is that the programs should remain usable with the new version. This will not happen if there is massive damage to the original installation, but in most cases all the programs will work fine with the refreshed version of Windows. Unfortunately, the problems with the original installation might be carried forward into the new one, and it could still be still be necessary to install Windows from scratch. A great deal of time can be saved if reinstallation on the old copy of Windows works, so it is well worth trying this method.

The process is very similar whether the operating system is installed from scratch or on top of an existing Windows installation. If Windows XP is already on the hard disc it will be detected by the Setup program, which can then reinstall Windows XP on top of the existing installation. Note that the versions of Windows XP supplied with some PCs do not have the standard installation disc. The methods described here are only applicable if you have the standard Windows XP installation disc. If your PC was not supplied with a standard installation disc it probably

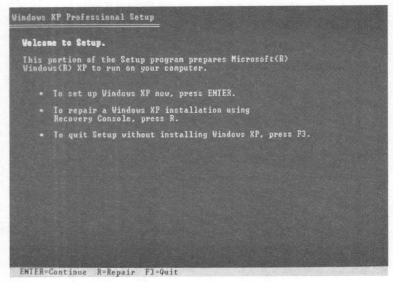

Fig.6.1 *The opening screen of the Windows XP Setup program*

came complete with a recovery disc that makes it easy to return to a basic Windows installation. With a PC of this type you should consult the instruction manual, and this should give concise information about reinstalling Windows.

Booting from CD

Whether reinstalling on top of the current installation or reinstalling Windows XP from scratch, the first step is to boot from the installation CD-ROM. The BIOS must be set to boot from the CD-ROM drive before it tries to boot from the hard disc. It is unlikely that the computer will attempt to boot from the CD-ROM drive if the priorities are the other way around, and it will certainly not do so unless the CD-ROM is set as one of the boot devices. If all is well, a message will appear on the screen indicating that any key must be operated in order to boot from the CD-ROM drive. This message appears quite briefly, so be ready to press one of the keys. The computer will try to boot from the hard disc if you "miss the boat". It will then be necessary to restart the computer and try again.

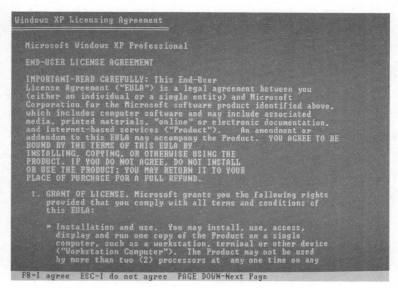

*Fig.6.2 You must agree to the licensing conditions in order to go
ahead with the installation*

After various files have been loaded from the CD-ROM, things should
come to a halt with the screen of Figure 6.1. The Setup program is
needed to reinstall Windows XP, so press the Enter (Return) key. The
Next screen (Figure 6.2) is the usual licence agreement, and the F8 key
is pressed in order to agree with the licensing terms. Note that Windows
XP can not be installed unless you do agree to the licensing conditions.
The installations on the hard disc are listed on the next screen (Figure
6.3), and in most cases there will only be one. Where appropriate, select
the installation that you wish to repair or replace.

Repair rather than replacement of the operating system will be considered
first. In other words, reinstalling Windows on top of the existing installation
rather than starting afresh. Press the R key to indicate that the selected
installation must be repaired. The Setup program then examines the
discs (Figure 6.4), and this process is usually quite brief. Next the Setup
program copies files from the CD-ROM to the installation folders on the
hard disc drive. This will take a few minutes, and the usual bargraph
display shows how far the copying has progressed (Figure 6.5).

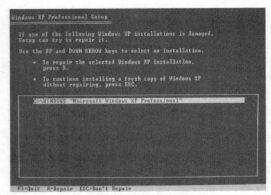

Once the copying has finished it is time for the computer to reboot for the first time. You can press the Return key to start the reboot (Figure 6.6), but after 30 seconds it will automatically reboot anyway. Make sure that there is no floppy disc in drive A:, as this would prevent the PC from rebooting properly.

Fig.6.3 Select the correct installation

Also, when the message appears on the screen, do not press a key to cause the system to boot from the CD-ROM drive. At this stage it must boot from the hard disc drive.

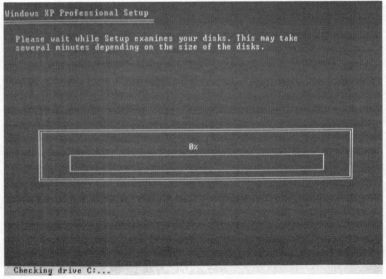

Fig.6.4 Setup will briefly examine the disc drives

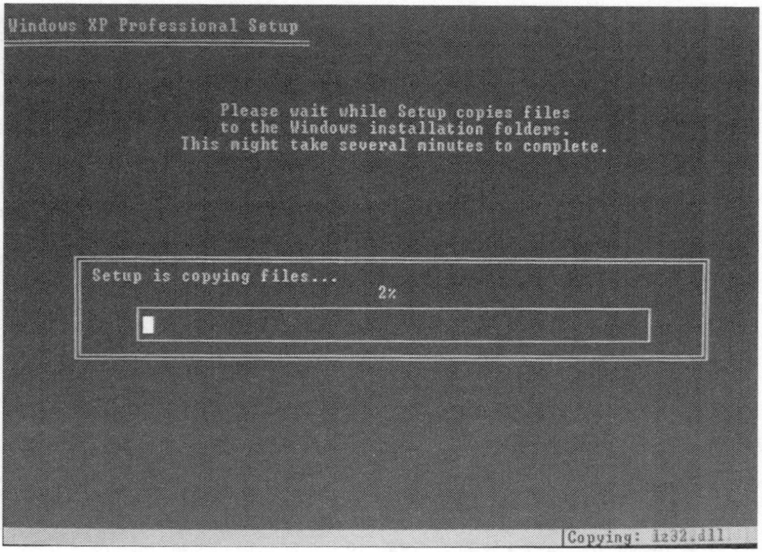

Fig.6.5 It will take some time for the files to be copied to the hard disc

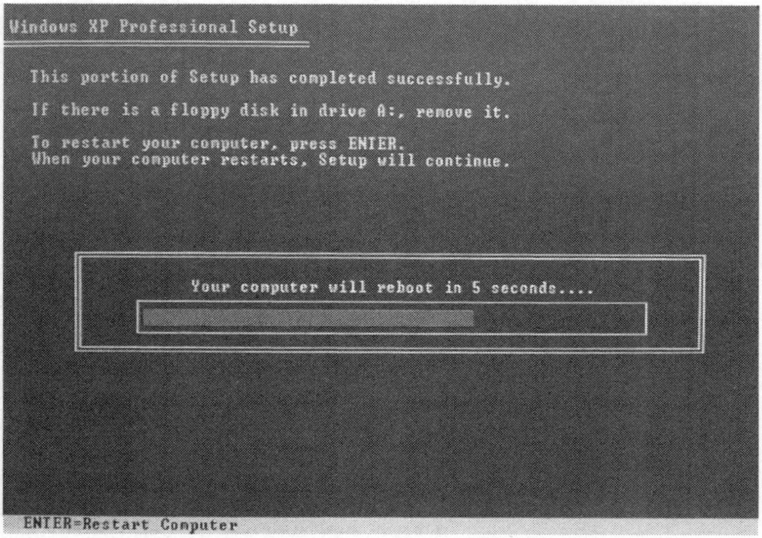

Fig.6.6 The computer will automatically reboot after 5 seconds

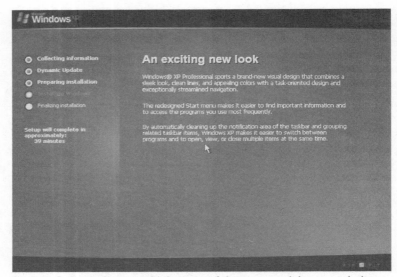

Fig.6.7 Setup indicates which stage of the process it is on, and gives an estimate of the time left until completion

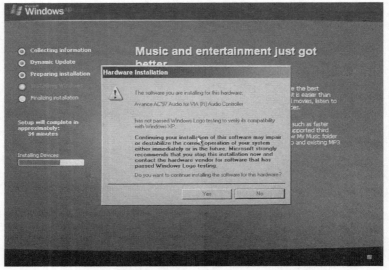

Fig.6.8 A warning message appears if a non-approved driver is found

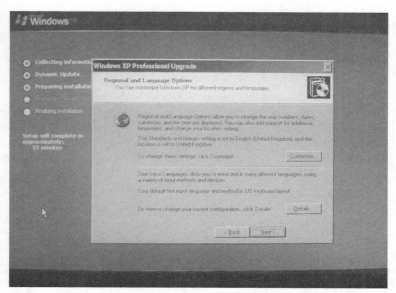

Fig.6.9 This window enables the language settings to be altered

A screen like the one in Figure 6.7 will appear once the reboot has completed, and this keeps you informed about the progress of the reinstallation. A warning message like the one in Figure 6.8 might appear during the reinstallation. This points out that one of the device drivers in use on the computer is not one that has officially passed the Windows XP compatibility test. This does not necessarily mean that it is the cause of the problems with Windows XP, but it is obviously a possibility that has to be given serious consideration. In this case the audio driver in question had been in use for some weeks without any problems arising, so it was not a likely candidate as the cause of the boot problems. However, if in doubt, operate the No button so that the driver is not loaded. It can always be loaded later if the problem is found to lie elsewhere in the system.

Language settings

Eventually a screen like the one in Figure 6.9 will appear. This permits the language settings to be customised, and it is advisable to operate the Customise button and check that the settings are suitable. This brings

6 Reinstallation

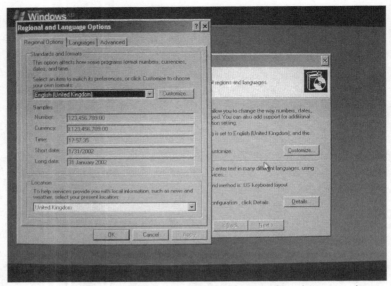

Fig.6.10 These settings determine such things as how large numbers and the time will be displayed

up an initial window like the one on Figure 6.10, but further windows and menus can be brought up by operating the Customise buttons and the tabs. Figures 6.11 and 6.12 show a couple of examples. Look through the various windows and menus, changing any settings that are incorrect. Mistakes here will not have dire consequences, but there could be a problem such as the keyboard producing some incorrect characters. It should be possible to correct any mistake of this type once Windows XP has been installed.

Even though Windows is being installed over an existing installation, it is still necessary to enter the product key when the screen of Figure 6.13 appears. The Windows XP installation disc is supplied in a cardboard folder rather than the usual jewel case. The 25-digit product key is on the rear of this folder. Keep the folder safe because it is not possible to reinstall Windows XP without it. With the correct product key typed into the textboxes, operating the Next button will produce a screen like the one in Figure 6.14, and the installation process will continue. The computer may then reboot, and the Welcome screen of Figure 6.15 will appear.

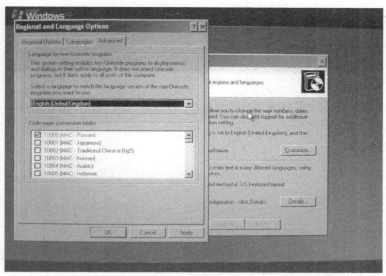

Fig.6.11 *Various Regional and Language settings are available*

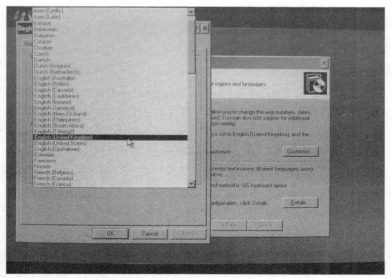

Fig.6.12 *Setting the correct region*

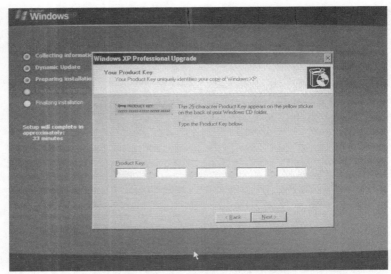

Fig.6.13 The product key is still needed when reinstalling Windows XP

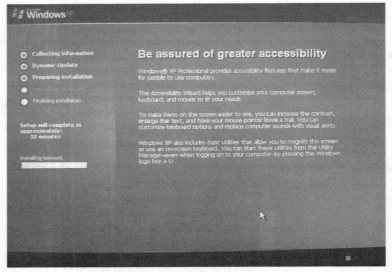

Fig.6.14 The reinstallation process resumes

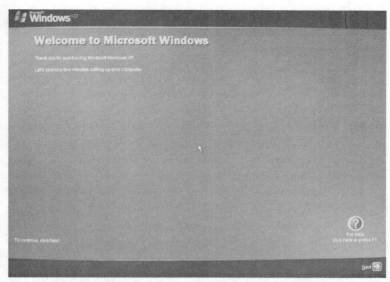

Fig.6.15 With reinstallation complete, the Welcome screen is displayed

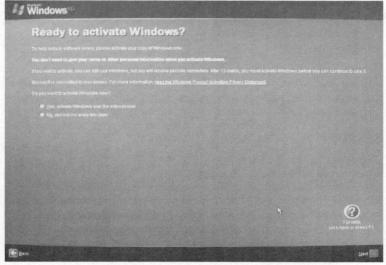

Fig.6.16 It is not essential to activate Windows XP at this stage

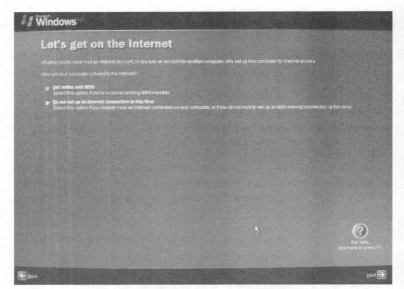

Fig.6.17 You are given the opportunity to get online with MSN

Operate the Next button to move on to the screen of Figure 6.16. Using the two radio buttons you can opt to activate the new Windows XP installation or leave this until later. As the computer is proving troublesome, it is probably best to defer the activation process. Activating Windows was described in a previous chapter and it will not be considered further here. At the next screen (Figure 6.17) you can sign on to MSN or continue with reinstallation. It will be assumed here that the second option is taken. The Windows reinstallation is then finished, and the screen of Figure 6.18 will appear to confirm that the process has been completed.

To try out the new installation, operate the Finish button. The computer should then boot into the usual login screen (Figure 6.19). Login using your normal password, and the computer should go into the Windows XP desktop (Figure 6.20). After reinstalling Windows 9x it is necessary to adjust some of the settings in order to provide normal operation. In particular, the reinstalled version of Windows uses very basic video settings, which have to be adjusted to your normal settings. As can be seen from Figure 6.20, Windows XP uses the previous video settings, and the new installation should be usable without any adjustments.

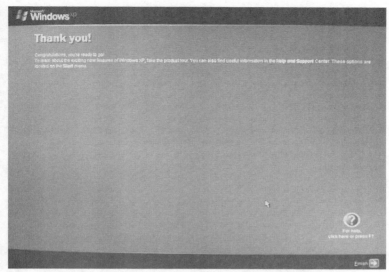

Fig.6.18 This screen confirms that reinstallation is complete

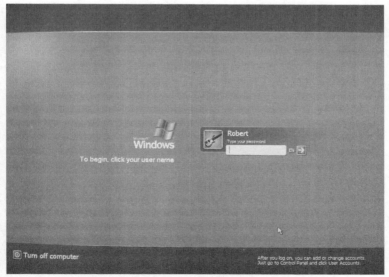

Fig.6.19 The next screen is the usual login type

Fig.6.20 The Windows desktop should look the same as it did before

The applications programs should remain installed and fully usable. Of course, if it was one of the application programs that was causing the problem, it might be unusable with the new installation. It is then a matter of uninstalling and reinstalling it. However, it would be as well to check with the manufacturer to see if there is a known problem when using the program with Windows XP. An updated version or a software patch might be available. If a program gives repeated problems with Windows XP, there is no point in installing and uninstalling it ad infinitum.

From scratch

The initial stages of installation are much the same if it is necessary to install Windows XP from scratch. As before, the computer is booted from the installation CD-ROM and it is only at the screen of Figure 6.3 that things change. It is a fresh installation that is required and not a repair, so the Escape key is pressed. This moves things on to the screen of Figure 6.21 where there are three options. Two of these permit the disc partitioning to be changed, and you will presumably wish to retain the existing set-up.

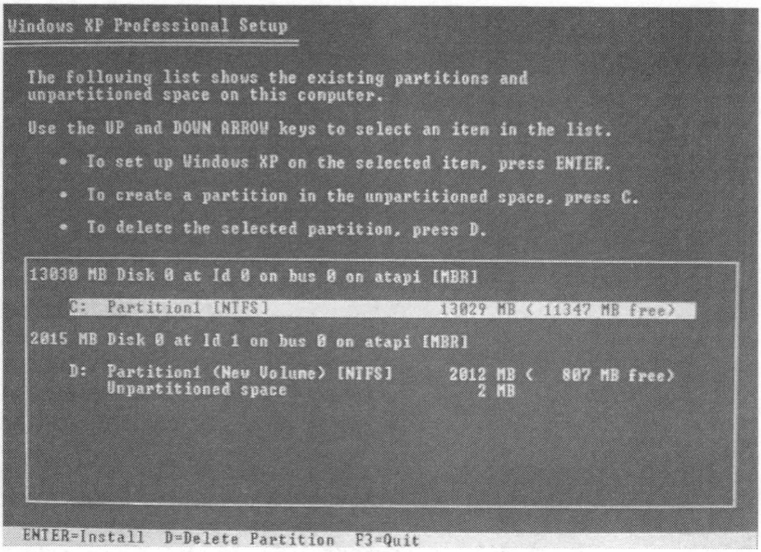

```
Windows XP Professional Setup

  The following list shows the existing partitions and
  unpartitioned space on this computer.

  Use the UP and DOWN ARROW keys to select an item in the list.

    • To set up Windows XP on the selected item, press ENTER.

    • To create a partition in the unpartitioned space, press C.

    • To delete the selected partition, press D.

  13030 MB Disk 0 at Id 0 on bus 0 on atapi [MBR]
      C: Partition1 [NTFS]                13029 MB < 11347 MB free>
  2015 MB Disk 0 at Id 1 on bus 0 on atapi [MBR]
      D: Partition1 (New Volume) [NTFS]    2012 MB <   807 MB free>
         Unpartitioned space                  2 MB




  ENTER=Install   D=Delete Partition   F3=Quit
```

Fig.6.21 Three options are available from this screen

On the face of it, the best course of action is to make sure that the correct partition for the installation is selected in the lower part of the screen and then press the Return key. However, this will produce the warning screen of Figure 6.22. Although you are not trying to install two operating systems on one partition, the existing Windows XP installation might give problems with the new one. After all, the idea is to completely do away with the old installation and start afresh with a new one. Therefore, the D key is pressed so that the partition used for Windows XP is deleted. This will delete everything in the partition, and a warning message to this effect appears when the D key is operated (Figure 6.23). Assuming that you have previously rescued any important data on the partition, press the L key to go ahead and delete the partition.

The previous screen then returns, but this time it indicates that disc C: has unpartitioned space (Figure 6.24). The next step is to create a partition for the new Windows XP installation, and to format that space. With the unpartitioned space selected in the lower section of the screen, operate the C key to create the partition. The next screen (Figure 6.25) enables the partition to be set at the required size. Presumably you will simply wish to reinstate the previous partition that used all the space just vacated.

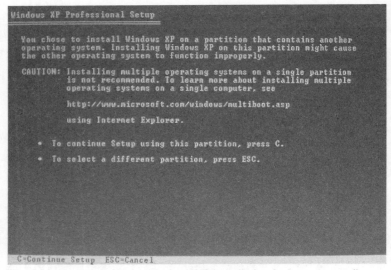

Fig.6.22 Remove the old Windows XP installation before proceeding

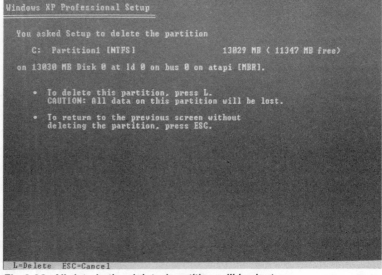

Fig.6.23 All data in the deleted partition will be lost

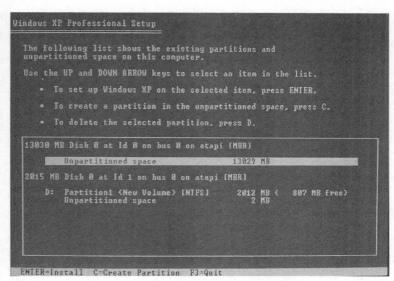

Fig.6.24 Disc C: now has unpartitioned space available

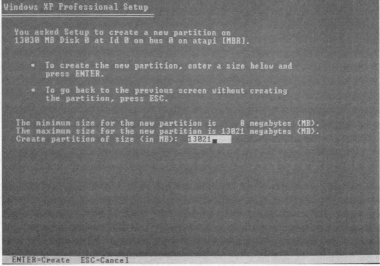

Fig.6.25 The partition will normally be set at the maximum size

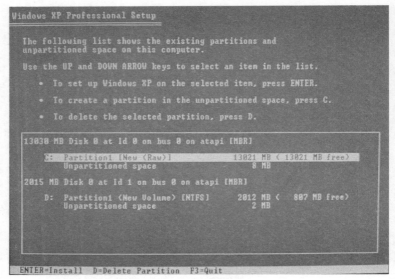

Fig.6.26 Drive C: now has an empty partition

In that case, simply press Return to accept the default partition size. This returns things more or less to the way they were originally (Figure 6.26), but the partition is now empty. It is not even formatted, which is why it is described as "Raw" in the partition table.

Formatting

Next press the Return key to go ahead and install Windows XP on the partition. This produces the screen of Figure 6.27, where the desired file system is selected. Unless there is a good reason to use the FAT or FAT32 file systems, such as compatibility with another file system, choose the NTFS option. This file system makes the best use of Windows XP's capabilities. Having selected the required file system, press the Return key to go ahead and format the partition. This brings up the screen of Figure 6.28, complete with the usual bargraph to show how far the formatting has progressed.

Once the partition has been formatted, the Setup program will start copying files to the hard disc, and thereafter the process is much the same as when reinstalling Windows XP on top of an existing installation.

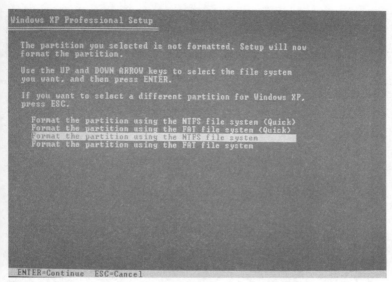

Fig.6.27 *The partition is formatted using the selected file system*

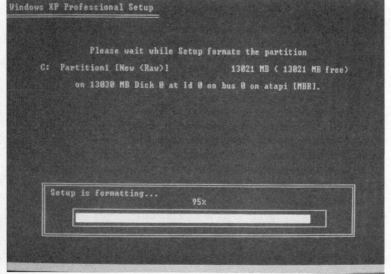

Fig.6.28 *Formatting a large partition can take a long time*

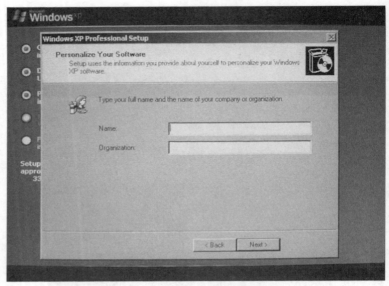

*Fig.6.29 Add your name and (where appropriate) organisation in
the textboxes*

There are one or two differences though. As the original installation has
been cleared from the hard disc, it is not possible for the new installation
to read any information from it. You must re-enter your details when the
screen of Figure 6.29 appears. The same is true of the passwords, and
a new administrator password must be used when the screen of Figure
6.30 appears. Some general information has to be entered at the screens
of Figure 6.31 and 6.32.

Near the end of the installation process there may be a small window
that asks if Windows can automatically adjust the screen settings.
Normally it is best to operate the OK button if this appears. Windows will
then start in something better than the basic 640 by 480 pixel resolution.
It will probably opt for only 800 by 600 pixel resolution, but this is still
much more usable that the basic 640 by 480 pixel mode. After negotiating
the usual login screen the computer should go into Windows XP (Figure
6.33). A window asking if you wish to activate Windows XP might appear,
but it is probably best to leave activation until you are sure that everything
is installed and working perfectly.

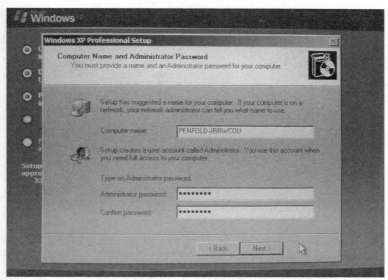

Fig.6.30 Type the administrator password into the textboxes

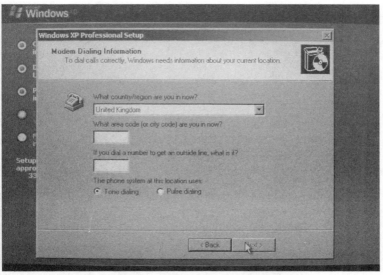

Fig.6.31 The modem dialling information is added here

Fig.6.32 Use this window to set the time zone, etc.

Fig.6.33 Finally, you are into the newly installed Windows XP

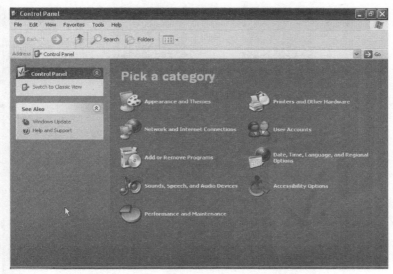

Fig.6.34 The default version of the Windows Control Panel

Hardware drivers

At this stage you have Windows XP reinstalled, but it is likely that some items of hardware will be either partially operational, or will simply be ignored by Windows. It is possible that Windows will detect all the hardware on the motherboard and install the necessary drivers. If the motherboard hardware is more recent than the version of Windows XP that you are using, then Windows is unlikely to have the correct drivers in its standard repertoire. It is virtually certain that proper video drivers will be needed. Even if the graphics card can be set to use high resolutions and colour depths, it is almost certainly using a generic driver rather than one designed specifically for the video card in use. Although high resolutions and colour depths can be used, the video system will probably be very slow in operation. There might be other items of hardware that Windows has missed completely, or has been unable to identify.

The first step is to go into Device Manager to look for any obvious problems with the hardware. First choose Control Panel from the Start menu, which will produce a window like the one in Figure 6.34. It is advisable to left-click on the Switch to Classic View link, which will change the window to the familiar Control Panel layout of Figure 6.35. This

Fig.6.35 The Control Panel using the Classic View

provides easy access to the hardware settings and other useful facilities. Launch the System Properties window by double clicking on the System icon and then operate the Hardware tab. Left-click the Device Manager button, and a window similar to the one in Figure 6.36 will appear.

The important thing to look for here is the yellow exclamation marks that indicate problems with the hardware. In this case the hardware appears to be trouble-free apart from the integrated audio system and the video card. It is worthwhile double-clicking some of the other entries to check that the hardware has been identified correctly. Internal modems can sometimes be troublesome, although the modem has been correctly identified and installed in this case.

If there are any problems with the main hardware on the motherboard, it is advisable to install the drivers for this hardware first. The main hardware means things like the IDE controllers and the PCI slots, and not integrated hardware such as audio systems and network adapters. Where appropriate, your PC should have been supplied with a CD-ROM containing the device drivers for the hardware on the motherboard. Next the video drivers should be installed, and then the device drivers for other hardware such as audio systems and modems.

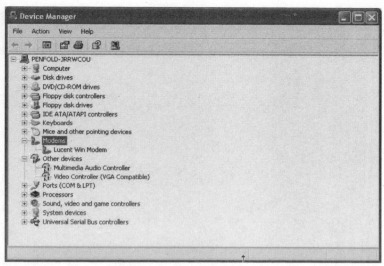

Fig.6.36 Check Device Manager for hardware problems

Driver installation

Windows has built-in facilities for adding device drivers, but few manufacturers seem to make use of these. Most hardware has its own installation program. This copies the device drivers onto the hard disc,

and then the computer is restarted. The device drivers are installed automatically during the boot process. The instruction manuals for the hardware should give concise information about installing the device drivers, and the installation instructions should be followed "to the

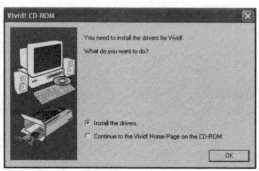

Fig.6.37 The initial screen of the installation program

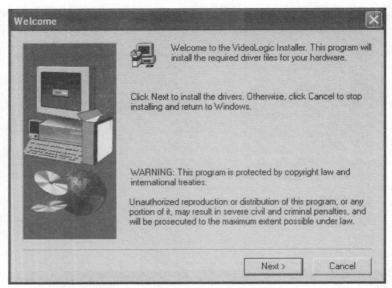

Fig.6.38 The Welcome window includes the usual copyright notice

letter". Note that the installation process is not always the same for each version of Windows, so make sure that you follow the right instructions and use the Windows XP device drivers. Fortunately, Windows XP will almost certainly display a warning message if you try to install inappropriate device drivers.

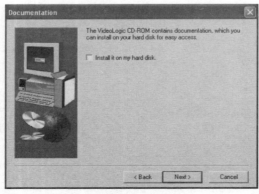

Fig.6.39 It is advisable to load the on-disc manual

In this example there is no need to install any additional drivers for the motherboard's system hardware, so the first task is to install the proper video drivers. The installation CD-ROM will usually auto-run,

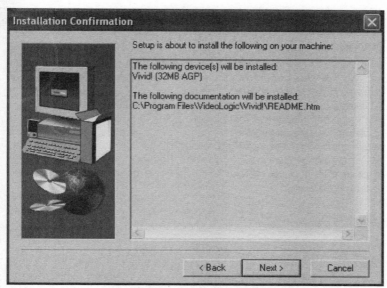

Fig.6.40 This window gives you an opportunity to review the options that have been selected

as in this case, and Figure 6.37 shows the initial window. This provides two options, and in this case is clearly the default "Install the drivers" option that is required. The next window (Figure 6.38) has the usual copyright notice, and operating the Next button moves things on to the licence agreement. Left clicking the Yes brings up a further window (Figure 6.39), and this one gives the option of loading the on-disc instruction manual onto the hard disc. Since the manual is unlikely to require much disc space it is

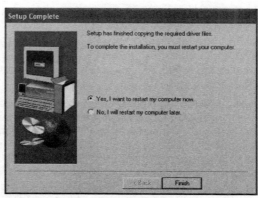

Fig.6.41 Restart the computer to complete the installation

a good idea to install the documentation onto the hard disc when this option is available.

The next window (Figure 6.40) simply shows the options that have been selected, and assuming everything is in order it is just a matter of left clicking the Next button to start installation. Once the files have been copied to the hard disc, the window of Figure 6.41 appears. It is definitely advisable to restart the computer immediately rather than waiting until later. This finalises the installation of the drivers and gives you an opportunity to check that they are functioning correctly. Installing several sets of device drivers and then restarting the computer might seem to be a more efficient way of doing things, because the computer only has to be restarted once. In practice it is not a good idea and is simply inviting problems.

Video settings

Windows will almost certainly detect that a new video card has been installed, and it will then produce the message window of Figure 6.42 when the reboot has been completed. Operate the OK button and then adjust the video settings using the Display Properties Window (Figure 6.43), which will be launched

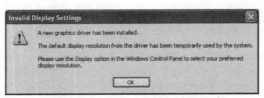

Fig.6.42 Windows will probably detect the newly installed video card

automatically. If the newly installed video card is not detected by Windows, the display settings window must be run manually. Launch the Control Panel, double-click the Display icon, and then operate the Settings tab in the window that appears.

Having set the required screen resolution and colour depth, operate the Apply button. It is likely that Windows is overestimating the abilities of the monitor if the screen goes blank or produces an unstable image. The screen should return to normal in a few seconds though. One way of tackling the problem is to operate the Troubleshoot button, which launches the Video Display Troubleshooter (Figure 6.44). By going through the questions and suggested cures it is likely that the problem would soon be solved. However, the most likely cause of the problem is Windows setting a scan rate that is too high for the monitor, and this is easily corrected.

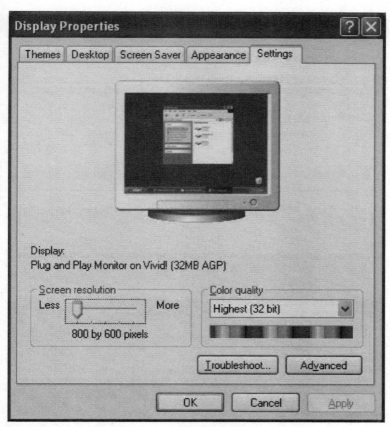

Fig.6.43 Set the required screen resolution and colour depth

First set the required screen resolution again, and then left-click the Advanced button to bring up a window like the one in Figure 6.45. Next, operate the Monitor tab to switch the window to one like Figure 6.46. Activate the Screen refresh rate menu, and choose a lower rate than the one currently in use. In this example the rate was reduced from 85 hertz to 75 hertz. Left-click the Apply button and observe the screen. With luck, this time a small window like the one shown in Figure 6.47 will be visible on the screen. If so, operate the Yes button to keep the new scan rate. If not, wait for a proper display to return and then repeat this process using an even lower scan rate. Note that the maximum scan rate for a

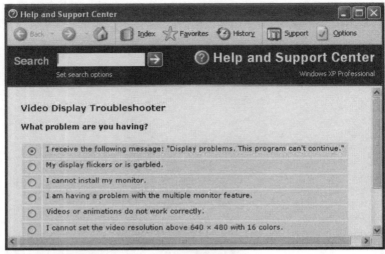

Fig.6.44 The Video Display Troubleshooter

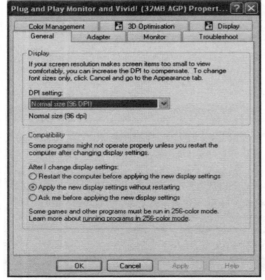

Fig.6.45 The Advanced Settings window

monitor generally reduces as the screen resolution is increased. Consequently, the higher the screen resolution used, the lower the scan rate that will have to be set.

Obviously the installation of the video card will vary slightly from one card to another, but most cards are installed using the general method outlined here. With the video card installed and set up

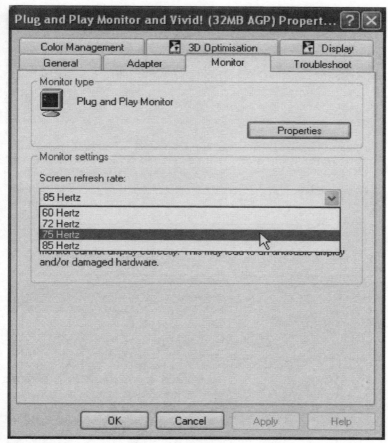

Fig.6.46 A lower scan rate should cure the problem

correctly, any further drivers that are needed can be installed. In this example it was only necessary to install the device drivers for the audio system. Device Manager then showed no problems with any of the hardware (Figure 6.48), indicating that the hardware was all installed successfully. With the hardware installed properly, it is then a matter of installing all the applications software, undertaking any customisation of the software, and then reinstating your data files. The PC is then ready for use again.

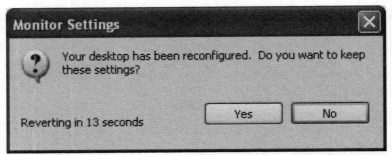

Fig.6.47 The settings return to normal unless the Yes button is operated

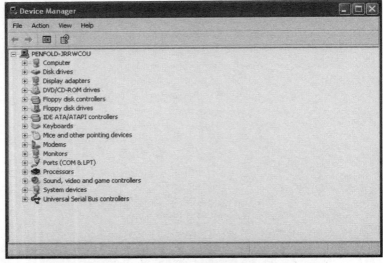

Fig.6.48 The problems with the hardware have been cleared

Correct channels

The installation CD-ROMs supplied with most hardware includes a Setup program. However, in some cases the disc contains device drivers but it does not include a program to install the drivers. If the instruction manual gives installation instructions, then follow them. With some low-cost hardware you are simply left to your own devices. One way of tackling

Fig.6.49 The Add Hardware Wizard

the installation of hardware of this type is to launch the Add Hardware Wizard. Go to the Control Panel, double-click the System icon, and then operate the Hardware tab in the System Properties window. In the upper section of this window there is an Add Hardware Wizard button, and operating this launches the wizard (Figure 6.49).

Heed the warning notice about using the manufacturer's installation program wherever possible. Check the installation CD-ROM to ensure that it does not contain an Install or Setup program. If you are sure that it does not, operate the Next button to move the wizard on to the next stage (Figure 6.50). The Add Hardware Wizard uses the normal technique of suggestions and questions to (hopefully) find the right answers. The first screen simply determines whether the hardware is already connected to the PC. Unless the manufacturer specifically advises otherwise, the hardware must be physically installed before the device drivers are loaded.

Assuming that the hardware is already connected, the next window provides a list of the detected hardware. Obviously the entry for the

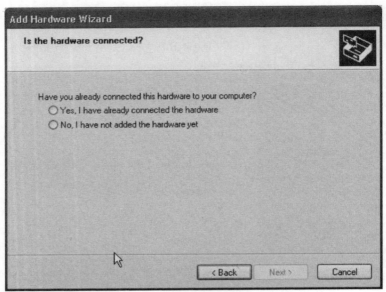

Fig.6.50 The first check determines whether the hardware is connected

hardware should be selected if it is found in the list. If it has not been detected and listed by Windows, select the Add a new device option

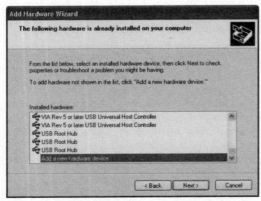

Fig.6.51 Select Add new hardware device

(Figure 6.51). The next window (Figure 6.52) gives the option of installing the device manually or having Windows try to detect it. There is no harm in trying the detection method, but it is likely Windows is incapable of detecting the hardware if it has not done so already. Taking the manual

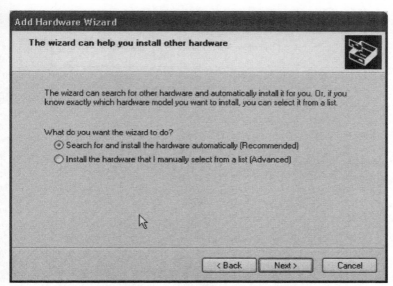

Fig.6.52 Manual installation is probably the best option here

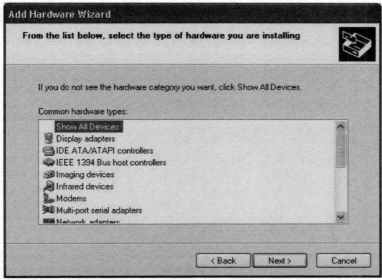

Fig.6.53 Select the correct category for the new hardware

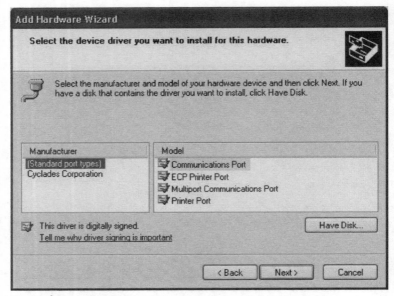

Fig.6.54 It is normally the Have Disk option that is needed here

route produces a window like the one of Figure 6.53). This gives a list of hardware types, and you must select the correct category for the device you are trying to install.

Moving on to the next window (Figure 6.54) gives a list of manufacturers in the left-hand section, and devices for the selected manufacturer in the

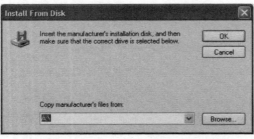

Fig.6.55 Give the location of the driver files

right-hand section. Obviously you should select the appropriate entry for your device if it is listed, but this is unlikely. It is normally necessary to operate the Have Disk button, which brings up a window like the one of Figure 6.55. Either type the path to the disc and folder containing the device drivers, or use the Browse option to locate the drivers. Having pointed Windows to the drivers, the installation process then follows along normal lines.

Language problems

Back in the days of MS-DOS it was often quite tricky to persuade the operating system that you were using a keyboard having the English

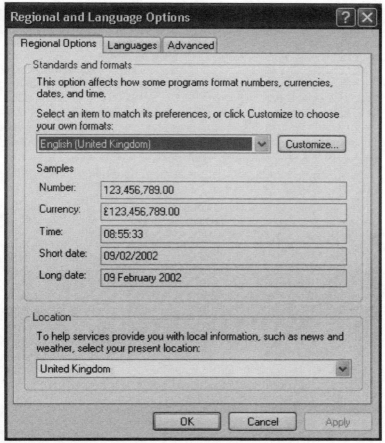

Fig.6.56 Check the the Regional and Language settings are correct

version of the English layout, rather than one having the US English characters and layout. The differences are quite minor, but they result in the double quotes and @ symbol being transposed. Also, the pound sign (£) tends to disappear or be replaced with the hash (#) symbol.

Some of the little used symbols also disappear or become assigned to the wrong keys.

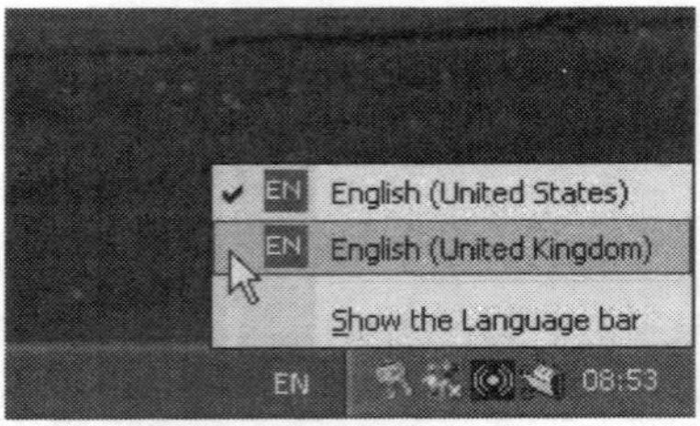

Windows XP can suffer from a similar problem after it has been reinstalled from scratch. The obvious first step is to go to the Control Panel and double-click the keyboard icon. This is the first thing to try if the keyboard is not working at all, but with a language problem it is unlikely to be of any

Fig.6.57 Choose the correct language version

help. It is better to start by going to the Control Panel and double clicking the Regional and Language icon. This produces a properties window like the one in Figure 6.56, which is essentially the same as the one that appears during the installation process. Check the various sections to make sure that the correct language is set.

If everything is correct, look at the bottom right-hand corner of the Windows desktop. Here there will be a button that indicates the language in use. This will usually be marked EN for English, but more than one version of the language will probably be available. Left-click the button to produce a small popup menu (Figure 6.57), and then select the English (United Kingdom) option. The keyboard should then function properly, producing the pound sign, etc. However, the wrong version of English will be set as the default.

Fig.6.58 Choose the Settings option from the popup menu

To correct this, activate the menu again and select the Show the language bar option. This removes the button and produces a small floating bar instead (Figure 6.58). Operate the tiny button in the bottom right-hand corner of the bar and select Settings from the popup menu. This launches the Text Services and Input Languages window (Figure 6.59). Use the pop down menu near the top of the window to select the correct default language. Next operate the Apply and OK buttons, and then restart the computer to check that the default has switched to the right language.

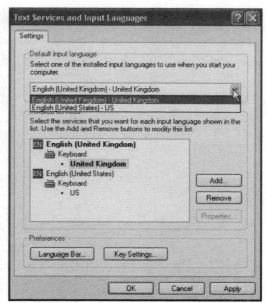

Fig.6.59 Set the correct default language

User accounts

At least two user accounts would have been produced automatically if the original Windows XP installation was an upgrade from Windows 9x, the Administrator account and one for the name used during the upgrade process. Both accounts are assigned the same password. Some computer retailers supply their PCs completely set up and ready for use, sometimes complete with one or more user accounts installed. Only an Administrator account is produced when Windows XP is installed from scratch. Any other accounts you require have to be set up manually.

The Administrator account is usually reserved for making changes to the system or troubleshooting, since it gives full control over the system. As a minimum, you should install one additional account for normal use. The first step in adding a new account is to go to the Control Panel and double-click the User Accounts icon. This launches a window like the one in Figure 6.60. Left-click the link for Create a new account, which switches the window to the one shown in Figure 6.61. Type a name for the account into the textbox and then operate the Next button.

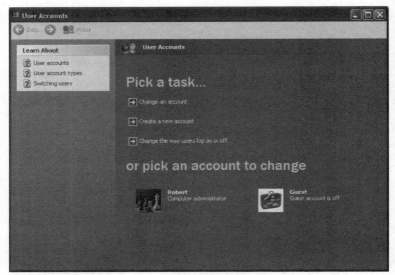

Fig.6.60 The initial version of the User Accounts window

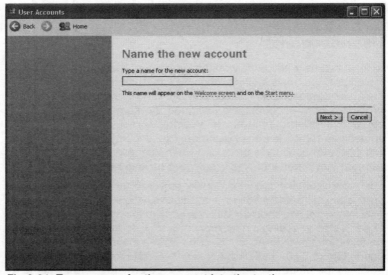

Fig.6.61 Type a name for the account into the textbox

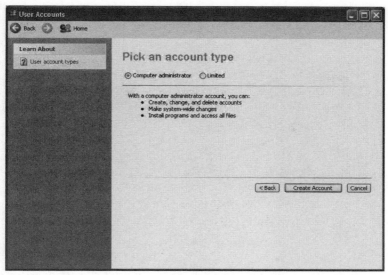

Fig.6.62 Use this window to select the most suitable type of account

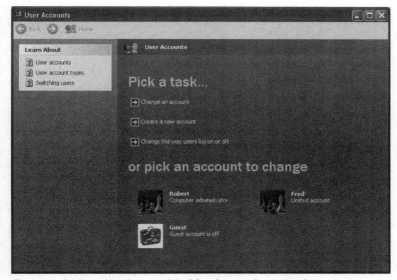

Fig.6.63 An icon has been added for the newly created account

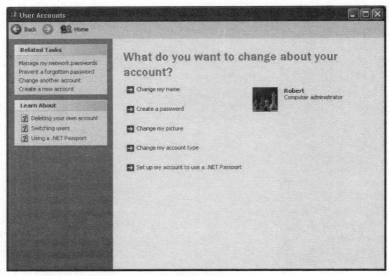

Fig.6.64 Operate the Create password link

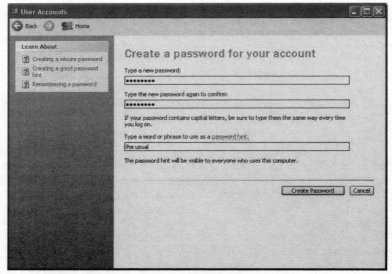

Fig.6.65 Type the password into the top two textboxes

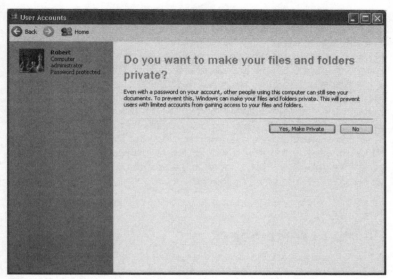

Fig.6.66 If desired, your files and folders can be kept private

The type of account is selected at the next window (Figure 6.62). An administrator account provides freedom to make changes to the system, but these abilities are not needed for day to day use of the computer. A limited account is generally considered to be the better choice for normal use, since the restrictions reduce the risk of the system being accidentally damaged. Note that you might not be able to install programs when using a limited account. Also, some programs produced prior to Windows 2000 and XP might not be usable with a limited account. Consequently, there is no alternative to an administrator account if maximum flexibility is required.

Having selected the type of account using the radio buttons, operate the Create Account button. The original User Accounts window then returns, but it should now contain the newly created account (Figure 6.63). There are other facilities in the User Accounts window that enable the login and logoff settings to be altered. By default, the Welcome screen is shown at startup, and you simply have to left-click the entry for the new account in order to use it. Note that the new account will start with a largely blank desktop. Each account has its own desktop and other settings, so each account can be customised with the best settings for its particular user.

Accounts are not password protected by default. To add a password, go to the User Accounts window and left-click the entry for the account that you wish to password protect. This switches the window to look like Figure 6.64, and here the Create password link is activated. At the next window (Figure 6.65) the password is typed into the top two textboxes, and a hint is entered into the other textbox. The hint is something that will jog your memory if you should happen to forget the password. Next operate the Create Password button, which moves things on to the window of Figure 6.66. This window explains that password protection does not prevent other users from reading your files. Operate the Yes Make Private button if you would like to prevent other users from accessing your files. This completes the process, and the password will be needed the next time you login to that account.

Points to remember

PCs that are supplied with Windows XP preinstalled are not necessarily supplied with a normal Windows installation disc. Windows then has to be installed in accordance with the computer manufacturer's instructions.

Installing Windows XP on top of an existing version might cure problems with the operating system, but it is not guaranteed to do so.

When reinstalling Windows XP from scratch it is not necessary to reformat the hard disc prior to reinstallation. The appropriate disc partition can be deleted and then added again during installation. This clears away any trace of the original Installation, but all data will also be removed from the partition.

Make sure that any important data is reliably backed up prior to installing Windows XP from scratch. Data should not be lost when reinstalling Windows XP on top of the existing version, but it is a good idea to backup any important data in case there are problems.

The Text Services and Input Languages window can be used to correct things if the computer defaults to using the US English keyboard layout.

Appendix 1

Useful web addresses

www.microsoft.com

This is the Microsoft web site, and a vast amount of Windows support is available here (see chapter 3).

www.shareware.com

A vast range of shareware, freeware, commercial demonstration software, etc., is available from this site. There are also useful links to other sites. Some useful utility programs and anti-virus software can usually be obtained from here, or via one of the links.

www.symantec.com

Symantec are the publishers of the Norton range of utilities. Their web site has demonstration versions of their programs plus some virus removal tools and general anti-virus information.

www.driverguide.com

www.windrivers.com

www.helpdrivers.com

The hardware manufactuer's web site is normally the first port of call when looking for device drivers. However, with generic hardware or if the manufacturer is no more, sites such as these can often help you to locate suitable device drivers.

Appendix 2

Windows XP Service Pack 2 (SP2)

Windows XP Service Pack 2 (SP2) is a major update to the original Windows XP operating system. Most of the changes are designed to address the numerous security issues that have plagued Windows XP since it was first released. Most of the changes operate unseen in the background, and do not alter the way in which Windows XP is used, or the way in which problems are dealt with. Installing the update is straightforward, and for most users there are no problems when utilising the updated operating system. Inevitably, there can be problems if you are unlucky.

Hardware related problems seem to be extremely rare, so you are very unlucky indeed if an item of hardware ceases operating when SP2 is installed. Unfortunately, it is unlikely that there will be a cure for the problem unless the hardware manufacturer produces a new version of the driver software or a patch for the old one. With reasonably modern hardware it is quite likely that the necessary update will be released by the manufacturer as soon as possible. The chances of obtaining a new driver or patch are slim when dealing with older hardware that the manufacturer may well consider to be obsolete.

Realistically, the only options will then be to obtain and install a more modern piece of hardware, or to uninstall SP2. Uninstalling the SP2 update is a way out of any problem that the new software causes, but it should really be regarded as a last resort. Uninstalling the update removes the added security it provides, and makes it more important to have good security software installed on the PC. Computer security is something that has to be taken very seriously these days, particularly when dealing with PCs that are used on the Internet.

Software compatibility

Problems with software are much more likely than difficulties with hardware. The most likely culprits are old programs, which are much more likely to ignore the correct Windows protocols than the latest Windows software. The situation with "ancient" software is much the same as it is with older hardware. You might be able to obtain an updated version or a patch from the manufacturer, but there is clearly no chance of this if the software is obsolete.

The manufacturer is unlikely to be very helpful in cases where you are (say) using version three of a program that is still being sold but as version eight. They will, quite reasonably, expect you to upgrade to the latest version that is fully compatible with modern versions of Windows. Unfortunately, this is likely to be quite costly as there will probably be no upgrade available for a really old program. You then have to buy the full-price retail version of the program. On the plus side, the new version is likely to have many new and improved features.

Before resorting to new software it is probably worthwhile trying to run the old program using an appropriate compatibility mode. In other words, try running the program with Windows XP set to be compatible with an earlier version of Windows. This process is covered in the "Software compatibility" section starting on page 56, so it will not be covered again here. There is no guarantee of success, but using a compatibility mode is quite likely to get older programs working again.

Firewall

Security programs are another common cause of problems with Windows XP SP2. There is a firewall program built into the original version of Windows XP, but it is not activated by default. A rather more advanced firewall program is installed as part of SP2, and it is switched on by default. Even if the firewall was not active when the SP2 update was installed, it will still be switched on by default on the updated PC.

This can cause confusion for some users, as warning messages can appear on the screen when programs are run. This occurs when a program tries to access the Internet, and its activity is detected by the firewall. In most cases the program will be something like a media player that is quite legitimately trying to use the Internet connection. When asked if you would like to go on blocking the program's Internet access or unblock it, choose to remove the blocking only if you are sure that the program is one that you are using, and that it has good reason to use the Internet connection. Backdoor Trojans, spyware, etc., gather information from a PC and try to send it to hackers via the Internet. The built-in firewall should detect and block most programs of this type provided you do not override it.

There is a potential problem in cases where the computer is equipped with a software firewall other than the built-in program. In theory it is possible to have two firewall programs running at the same time, but in practice it might cause problems. It is probably pointless to use two firewall programs, since they provide the same function. Two firewalls will drain the computer's resources more than using just one, but little additional protection will be provided. Uninstall the existing firewall program before updating Windows XP if you wish to switch over to the new version of the built-in program.

The new Windows XP firewall is better than the original, but it is not as good as most third-party firewall programs. Consequently, in most cases the existing firewall will be retained and the built-in program will have to be switched off. The SP2 update adds a new feature called the Security Center, and this can be accessed via the Windows Control Panel. At the bottom of the Security Center's window there is a Windows Firewall link, and left-clicking this produces a new window. The radio button near the bottom of this window enables the firewall to be switched off.

Antivirus

There are two main problems that occur when using Windows XP SP2 with antivirus software. One is that a few of these programs do not do things using the approved methods, which can result in Windows "thinking" that the antivirus software is attacking rather than protecting the system. It is likely that the only way around this problem will be to obtain an updated version of the program or to switch to different antivirus software. Software patches should be available for any major antivirus programs that have this problem, or the manufacturer's web site might give details of a way around the problem.

A more common problem is that of the antivirus software not being recognised by the new Security Center feature (Figure 7.1). It is important to realise that although the antivirus software appears to be non-operational, in the vast majority of cases it will still be working normally. The problem is simply that the Security Center has failed to detect and link to the antivirus program. Most antivirus programs try to protect themselves from harmful programs such as viruses, and this can result in them blocking Window's attempts at detection. With lesser known antivirus software the problem can simply be that Windows does not recognise that particular program.

Windows XP SP2 adds a pop-up blocker to Internet Explorer, and it seems to be very effective. In fact it can be too effective, causing it to block some features such as automatic updating facilities. No doubt the relevant features will be updated in due course, but that leaves a problem in the

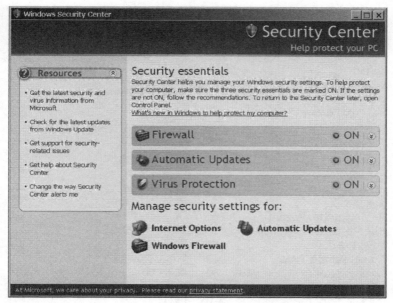

Fig.7.1 The Security Center is new to Windows XP SP2

mean time. Blocking can be switched off of course, but a better solution is to enable pop-ups when using the relevant web addresses. From within Internet Explorer, select Pop-up Blocker from the Tools menu, followed by Pop-up Blocker Settings from submenu that appears. Type the URL into the textbox near the top of the new window that appears and then operate the Add button. The URL should then be added to the "Allowed sites" list in the middle part of the window.

Finally

Bear in mind that any Windows update can result in changes to the exiting settings of Windows itself and the programs that are supplied with it as part of the system. This can give the impression that something has gone wrong, but it is just a matter of restoring any changes to the original settings.

A great deal of useful advice about SP2 problems can be obtained from the Microsoft web site at http://support.microsoft.com. Click on the link for the Windows XP Service Pack 2 Support Center.

CAW

Index